Further praise for *Over the Beach*

"Although *Over the Beach* somehow seems to get its arms around all the major issues of the air war in North Vietnam . . . the story comes together in the character studies of the men who flew."
    —Adm. James Bond Stockdale, USN (Ret.), *Wall Street Journal*

"First rate. . . . History as it should be: well-rounded, human, understandable, exciting and moving. . . . Grant puts living flesh on historical bones through exceptionally candid interviews with the pilots. . . . The interviews are poignant. . . . The detailed descriptions of the unbelievable physical force and the danger of aircraft and pilot launching from a carrier are finely wrought, some of the best such descriptions to be found anywhere."   —*Kirkus Reviews*

"As a *Time* correspondent, Grant frequently visited the fighter pilots who flew missions over North Vietnam from the carrier *Oriskany,* and interviewed many of them anew after the war. The material he collected, combined with diligent research and considerable journalistic talent, comprises a first-class account of an important aspect of the war that has not received major attention. The pilots are portrayed in a dimensional way rarely found in war literature, and Grant conveys vividly what it was like to live through intense anti-aircraft fire, dogfights with MIGs, downing and rescue (as well as downing and capture) and psychic burnout. This is more than an air-combat book, however: the author follows the course of disagreements between the high command and Defense Secretary Robert McNamara over the usefulness of the air w——— ———n of the pilots to charges of bombing civil——— ———ι pilot's widow to confirm that he——— ———cile herself to his death."

"In this sympathetic and penetrat——— ———ο of a fighter squadron aboard the U.S.S. *Oriska.* ———ιe the internal politics of their unit, their own doubts about the Vietnam War, and fears for their safety, while acting like fighter jocks, all bravado and hard living. Laced through this diverse, personality-filled work are the words of wives and many of the pilots themselves and the author's telling assessment of the bombing policy, which was tentative and ineffective despite the courage and skill of the men who carried it out. . . . This is a valuable examination of the Navy's bombing of the North, with less emphasis on hardware than a pilot might wish, but biting and insightful. A gem."   —*Library Journal*

OVER THE BEACH

OVER
THE
BEACH

Zalin Grant

W·W· Norton & Company

NEW YORK   LONDON

Copyright © 1986 by Zalin Grant and Claude Boutillon
All rights reserved.
Printed in the United States of America.
First published as a Norton paperback 2005

For information about permission to reproduce selections from
this book, write to Permissions, W. W. Norton & Company, Inc.,
500 Fifth Avenue, New York, NY 10110

Manufacturing by The Courier Companies, Inc.
Production manager: Amanda Morrison

Library of Congress Cataloging-in-Publication Data

Grant, Zalin.
Over the beach.
Includes index.
1. Vietnamese Conflict, 1961–1975.
I. Title.
PS3557.R27608   1987   813'.54   86–5320

ISBN 0-393-02332-X (hardcover)
ISBN 0-393-32727-2 pbk.

W. W. Norton & Company, Inc.
500 Fifth Avenue, New York, N.Y. 10110
www.wwnorton.com

W. W. Norton & Company Ltd.
Castle House, 75/76 Wells Street, London W1T 3QT

1 2 3 4 5 6 7 8 9 0

To Frank McCulloch

Contents

Acknowledgments

MY FIRST WORDS of thanks go to those who are not often mentioned in these pages, although their role was of primary importance—the officers and men of the United States Air Force. As a journalist covering the war, I put myself in their capable hands countless times. I remember the C-130 pilot who landed us under rocket fire at Khe Sanh as calmly as if he were flying the Washington–New York shuttle. Also the forward air controller who, on his final mission over the DMZ, in a flimsy Cessna, decided to bend the rules and show me the effects of the bombing on the southern panhandle, giving me the distinction of being perhaps the only journalist of the war to fly over North Vietnam in combat. (After we landed he asked my impressions. I could sum them up in one word: Terrifying.) Some of my more pleasurable hours in Saigon were spent in the company of the Seventh Air Force's public affairs officer, Colonel Bill McGinty, who was as witty as he was effective, and his deputy, George Weiss. I met pilots such as Robbie Risner and James Kasler, who flew north and were later shot down and held prisoner, truly remarkable men of courage and dedication.

But this is a book about the war as seen from the perspective of a naval air squadron, and so my gratitude must be directed specifically to the following former officers of the United States Navy. Several of them, such as Wynne Foster, who lost an arm in combat but successfully fought to remain on active duty, and Richard Mullen, who was a prisoner of war, do not appear in this story, but all of them made an invaluable contribution to my understanding of the air war: Robert (Rick) Adams, Jerry Breasted, Ronald Coalson, Patrick Crahan, Leabert Fernandez, Wynne Foster, John Hellman, John Iarrobino, John MacDonald, Richard Mullen, James Nunn, Robert Punches, Charles Rice, C. A. L. Swanson, Charles Tinker, Demetrio Verich, Richard Wyman. My thanks to Marilyn Elkins and Nell Swanson, wives of naval aviators, both pacific by nature but as honest and brave as any warrior. Anna C. Urband of the Pentagon's magazine and book branch responded quickly and effectively to my numerous requests. Captain Gary Hackanson, commanding officer of the Miramar Naval Air Station in San Diego, graciously took me on a personal tour of the base. My thanks to Dr. Wayne Thompson of the Office of Air Force History and to Mr. Wes Pryce of the Naval Historical Center for giving a reading to this work and making suggestions. Responsibility for everything written here is, of course, mine alone.

I would also like to express my appreciation to a few confirmed civilians who were professionally or personally helpful: Starling Lawrence and Jeannie Luciano of W. W. Norton & Company; Peter Shepherd of Harold Ober Associates; in Paris, Annie and Jacques Belaiche, Philippe Muller, Deborah Palmer, Sultana Belaiche; also, my mother, Barbara Smith Grant, wife of the late Thurman B. Grant, who served with the most decorated infantry regiment of World War Two; Thurma Dean and David Smith; and a friend from our sunny days in Spain, Sally Ann Palmer.

Janice and Wallace Terry deserve the medal of friendship with three gold stars.

The day I finished this book, Claude, who not only sparkles with intelligence and cheerfulness but is usually the soul of modesty, was fishing for a compliment, and she asked in the French approximation of my Southern accent, "Do you zhink I have helpt?" The answer is yes, I do, mon amour. Je te remercie infiniment.

ZALIN GRANT
Paris

OVER THE BEACH

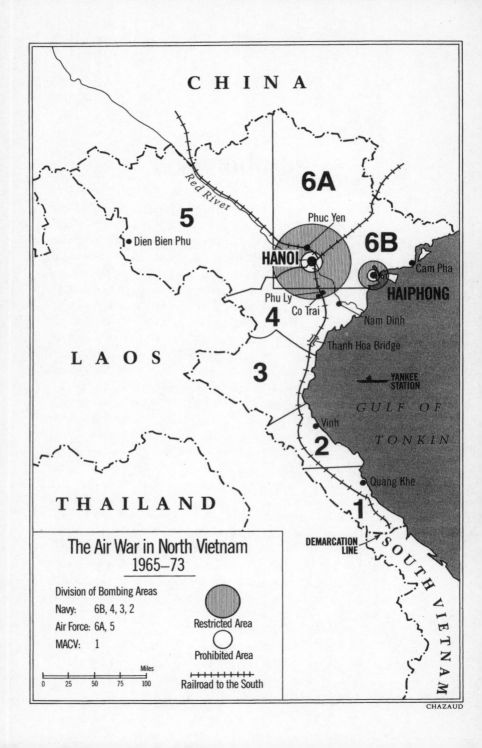

CHINA

6A

5

Dien Bien Phu

Phuc Yen

6B

HANOI

Cam Pha

HAIPHONG

Phu Ly

Co Trai

Nam Dinh

4

Thanh Hoa Bridge

LAOS

3

YANKEE
STATION

GULF OF

TONKIN

Vinh

2

Quang Khe

THAILAND

1

DEMARCATION
LINE

SOUTH VIETNAM

The Air War in North Vietnam
1965–73

Division of Bombing Areas

Navy: 6B, 4, 3, 2

Air Force: 6A, 5

MACV: 1

Restricted Area

Prohibited Area

Miles

| 0 | 25 | 50 | 75 | 100 |

Railroad to the South

CHAZAUD

Prologue

THE SKIPPER raised his binoculars and saw the USS *Oriskany* on the horizon. The aircraft carrier looked massive in his glasses, although he knew it to be one of the smallest of the fleet. The skipper was a big man, barechested and hairy. He wore faded blue shorts. A white cloth covered his head from the sun. He watched as the *Oriskany* approached another vessel from astern, an ammo supply ship. From where he stood near the deckhouse, the skipper could see that many of his thirty-five-man crew were working on their tans or swimming off the port side. He finished his cigarette and went below to get a radar fix on the *Oriskany.* On the way, he told the first mate to make ready to depart.

Moscow had sent the skipper to spy on the U.S. Seventh Fleet in the Gulf of Tonkin. This was his second tour on "Yankee Station," as the Americans called that locus of the gulf where they waged their imperialist air war against the Democratic Republic of Vietnam.

The *Gidrofon,* a one hundred and fifty-foot trawler, could do but thirteen knots, less than half the speed of the three aircraft carriers and thirty support ships that made up Task Force Seventy-Seven. Yet the skipper had no trouble keeping close watch on the Americans. The *Gidrofon* pretended to be making hydrographic surveys—a cover story that neither the Russians nor the Americans took seriously. The trawler was equipped with the most advanced electronics the Soviet Union could provide.

Still, it wasn't just the technology that made the skipper's job easy. The Gulf of Tonkin was only about one hundred and fifty miles wide and three hundred miles long. The U.S. operational area was limited on the west to three miles offshore North Vietnam; on the east, to three miles from China's Hainan Island; and the north-south boundaries stretched a hundred miles or so. Yankee Station was, in effect, if one considered the number of ships involved, no more than a small lake. To launch and recover aircraft, the carriers needed a thirty-five knot wind blowing over their flight decks. They were constantly steaming up and down, making frequent course changes in search of the right breeze. The skipper could sit at 18° north—108° east and watch the Americans go by. In an average month, the *Oriskany* might log twelve thousand miles, while the skipper, lying dead much of the time, ran up seven hundred. The *Gidrofon* could remain on station for weeks, or even months, without being resupplied.

The skipper knew more about the *Oriskany* than did many of the thirty-five hundred Americans who manned the carrier. The ship had seventy aircraft. Its air wing was made up of two twelve-plane squadrons of F-8 fighters, two fourteen-plane squadrons of A-4 bombers, ten aging "Spads," three A-3 refueling tankers, several photo recon birds, and a couple of E-2 radar planes. By now, the Russians could recognize the radio voices of the *Oriskany*'s pilots.

In the early days of the air war, the skipper had been wary. He suspected the imperialists' strategy of being an elaborate trick. Why else would Washington draw a circle around Hanoi and Haiphong and not allow American planes to bomb within those prohibited zones— the very places where most of the DRV's critical industrial targets were located? If the capitalists had nothing up their sleeves, why, then, did they look on benignly as the North Vietnamese installed surface-to-air missiles and make no attempt to hit the sites until months after they were first photographed? With that kind of reaction on the capitalist side, and with generous help from the socialist camp, the Vietnamese comrades were able to construct the most deadly antiaircraft defense system ever devised.

And if Washington's policy truly was to stop Hanoi from sending war material to South Vietnam, why did the Americans wait more than a year after the bombing campaign began before they tried to wipe out the DRV's gasoline supplies? Fortunately, by then the Vietnamese freedom fighters had hidden in caves, or buried, much of their gasoline, making it impossible to find from the air.

The skipper discovered that manifestations of this odd strategy extended to him. The Seventh Fleet commander assigned a salvage tug to shadow him full-time, and U.S. destroyers were called in to give chase when he evaded the tug. In spite of this, an American supply ship recently circled the *Gidrofon,* with the ship's band playing and a

singer giving the Russians a selection of decadent rock 'n' roll. Then a
U.S. helicopter swooped low and offered the crew some strawberry ice
cream.

Strange, these Americans—crazy, even!

Moscow had laid down guidelines for the *Gidrofon's* conduct on
Yankee Station. The skipper was encouraged by his superiors in the
Kremlin to harass U.S. warships, so long as he did it while following
the international rules that governed sea travel. An excellent shiphan-
dler, he tried always to approach American ships from their starboard
side at a perpendicular, thus giving him the right of way and making
them yield. Sometimes, when he couldn't manipulate the rules to his
advantage, he simply ignored them. It broke the boredom.

The *Oriskany* was a particular favorite for harassment. The ship
itself was not very interesting—a leftover from World War Two. But
there was something different about the pilots and men of the *Oriskany,* a certain spirit, a willingness to take risks, which made them a
deserving adversary. If someone had told the skipper that the *Oriskany*
would see more action and suffer more losses than any aircraft carrier
of the Vietnam War, he would not have been surprised.

The skipper returned topside and took a look once more through his
binoculars. Then he set the *Gidrofon* on a collision course with the
Oriskany.

I

July 19, 1966

Attack on Co Trai

1

EARLY ON TUESDAY MORNING, July 19, 1966, the pilots of Squadron 162 began to assemble in Ready Room 4, which was located on the level below the hangar deck of the USS *Oriskany*. The *Oriskany* was one of three aircraft carriers assigned by Washington, along with air force planes flying from land bases in South Vietnam and Thailand, to participate in an air war against the Democratic Republic of Vietnam, in order—said official pronouncements—to help bring the ground war in South Vietnam to a successful conclusion by forcing the North Vietnamese to cease their aggression in the South; or, at least—as time went on and the war became unpopular in America—to make them agree to a negotiated settlement. After U.S. government officials debated strategy and targeting, after they exchanged and reviewed memoranda discussing how best to pressure Hanoi into acquiescence, it was American pilots like the fifteen naval officers of Squadron 162 who carried out Washington's orders and dropped the bombs on North Vietnam.

A major strike was scheduled at noon on the railroad bridge at Co Trai, twenty-five miles south of Hanoi, and the pilots of 162 who were taking part in the attack wanted to acquaint themselves with the map coordinates of the target before the formal briefing began in the strike operations room. A transit point on the railway to the South, Co Trai was heavily defended by missile and flak sites and would be the first important target for many of the *Oriskany*'s pilots since they arrived on Yankee Station eleven days before. A sliding panel of maps at the front of the ready room showed North Vietnam in varying degrees of close-up.

When the bombing campaign had begun more than a year earlier, on March 2, 1965, farmers made up 80 percent of North Vietnam's laborers and agriculture accounted for nearly half the gross national product, estimated at 1.5 billion dollars, an amount much less than the annual revenues of any of a dozen American corporations. In a country of nineteen million inhabitants, rice was the chief crop, and since rice needed an abundance of water in its early stages of growth, the impression an American pilot got of the country from the air, on the east, was of watery green fields divided into checkerboard patterns by dirt embankments—dikes molded by hand to hold water in the ricefields, connected by ditches to drain them. The dikes also protected the mature rice from the flooding caused by the country's many rivers during the downpours of the monsoon season, between October and May, when 85 percent of the high annual rainfall occurred. Fertilizer was second in importance only to water in growing rice, and because of the scarcity of chemicals, animal and human excrement were used in the ricefields, which produced a pervasive odor of night soil unnoticed by the Vietnamese but immediately apparent to the Americans who were forced to bail out after their planes were hit by antiaircraft fire. In the ricelands, strange-looking limestone hills and ridges jutted up in unexpected places. The delta formed by the Red River gave way on the north and west to mountains covered by jungle.

Despite the primitive aspects of the economy, there was nothing underdeveloped about the antiaircraft system the North Vietnamese had installed in their ricefields and villages with the help of Russian and Chinese technicians. The Soviet SA-2 Guideline missile, thirty-five feet long and carrying a warhead of three hundred and forty-nine pounds, exploded in an orange fireball that could be seen for miles around. The number of missile battalions was steadily growing in 1966. Each unit contained six missiles, plus radar, computers, and generators. The assemblage was mobile enough to be moved to a new position within twenty-four hours, and the missiles were rotated among three hundred different sites. The SAMs, as pilots called the missiles, were psychologically the more frightening—you could watch them coming and coming—but the flak, or shellbursts from antiaircraft guns, was the more effective in bringing down American planes. Already, there were seven thousand antiaircraft installations, firing a total of eighteen thousand tons of ammunition at U.S. planes each month. It seemed to the pilots, moreover, that everybody in the country, from young girls to old men, had a rifle pointing skyward when they flew over.

Ready Room 4, which smelled vaguely like an athletic locker room because of the sweat-damp flight suits hanging on the walls, served as a squadron office and a family room for the pilots of 162, where bombing raids were planned by day and a Hollywood movie, with popcorn, was shown each night. An astrological sketch of Orion the Hunter decorated the outside door. Inside the room were sixteen brown leather airplane chairs, grimy and worn. The front wall was a complex of maps and screens. A twenty-three-inch TV monitor, connected to the ship's closed circuit, showing takeoffs and landings on the flight deck, overlooked the room from the right. A woodcarving of a headhunter stood between a coffee urn and a ten-gallon water can. Most naval air squadrons had nicknames as a morale factor and 162 was known as "The Hunters," although the squadron had written to ask Charles Schulz, creator of the *Peanuts* comic strip, for permission to use the drawing of his Snoopy character as the squadron insignia on the tail of its airplanes.

On the morning of July 19, 1966, Richard Bellinger, the commanding officer of 162, was the first to arrive in Ready Room 4. Bellinger was annoyed to find that once again two folding cots had been left open by junior officers who had passed the night on standby alert. The ready room, unlike the junior officers' personal rooms, was air conditioned; and the younger pilots enjoyed getting the chance to sleep there. The night before, the *Oriskany's* passageways had registered ninety-four degrees Fahrenheit at 10:00 P.M. Bellinger began to dismantle the cots, and Rick Adams, a junior officer who had used one of the beds, returned from breakfast and finished the work.

It was difficult for Bellinger to stay angry with Rick Adams for very long. Bellinger and his wife had no children, and Rick, who was twenty-five, had become almost like a son. Navy pilots flew under a two-plane buddy system for mutual support, usually linking a senior officer to a junior officer, and Rick had been Bellinger's wingman on the *Oriskany's* first combat cruise in 1965. Adams had dropped out of the University of Minnesota after majoring in philosophy for three years and had spent time in Aspen skiing before he signed up for the Naval Aviation Cadet program. On one of their first strikes near Hanoi, Rick had calmly radioed Bellinger, "Hey, Belly, look behind you." Bellinger looked, just in time to see two missiles hurtling up toward him. He went into a sharp turn and they missed. "You could at least get a little excited," Bellinger told Adams. That flight cemented their friendship, and at the end of the cruise when Bellinger, as the new squadron commanding officer, had the opportunity to select six veterans to return for the 1966 cruise, Rick was the first one he chose. The rest were sent to teach tactics at naval air stations in the States, and the squadron was filled out by new men, pilots such as Dick Wyman and John (Black Mac) MacDonald, who, along with Rick, were to become known as some of the best on Yankee Station.

Rick had found the 1965 cruise a little disappointing. He had been trained as a fighter pilot, and he went on his first flight over North Vietnam fully expecting to fight MiGs. He scanned the skies, looking for a smoke trail, a glint of canopy, anything that would reveal the presence of an enemy plane. But the North Vietnamese had few MiGs and even fewer well-trained pilots. They quickly lost five planes when they first challenged the Americans in the summer of 1965, and they just as quickly changed their tactics. Instead of confronting the Americans directly in air-to-air combat, they mainly used the MiGs for psychological purposes. The presence of a MiG in the sky forced American tactical bombers to jettison their bombs to evade or fight more effectively and caused them to dive into the range of antiaircraft fire. Thus the MiGs could often thwart an American mission simply by taking off. Frustratingly for Rick Adams, the enemy planes remained ghosts.

In October 1965, Adams had been hit by a missile. He and Bellinger were separated from the strike group, flying over a small valley, hoping to catch a MiG by surprise. Rick saw the flash and felt a sharp thump. It was, he said, like being in a car when someone kicked on the side. He looked in his mirror and saw that his right wing was on fire. The normal way to eject was to reach up with both hands and pull the face curtain down, triggering a charge that shot the pilot and seat out of the cockpit. Adams pulled the curtain down with one hand almost to the point of ejection and continued to fly as long as he could.

"The number of Americans who jumped out of airplanes prematurely was endless," said Adams, explaining his decision years later. "They caught on fire. Someone yelled 'Eject!' And out they went to become prisoners of war."

He made it back to sea, suffering only burned hands before he was forced to eject, and was picked up by a helicopter and taken to a destroyer. He was the first pilot hit by a missile to escape death or capture. The tale of his panache in riding out a burning airplane spread throughout the fleet.

On the morning of July 19, 1966, Rick Adams was not scheduled to fly against the bridge at Co Trai. Nor was it likely he would fly any more strikes against North Vietnam. The week before, four days after the *Oriskany* arrived on Yankee Station, Rick had been shot down for the second time, on this occasion by antiaircraft fire. He was the first American of the war to be downed twice and rescued, and the navy had decided that was enough.

To the other pilots, Rick had become a Saint Christopher, a four-leaf clover, a rabbit's tail, a good luck charm to be touched before a mission; and as Squadron 162 gathered in Ready Room 4, he was the center of attention. By 9:00 A.M., Dick Wyman, Black Mac, Jim Nunn, Terry Dennison, and the rest, all the pilots but one, had taken their assigned chairs and were sipping coffee and talking quietly. Cal Swanson, the squadron's executive officer, the only one missing, was the flight leader of the men from 162 who were taking part in the Co Trai raid.

2

IT WASN'T the ambient noise of the aircraft carrier, the whir and clank of machinery, or even the sticky heat that had kept Cal Swanson awake the night before. Swanson tossed and turned, thinking about the bridge at Co Trai. This would be his first strike on North Vietnam. Normally, he picked up a book, read for a couple of hours, and fell asleep. But Swanson, who was analytical, recognized his prestrike anxiety, and finally, in the early morning hours of Tuesday, he lay without moving, his arms folded under his head, staring into the darkness.

Commander Charles A. Lindbergh Swanson was the way he was listed in U.S. Navy records, service number 508275/1310. The rank of commander was equal to that of lieutenant colonel in the army or air force. Born five months after the first solo flight over the Atlantic, he was named by his Swedish immigrant parents, farmers who'd settled in Greeley, Colorado, in honor of the Lone Eagle, who was also of Swedish descent. But Lindy, as he was called when he was growing up, bore little physical resemblance to his namesake. He stood five foot, eight inches. He had a round, bland face and the beginnings of a slump. His closely-cropped blond hair looked white, adding to the impression that he was older than thirty-nine. Being picked as the executive officer of Squadron VF-162, the navy's newest fighter squadron, he considered the luckiest thing that had ever happened to him. If he did well as the number two officer during 1966, he would be promoted to squadron commander for the 1967 cruise. From there, anything was possible, even two stars. Making admiral was not something Swanson allowed himself to think about, but he was determined to succeed in his new job. Only a year ago, his career had seemed at an end. The trouble stemmed from his tour on the USS *Midway* as the catapult officer. The catapult was a monster piece of machinery concealed under the flight deck that was used to hurl an airplane off the carrier at 190 miles-per-hour in two and a half seconds. Many things could, and often did, go wrong with the catapult.

The *Midway*'s skipper called Swanson to the bridge and said, "We're going to make a change. I'm not satisfied with the catapult situation, and I'm relieving you at this time." Cal knew the navy well enough not to try to argue. He returned to his cabin feeling as though the sky had fallen in. Getting fired from his job could have been a disaster had it been entered on his permanent record. But Swanson was near the end of his tour on the *Midway*, and the skipper chose to treat the relief as a normal transfer of duty stations. Although it could have been worse, Swanson knew he would not escape certain consequences. Naval aviation was small enough so that one's service reputation, which rose and fell on gossip at the officers' club, was as important as a fitness report. Sure enough, when the promotion board met, Cal was not promoted to the rank of commander with his contemporaries. If he were passed over a second time, he could start looking for a job in civilian life. That would be the end.

To his wife, Nell, there were two Cal Swansons—one before and one after the *Midway* incident.

When they met, Nell had been a navy lieutenant in charge of personnel at Patuxent River, in Maryland. Cal, a young lieutenant, was going through the test pilot school there. She stood five-one, weighed ninety-six pounds, and spoke in an odd little girl's voice, using giggles as punctuation marks. Underneath the disarming exterior, though, was a shrewd and tough woman who had lost her father when she was fourteen and had worked after school every day in order to escape a Massachusetts mill town. She was pretty and had appeared on a U.S. Navy recruiting poster.

"That was a humbling experience for my husband to be passed over," Nell said. "It matured him very quickly. His attitude now I call 'blood-and-guts.' He didn't have that then. He was just a flyboy and la-de-dah. But he became a really good naval officer."

Swanson already had been assigned as the executive officer of a squadron commanded by Jim Stockdale on the USS *Ticonderoga* when he learned he had been passed over. Jim Stockdale was an up-and-comer, a good man to be associated with, which added to Cal's humiliation that he couldn't take the job. Depressed, Swanson left the States on assignment to Japan. Soon after he got there he heard that the Military Assistance Command, Vietnam, was looking for an air officer. MACV was expanding and needed someone with a reconnaissance background to help coordinate surveillance missions over Laos. Swanson had no recon experience, but when no one in Japan wanted to go, he volunteered and was accepted.

He arrived in Saigon in July of 1964. MACV was located in a French-style colonial building on Pasteur Street. It was a time of confusion, which presented an opportunity for quick advancement to an officer ready to work hard. In the topsy-turvy way MACV had grown, an army colonel was in charge of coordinating out-of-country air operations. The colonel was not an aviator. Cal became his assistant and made himself indispensable. When the colonel's tour was up, Swanson took over his job. He was in the combat operations center at MACV when the Gulf of Tonkin incidents occurred in August 1964 and led to the first American air strikes on North Vietnam.

Jim Stockdale was in the thick of things in the gulf. Maybe Swanson, too, would have been there had his *Midway* tour turned out differently. By now, though, Cal was happy with his work, and so were his superiors. He was awarded a Legion of Merit and received a personal letter of commendation from General William Westmoreland, the MACV commander.

One day Swanson went down to greet an old friend who was skippering a minesweeper that had just arrived in the Saigon harbor. "Hi, Pete, how you doing," said Cal.

"Congratulations, Commander," replied Pete.

"You've got to be kidding," said Cal.

"No, it's been on the wires for four days."

They returned to the minesweeper and went through the wastebasket in the radio room. There it was. Commander C. A. L. Swanson. He would take an F-8 training course at the Miramar Naval Air Station in San Diego, California, and then be assigned as the executive officer to Commander Richard Bellinger in Squadron VF-162 on the USS *Oriskany*.

It was 1965 and the *Oriskany* was deployed on her first combat cruise on Yankee Station, with Jim Stockdale as her air wing commander. By the time Cal finished training in the F-8 Crusader, the ship had returned to San Diego and was preparing for her second combat cruise, to begin in mid-1966.

The F-8 Crusader was a long-tailed fighter with a fuselage stretching a little over fifty-four feet. The swept-wing plane was slung low to the ground and had a jet intake that gave its nose a deadly, sharklike appearance. Despite the plane's size, the cockpit was cramped. The pilot sat with his left hand gripping the throttle, a short lever on the port side. His right hand held the stick—the steering mechanism—between his legs. On the floor were the rudders, looking like two oversized brake pedals, which helped make coordinated turns. In front of him and on both sides were switches and dials, including the gyro, compass, air speed, altitude indicator, oil pressure, exhaust gas temperature, fuel flow, radar scope, angle of attack, and numerous others.

The F-8 was put into service by Chance Vought in 1955 as a pure fighter. The handgrip of the stick had a trigger similar to one found on a rifle, which was used to fire the four 20-mm guns. Two air-to-air missiles, the AIM-9 Sidewinder, an inexpensive rocket with less than two dozen moving parts, were set on fuselage rails. Later, a number of F-8s were modified by adding two wing pylons to carry external ordnance: bombs, missiles, and air-to-ground rockets. By punching a button on the stick, the F-8 pilot triggered a small explosive charge—an ejector cartridge—in the bomb rack, which pushed the bomb away from the plane and sent it on its way to the target.

The value of the F-8 as a bomber was disputed among pilots. It was not as good as the F-4 Phantom, which was developed by the navy after the F-8 as a pure fighter and then modified to carry bombs. The

F-4 was adopted by the air force and had become a mainstay of the U.S. arsenal. It flew from a number of the newer carriers, but was too large and heavy for use on the *Oriskany*. The F-8 did not even match the much smaller A-4 Skyhawk, a McDonnell Douglas light attack plane initially developed as an expendable carrier-based nuclear bomber but now used as the *Oriskany's* primary conventional bomber.

Adding to its liabilities, the F-8 was also the most dangerous plane ever brought aboard an aircraft carrier. The Crusader was nearly three times as likely to have a major accident as the F-4 Phantom. A pilot who let his attention wander was gone. The plane was, said the pilots, "unforgiving." You had only ten feet of ramp clearance to land the F-8 on the *Oriskany,* and it was easy to misjudge the approach and hit the back edge of the flight deck, especially on a rainy night, when a turbulent sea made it like trying to land on a rocking chair. The danger, however, appealed to many pilots. And the F-8 was a single-pilot fighter, unlike the F-4 Phantom, which had a radar intercept officer riding shotgun, a GIB, pilots condescendingly called him—Guy in Back.

That they were considered second-class bombers and often used to knock out antiaircraft sites while the A-4s hit the main target did not bother the pilots of Squadron 162. They thought of themselves with no little pride as the only "gunfighters" in the navy, honest-to-God fighter pilots. They liked the F-8. It was fast. John Glenn, later a U.S. senator, had set a coast-to-coast speed record in a Crusader in 1957, flying from San Diego to New York in three hours and twenty-three minutes. To them, bombing was a sideline brought on by the requirements of the Vietnam War.

Cal Swanson was pleased to be assigned to Squadron 162. The only jarring note came from Nell, which caused arguments between them. Nell liked most of the fifteen pilots in the squadron. She was especially fond of Dick Wyman, a young lieutenant from Kittery, Maine, who was handsome and polite. Nell could tell by his ruddy, windburned face that Dick Wyman had been around the sea all his life; and he had that combination of masculinity and sensitivity women found attractive. But Nell could not abide Richard Bellinger, Cal's new squadron commander, "Belly," they called him.

No, that was not exactly true. Bellinger could be charming. He was always pleasant to her, always smiling and joking, never seemed to be depressed or in a bad mood. He was intelligent and had an advanced degree in political science from Boston University. But Bellinger drank like no one Nell had ever seen. And she resented him for cheating on his wife, Norma, a loyal woman, exuberantly, without apology. All fighter pilots were flamboyant—certainly, most of them. They were relentless in paying homage to their self-image, and over the years Nell had learned to accept that. But *flamboyant* wasn't the word for Bellinger. In the United States Navy, there was no one quite like Commander Richard M. Bellinger. Cal, for his part, told Nell he didn't want to hear a word of criticism of Belly. He was going to be the loyal subordinate. That's the way the game was played.

On the morning of July 19, 1966, as the other pilots gathered in Ready Room 4, Cal Swanson got up and dressed and went to get something to eat. He wore a set of green jungle fatigues he had brought from Saigon. He was probably the only pilot to have served on the ground in South Vietnam. The traditional fighter pilot breakfast was a Coke and a cigarette, but Swanson liked something more substantial—though light—before he flew, and the food on the *Oriskany* was excellent, the best in the fleet.

3

NEITHER HAD JOHN IARROBINO gotten much sleep the night before. As the *Oriskany*'s captain, he seldom spent more than three hours a night in his bunk, and that was usually divided into fifteen-minute catnaps, taken in his uniform with shoes off, in the small sea cabin to the rear of the bridge. A well-knit man with massive hands, Iarrobino had the dark features of his Italian father and the warm blue eyes of his Irish mother. The captain years ago had given up cigarettes and coffee. He relied on fruit juice and his own equanimity to see him through the long hours on the bridge.

The *Oriskany*'s flight deck, which stretched nine hundred and eleven feet, was oblong, had a tapering bow and stern, and was covered with a black nonskid material. Most of the equipment on the flight deck could be retracted and stowed, although the deck was usually full of tightly parked airplanes, their wings folded, the long tails of the F-8s sticking over the ship's sides. Standing on the flight deck when it was empty of airplanes, one was only dimly aware of the angled deck, the two catapults, the elevators from the hangar deck, the arresting wires, the barrier net, and the jet-blast deflectors. The ship's dominating feature, the only thing that caught the eye, was the superstructure called the "island." Located on the starboard side, about the middle of the ship, the island was tapered at the bottom and rose high into the air, its greatest bulk appearing at the top, an erector-set assembly of cylinders, rectangles, balconies, ladders, pipes, hatchways, topped by radar and radio antennas. The main row of windows belonged to the bridge. Here Captain Iarrobino sat in a black elevated barber's chair, which swiveled to give him a commanding view of the ship. Above him, in a glass-enclosed compartment, was the air boss, who controlled the action on the flight deck with an impatient voice blaring through loudspeakers.

The *Oriskany's* heavy operating schedule pushed the carrier to her limits. Much of the burden fell on the ship's company—or permanent crew—which was distinct from the smaller group of men who served the airplanes and who left the ship when a combat cruise was completed and the air wing was stationed at a land base. On the flight deck they wore bulky "Mickey Mouse" headsets for radio communications and to protect their ears from the engine noise; they also wore bright jerseys color-coded to their work—red, green, blue, yellow, brown, white with black checks—so that an officer could tell at a glance if anyone was out of place. Despite the precautions, accidents still occurred. The crew's average age was twenty. The stronger and less educated were assigned to the flight deck, just as their army counterparts in the South were assigned to infantry companies. A kid got sucked up in a jet intake or crushed by an airplane more frequently than the navy liked to admit.

Captain Iarrobino had asked the officer of the deck to alert him when the *Oriskany* began her approach on the ammunition supply ship. The daily twelve hours of air operations used up more bombs and ammunition than the *Oriskany's* storage magazines could hold, and it was necessary to get resupplied at sea nearly every other day. Iarrobino liked to be on the bridge when underway replenishment took place. Actually, underway rep wasn't so hard once you got the hang of it and he enjoyed teaching his senior officers how to do it, the same way he took pleasure in showing civilian visitors the *Oriskany*'s bridge and watching their faces when he told them that the small brass wheel there in the center, no bigger than a car's steering wheel, was what turned the aircraft carrier. In this modern age ships had power steering.

"Get yourself positioned several hundred yards astern from the supply ship," Iarrobino said to the officers he was teaching. "Reverse engines to stop your forward momentum. Then pick up the same speed as the supply ship and throw your lines over to her decks." It sounded easy, but learning when to back down—reverse engines—was difficult. "It's just a matter of feel," Captain Iarrobino would say, "like putting the brakes on an automobile." Returning to his seat, he would add, "It's yours. I'll stay here and watch you. Just relax and do the best you can."

The senior officers appreciated his training. They knew that other skippers, many of them, wouldn't take the time to bother. The young sailors also liked the captain and the way he shambled across the flight deck saying "hi" to everyone in sight. When the ship put in at the Philippines, Iarrobino invited all ranks above lieutenant to a barbecue that he prepared himself.

Today, however, was not the time to teach anyone the techniques of underway replenishment. Iarrobino had been told by his staff that the Russian trawler, the *Gidrofon,* was trying to make trouble. He would direct the resupply operation himself. He was determined that nothing should happen to the *Oriskany*. His brother Charles had been the *Oriskany*'s skipper three years earlier, and Charles, now working for the Joint Chiefs of Staff at the Pentagon, had telephoned when he heard the news of John's selection and said, "Make sure you take good care of the Iarrobino yacht." Charles and John were the only two brothers in U.S. Navy history to skipper the same capital ship. Not bad for the children of an Italian immigrant from a poverty-stricken village outside Naples who had settled in Massachusetts and become a chauffeur. Not bad, either, for a guy who had attended Boston College for two years. Most aircraft carrier skippers were U.S. Naval Academy graduates. Cal Swanson believed that Captain Iarrobino would easily wind up an admiral. He would be one of those officers made by the Vietnam War.

The *Oriskany* too seemed to have been waiting for Vietnam to come along. Her history was as near a blank page as a U.S. aircraft carrier's

and Stockdale radioed, "All boats hit, two still underway toward the coast, one dead in the water and burning."

On Tuesday morning, August 4, 1964, Stockdale read newspaper reports wired to the carrier that said President Lyndon Johnson had met with State Department and Pentagon officials. They had decided not to retaliate for the attack, choosing to consider it an isolated incident caused by an impulsive PT-boat commander. Another destroyer, the USS *Turner Joy,* joined the *Maddox,* and Stockdale spent most of Tuesday afternoon flying guard duty over the two ships. When he left the destroyers at about 6:00 P.M., the cloud cover was dropping and the sea becoming choppy with whitecaps. As he parked his airplane on the *Tico,* Stockdale could see lightning flashes in the northwest. He finished dinner in the wardroom, conferred with his maintenance officer, and then walked into the squadron ready room. No flights were scheduled that night. Two Crusaders were on ready alert, spotted on the catapults, fueled and armed, engines not running but with pilots in the cockpits, ready to be launched. It was hot and muggy. The ready room's air conditioner was chuffing out waves of damp air, engaged in a losing battle. Stockdale knew that the lightning-charged sky in the Tonkin Gulf could be expected to play tricks on old-fashioned radar. He was talking to one of his pilots when he realized that a couple of propeller-driven Spads were tuning up to be launched. An officer from the combat information center stuck his head into the ready room and motioned Stockdale outside. "Are they ready?" he asked. Stockdale said he didn't know what was going on. The officer told him that radio intercepts suggested the *Maddox* and the *Turner Joy* might be attacked and that the admiral's staff had ordered the Spads out to cover the destroyers. After the two Spads were launched, the two F-8s on ready alert would follow.

Stockdale grabbed his gear and ran to the flight deck. The dark night, the bad weather, and the Crusader's high accident rate made him think that as the squadron commander he should be the one to go. Only he knew how the North Vietnamese PT boats maneuvered and how they looked up close. Neither of the two pilots who were seconds from being launched had been on Sunday's action. And Jim Stockdale was just plain aggressive—he wasn't about to miss this chance. He climbed on one of the F-8s and shouted above the noise of the jet, "Unstrap and get out! I'm getting in!"

At 9:35 on that August night, there was constant radio talk between the two American destroyers about radar contacts closing from the east, followed by torpedo warnings and sightings. Both ships were taking evasive action, turning frantically, and the *Turner Joy* began firing her guns at the presumed PT boats.

"I had the best seat in the house from which to detect boats—if there were any," said Stockdale. "I didn't have to look through the surface haze and spray like the destroyers did, and yet I could see the destroyers' every move vividly."

When one destroyer radioed that she was taking fire from a PT boat two thousand yards to the left, Stockdale swung around and fired his rockets and guns at the spot. He was trying desperately to find the targets and sweating heavily. "Now calm down and think, Jim," he told himself, after an hour of fruitless search. "You're getting caught up in this thing. Watch that altimeter. There's something wrong out here. Those destroyers are talking about hits, but where are the metal-to-metal sparks? And the boat wakes—where are they? And boat gun flashes? The day before yesterday I saw all those signs of small-boat combat in broad daylight! Any of those telltale indicators would stand out like beacons in this black hole we're operating in."

When he landed on the *Tico*, he was met by ten officers in the ready room. Someone asked what the hell was going on out there. Stockdale replied that he had seen nothing but black sea and American firepower. The mood of the debriefing turned hilarious, with Stockdale illustrating the fiasco with elaborate gestures, playing the role of the destroyers and his Crusader.

"Have a look at this," someone said. "This is what Herrick, the commodore on the *Maddox*, has been putting out, flash precedence, plain language, to Washington and the world in general tonight."

It was a communication log. On it were all the messages the *Maddox* had dispatched since Stockdale left the *Ticonderoga*. At first glance, it looked like the stuff he had heard on his radio, the feverish reports of two victimized destroyers being attacked. Then on the last page and a half, the log did an abrupt turnaround. Messages expressed doubt about the validity of earlier messages. There was skepticism that the PT boats had actually existed. It was clear to Stockdale that Commodore Herrick, the commander of the two destroyers, had finally realized that the incident was the result of confusion and was cautiously trying to set the record straight without making himself and his staff look like dolts. Herrick urged his superiors to make a complete evaluation of the mixup before any further action was taken.

The next morning at five, Jim Stockdale was awakened by the junior officer of the deck. The ship's captain sent him to tell Stockdale to get ready to lead a reprisal attack on North Vietnam, ordered by Washington.

"Reprisal for what?"

"For last night's attack on the destroyers, sir."

In SEPTEMBER 1965, Rick Adams heard that the North Vietnamese had announced they'd shot down and captured James Bond. Adams chuckled. It was the first indication that Jim was okay. The name was James Bond Stockdale. He used Double-Oh-Seven as his radio call sign. The *Oriskany's* crew had painted 007 on all their tow tractors, starter jeeps, forklifts, and crash cranes. The North Vietnamese, Rick Adams said, would have their hands full with James Bond. He might be tortured and forced to talk. But he would never disclose any big secret. You could bet on that.

Captain John Iarrobino did not know Jim Stockdale. He had taken command of the *Oriskany* a few months after Stockdale was shot down. But he felt Stockdale's spiritual presence, his aura, on the ship. The *Oriskany's* pilots were giving it their all—which didn't necessarily mean you had to like the way the war was being fought. Iarrobino often talked to Commander Spruett, the air wing commander who replaced Stockdale. The captain made it clear that what was said shouldn't go any farther, because it would be bad for morale. They spoke about how stupid it was to expose their pilots to killing antiaircraft fire to hit a dumpy bridge like Co Trai.

"Knock it out today," Captain Iarrobino said. "And they'll repair it tomorrow."

4

TARGETING. The whole mess could be summed up by the way targets were selected, so far as Grant Sharp was concerned. Admiral Ulysses S. Grant Sharp, Jr., was commander of all American forces in the

Pacific. A short, thin man of fifty-eight, Sharp seldom raised his voice. About the strongest expletive he used was "doggone." But Grant Sharp could get exercised when he thought about how Washington was tying down his pilots with restrictions that, in his opinion, violated the principles of warfare. Washington approved targets to be hit on a two-week basis. Sharp thought this was a dumb way to run things. But at least it represented an improvement over the first days of the air war, when strikes were directed to take place on a certain day, with no consideration given to weather conditions, to whether the target was socked in or not. The way it worked now, Sharp talked to the air force and navy in Vietnam and forwarded their recommendations to the Joint Chiefs of Staff in the Pentagon. The JCS added or deleted targets and sent the list to the secretary of defense. Before it got to the secretary, however, a bunch of "whiz-kid" civilians at defense and state added their comments and suggestions for changes. When the list finally reached the president, he decided which targets would be hit, and he did this at a Tuesday luncheon at the White House, attended by the secretaries of state and defense, the national security adviser, and the presidential press secretary. No military man, not even the chairman of the Joint Chiefs, was usually present until late 1967. Lyndon Johnson was there poring over a map with names he could never pronounce correctly, putting his big thumb down, saying ya'll can hit this, or ya'll can't hit that.

Lyndon Johnson wanted to maintain tight civilian control over the military, which was fair enough, but Sharp suspected that his attitude was greatly influenced by Robert McNamara. The secretary of defense may have been a highly regarded executive of the Ford Motor Company and a brilliant guy with statistics, but to Sharp, McNamara was the king of ambivalence, a man of stern visage and imperious manner, yet essentially a muddlehead who wanted it both ways. After the war, Sharp was not surprised to read a memo Robert McNamara sent Johnson in mid-1965, in which he advised the president how the air war should be fought.

"Emphasize the threat," McNamara told Johnson. *"It should be structured to capitalize on fear of future attacks. At any time pressure on North Vietnam depends not upon the current level of bombing, but rather upon the credible threat of future destruction which could be avoided by agreeing to some settlement in negotiations.*

"Minimize the loss of North Vietnamese face. The program should be designed to make it politically easy for North Vietnam to enter negotiations and to make concessions during the negotiations. It may be politically easier for North Vietnam to accept negotiations and / or to make concessions at a time when bombing of their territory is not currently taking place. . . .

"Avoid undue risks and costs. The program should avoid bombing which runs a high risk of escalation into war with the Soviets or China, and which is likely to appall allies and friends."

In other words, McNamara, Johnson's chief military adviser on the civilian side, was saying that the United States should do just enough bombing to frighten the North Vietnamese into possible concessions, stopping periodically to see if they were ready to give up.

That was not the way Admiral Sharp, as one of America's top-ranking military men, thought the air war should be fought. North Vietnam was underdeveloped, with a weak economy based on growing rice. The Pentagon could find only ninety-four significant military targets in the whole country. Baltimore probably had more than that. In Sharp's opinion, it didn't require much complicated thought to plan an effective air campaign. North Vietnam was not exactly Germany during World War Two.

There had been several retaliatory attacks after the Tonkin Gulf incidents in 1964 and later, in 1965, after the Viet Cong hit a U.S. barracks in South Vietnam. Then, on March 2, 1965, the first attack of the official air war, code named Rolling Thunder, took place. The strike by one hundred and four American and nineteen South Vietnamese planes hit an ammo dump and small naval base in the southern part of North Vietnam at Quang Khe. The military establishment considered the target insignificant, and fifteen days later the Joint Chiefs of Staff submitted a four-phase bombing program to Secretary of Defense McNamara. It would take twelve weeks, they said, to isolate North Vietnam and stop Hanoi from being supplied by China and Russia and then to destroy the country's military and industrial capacity. The first phase would be aimed at blocking North Vietnamese lines of communication—railroads and bridges—in the southern part of the country. The second phase would destroy overland links with China. The third phase would close North Vietnam's sea ports—the mining of Haiphong a priority—and the final phase would be a windup period, devoted to restriking all previous targets as necessary.

Twelve weeks. If you were going to use air power, said the Pentagon, that's how it should be done. It was not the military's job to consider the political implications of such a campaign, and Admiral Sharp and other uniformed leaders would never change their minds as to the most effective way to bring Hanoi to heel, as they watched their recommendations being ignored or postponed by civilian leaders.

At the beginning of the air war, U.S. planes flew roughly every other day, hitting targets only in the southern part of North Vietnam, mainly the transportation network. By the summer of 1965 they began to strike north of Hanoi. In August 1965, about sixty-five planes were taking part in the strikes; the following month the figure reached one hundred and twenty. The tempo of the air war grew until Christmastime, when a thirty-seven-day bombing halt was called to see if the North Vietnamese were ready to give in.

They weren't.

The attacks resumed on January 31, 1966, and by the time Cal Swanson and Squadron 162 arrived on Yankee Station, on July 8, 1966, the Uong Bi power plant, the Hanoi-Haiphong Highway, and various petroleum supply dumps had been hit for the first time. The Co Trai bridge was one of the targets parceled out to American pilots as part of Washington's campaign to put pressure on Hanoi while avoiding, in Robert McNamara's words, "undue risks and costs."

5 · Dick Wyman

I GOT AIRSICK in primary flight training. My instructor threatened to wash me out of the program. I said, "No, I love flying; it's just that, well, I get to flipping upside down in that thing, and I have to barf." He ordered me to go to sick bay. I said, "Yessir," but didn't go. In those days, right before Vietnam, they didn't need many pilots, so they were really tough, and if you went over there twice for airsickness you were out the door. I used to roll up the edges of the barf bag and hide it under my seat. I got so I could throw up and keep flying without missing a beat. The airsickness was psychological, I think. I overcame it and wasn't sick again, until I got to advanced training, and then I got sick the first time I flew with an oxygen mask on.

I entered flight training as an ensign. My brother went to the Maine Maritime Academy, and I followed him there—that's how I got the rank. We've been New Englanders for generations. My father's grandfather was a shipwright. I'd always piddled around the water. I was a lobsterman as a kid, used to make a lot of money from it after school. Actually, my brother Harry accused me of coming along behind and trying to outdo him. I didn't consciously do that, but looking back now, I might have. There's eleven months' difference between us, and we fought all the time; Mother just finally gave up and let us go to it. I emerged second-best but I always tried. As a matter of fact, I did beat Harry when I got to school. My last year I was selected as the academy's battalion commander, the top-ranking cadet.

You graduated from the maritime academy either as a third assistant engineer in the merchant marine, or as a third mate. I was an engineer because I used to tinker with cars and everything. But I decided engine rooms were miserable to work in—hot, steamy, horrible—and I wasn't going to sea like that. In those days you had to accept five years in the naval reserve. I'd read some books about flying, so I decided to try for naval aviation. I'll be honest with you. I was after the thrills. I've always liked to dare the edge. When I was a freshman in football, I was a small guy, at least compared to the others, but I could tackle and hit with the best of them. I never thought of getting hurt.

In flight school you got academic and flying grades, and the two scores were combined. I was a good pilot and had very good flight grades, but my academic grades were terrible. I hated studying. I'd been in school all my life. I said, well, now I'm going to raise a little hell—stand at the bar, make fighter pilot talk, chase beautiful women, that kind of stuff. After primary they assigned you either to prop-driven planes or jets. When I got to the assignment office in Corpus Christi, ten guys were already waiting outside and others coming. They told me only two jet slots were available and that I didn't have a prayer of getting one.

The assignment officer asked everybody the same question: "Why do you want to go to jets?"

"Sir," I said, "what I love about flying is air-to-air gunnery, acrobatics, and formation flying. Props don't do that. I want one of those jet seats, and I want it bad."

He said, "How long do you think it will take you to get over to Kingsville?"

"Sir, I'll leave in five minutes."

"Don't you have a family?"

"I'll be gone in ten minutes, I promise you."

"Okay, if you get there in time to check in by noon, you can have that seat."

I had a wife and daughter. We'd just moved into an efficiency apartment. I opened the door and told Ardyce, "Pack everything. We're leaving."

She said, "What?"

I said, "We're going to Kingsville, Texas, right now." Within five minutes we were out and gone. I broke the speed limit all the way.

I was two-thirds the way through advanced training before I had an unsatisfactory flight. The instructor would take you up in an A-4 and do all kinds of maneuvers to confuse your inner ear and then suddenly say, "Okay, you've got it." The airplane might be going straight up and you were supposed to recover it. That got to me; I became nauseated. What I loved were my solo flights. The excitement of graduating from flight school was not, hey, I'm a big man now that I've got my wings. For me, it was getting rid of that guy sitting in my backseat grading me all the time.

I was sent to a utility squadron in Puerto Rico. That was a disappointment. I wanted fighters. You never told anyone you were in a utility squadron. It was embarrassing. Our job was to fly drones to check radar patterns for surface-to-air missiles. The drone was an old airplane under remote control. You'd come along in an F-8 and pick up control from the guy on the ground and fly the drone out to the ship where they were going to shoot at it. Then you'd turn control over to the ship's remote station, and they'd take their shot.

This was 1964, at the time of the Tonkin Gulf incidents. I wrote a letter to navy headquarters in Washington and asked to be sent to a fighter squadron. I said I thought my place was in combat. Well, they gave me fighters fifteen months after I was assigned to the utility squadron, which was unusual since you normally had to stay three years in your first squadron, but they didn't send me to the West Coast, where

I wanted to go. I was assigned to Jacksonville, Florida. If anyone was going into combat, I knew, it would be the West Coast pilots. There were two air navies at the time—East Coast and West Coast. And they didn't mix. West Coast aviators thought pilots from the East Coast did not fly well and were losers, to put it mildly.

In Jacksonville I let it be known I wanted to go west. I got a phone call on Christmas Eve, 1965. My commanding officer: "I've got some real bad news for you, Dick."

"What's that, Skipper?"

"I hate to break it to you on Christmas Eve. You're going to an F-8 squadron on the West Coast. And from there to Vietnam."

"Great!"

"You mean you're not upset?"

"Best news I've heard, Skipper."

He planned to call Commander Bellinger to tell him I was coming. I said, "When you talk to him, please ask if there's any big rush for me to report in, because if not, I'll go home to Maine on leave and then head west."

He talked to him and Bellinger said, "No, we don't have any planes right now and we're not doing much. Tell him to take some leave." I took thirty days; then Ardyce and I loaded our daughter and new son into a blue Chevy stationwagon and swung south to avoid as much of the winter as we could and soon arrived in California.

The Miramar Naval Air Station was right outside San Diego. The temperature was pleasant. My first thought was, "There's no trees or grass around here." It looked like a desert, a shock after Maine and Florida. But I didn't really care. I hate to say this, but it's true, and Ardyce will be quick to tell you: at that time, when I was twenty-seven, my family, my kids—everything but flying was incidental to me. I was after that thrill. I had spitshined boots and a spotless flight suit. To climb into the cockpit of an F-8, you had to use spring-loaded steps on the side. I'd put my foot in the step with my glove, so it wouldn't mess up the shine on my boots. That's the way I was.

There were a couple of massive hangars at Miramar. Around the sides, on the upper levels, was office space for the squadrons. We were in Ready Room 285 of Hangar Two, on the left side, two flights of stairs up, on the south side of the runway. It was really noisy. I thought there was no rush to check in, so I helped Ardyce find us a place to live, a house near Cal Swanson's in the University City part of San Diego, and then reported to the squadron at nine the next morning.

The ready room was filled with old school-desk chairs. A blackboard was at the front. On the right side was a bar area with cups and donuts and stuff. Several guys were standing around drinking coffee—John (Black Mac) MacDonald, Lee Prost, and Jack Kilpatrick. All of them were from the East Coast and I'd met them before.

I said, "How you guys doing?"

Black Mac looked at me solemnly and said, "Boy, Wyman, are you in a world of shit. The skipper is really pissed off."

I said, "What's he got against me? I don't even know him."

Rick Adams was the duty officer. He said, "Yeah, the skipper's mad because you took leave and were so long in getting here."

I said, "Well, I had a great time."

Rick said, "What did you do?"

"Went skiing."

"Hey, you ski? Let's go some weekend. There's some great places I know."

Commander Bellinger walked in to refill his cup. He didn't fit my image of a fighter pilot. He was six feet tall and way over two hundred pounds. Most of it sagged in the middle. That was his radio call sign: "Belly-One." He looked like a big Irish cop. Bellinger gave me a dirty look and said, "Where the hell have you been?" He got some coffee and told me to come to his office.

I entered and he started, "Goddammit, we've been out here trying to get ready to go to war, and you've been somewhere screwing off."

"I beg your pardon, sir. My commanding officer talked to you on the phone and you said there was no rush. I took leave because I thought I wasn't going to be able to fly if I arrived earlier."

He calmed down a bit but then started yammering about East Coast pilots. "You guys don't know how to fly. We're gonna have to teach you how to be fighter pilots. East Coast pilots are the dregs of naval aviation. If you guys don't shape up, I'll get rid of you pretty damn fast."

That got to my knickers, 'cause I could fly that airplane. But I stood at attention and didn't say a word. Every year a pilot had to pass a written, oral, and flying exam. I'd just got through taking mine. He told me I had to take it over.

42

"As far as we're concerned you guys know nothing."

Four of us were from the East Coast. Cal Swanson had been in Asia and he didn't go either way, just kept quiet. Of the other ten pilots, Rick Adams and another junior officer wanted to be friendly to us but had to hold back. Everybody else was down on us and wanted to see us humiliated. They put instructors in the cockpits with us, said they were going to grade us on how well we did. It was like being back in flight training as raw recruits. I was a lieutenant, the equivalent of captain in the army or air force, but Black Mac was older and a lieutenant commander, and they were doing it to him, too.

Black Mac withdrew socially and wouldn't have anything to do with them after working hours. That wasn't my style. I said to myself, "You aren't going to get me down. I'm going to win this thing." I went to the officers' club, went to parties, drank with them. I never tried to break through the barrier. I just pretended it wasn't there. Butter wouldn't have melted in my mouth. But was I waiting! I knew my number would come up.

They screwed us over for some time. Then one morning Bellinger said he was going to give me an orientation flight, and, afterward, we would go out over the water and have a dogfight. This was what I'd been waiting for. Fighter pilots constantly engaged in air combat maneuvers, practice dogfights. You went up, separated, and came at each other head on. When you passed each other going the other way, that was the signal the fight was on. The first pilot to get on the other's tail—that is, in a position for a shootdown—was the winner. The dogfights established the pecking order of who were the best stick-and-throttle men in the squadron.

So Belly and I went up. What I did was throw some high yo's and then some barrel rolls on him. It didn't take but seconds and I was on his tail. And I just sat there. He kept saying, "Where are you?"

I said, "I'm right here, Skipper."

"Well, where are you?"

"I'm right on your tail."

"Show yourself."

I moved out so he could see me.

"Why didn't you tell me you were that close?" he said gruffly.

We separated and I won again. Three times. I almost stressed my airplane doing it, but I didn't care. I would've pulled the wings off to beat him. Finally he said, "I'm tired of this. Let's knock it off."

Black Mac was a fine pilot. He and the other guys from the East Coast challenged the veterans and beat them in dogfights. All of a sudden we were accepted by the squadron. It was as though we'd been there forever.

Three weeks before leaving for Vietnam, we were scheduled to make a four-plane flight to Chocolate Mountain, a training range near Yuma, Arizona. Belly was supposed to lead, and I was flying his wing. We were assigned to make a low-level high-speed run to the target, drop our bombs, then return to Miramar. We had a precise time to hit the target because other flights were also using the range.

Belly's plane had a malfunction on the runway. We waited for him past the time we should have left to make our schedule. At the last minute Belly said, "Wyman, you've got the lead. Take the flight to Chocolate Mountain." I said, "Roger," and we took off. This was the first low-level flight I'd ever gone on. I wanted to say to the others that "By God, an East Coast pilot can fly as low and fast as anybody." At the same time, I was trying to find a short cut to Yuma, to make up for the time we'd lost. I was down low, blowing sand, flying like a son of a bitch, glancing at the map in my lap to try to find a navigation checkpoint, to see where I was.

I looked at the map and said, "There are some electric power lines running through this area. I'll use them as a checkpoint." Then I looked up and—holy shit!—right in front of me, ready to yank my head off, were those power lines. I pulled back on the stick hard as I could. One power line broke on the side of the intake duct. The next one slashed open the airplane's belly and drove the missile transformers into the nose wheel well. The fire warning lights blinked on. The airplane was making a horrible noise. I radioed one of the other pilots and said, "I got a fire warning light. Check me over."

He moved up beside me. "Hey, you're on fire!"

"What? You sure?"

"Wait a minute. No, I don't think so. It must have been the sun glinting off the titanium."

"Take a look and see what I've got."

"Ah, you got a few holes. And your left wing tip is gone. Do you think you can fly it?"

"Roger."

Miramar was about the same distance as Yuma. We decided to return to home base. I called the tower and said I was coming back with a damaged plane. I got over the field and tried to drop my landing gear. The nose wheel wouldn't come down. I asked the tower for suggestions but they couldn't tell me anything I hadn't already tried. I was going to land and keep the nose up, just ease it onto the runway, and maybe the airplane wouldn't explode. I wasn't scared. Just embarrassed I'd smashed the airplane. I was concerned about what everybody was going to say. It was a good landing. I put it down exactly the way I wanted. I could smell the fumes as the titanium ground off underneath my feet. Before it stopped, I was unstrapping. A crash crewman ran up and said, "That's the fastest I ever saw anybody get out of an airplane." I looked at the mangled thing and shook my head. Then I saw Bellinger walking across the ramp toward us, arms swinging, fists clinched. I said, "Oh, Jesus, I don't want to talk to him now."

An ambulance had arrived in case I was injured. I told the medics, "Quick! Give me a ride to the hangar." I jumped in back and hunkered down. We passed Bellinger going the other way without his seeing me.

Cal Swanson, the executive officer, was at the squadron office. He was nice about it. He wanted to know where the accident had occurred so he could telephone and tell them, yeah, we'd cut the power lines. Some small town in Arizona was plunged into darkness for ten hours.

Commander Bellinger soon returned. He walked in and said, "Stand at attention, right there!"

I braced.

"You've really screwed up our safety record, Wyman. We had a good record till we got you guys from the East Coast." He went on about how lousy we were as pilots and then said, "What do you think we ought to do about this?"

I said, "Sir, I think you ought to do whatever is best for the squadron." I felt like duckshit. I didn't want to lose my wings, but I knew I deserved it.

"What's best for the squadron is that you didn't hit the goddamn power lines to start with."

"Yes, sir."

"Have you ever considered being a shoe salesman?"

"No, sir."

"Well, mister, when I get through with you, you're going to wish you had. Now get out of here."

I changed my clothes and went home.

"Ardyce," I said meekly, "have you ever considered our being civilians and living somewhere else?" Then I told her what the skipper had said.

"What are you going to do, Dick?"

"They'll have to throw me out," I said. "I'm certainly not giving up. I'm going to prove to those guys I'm a good pilot."

6

CAL SWANSON arrived at Miramar in early 1966 full of enthusiasm and anxious to teach navy pilots the new fighter pilot doctrine being introduced to the U.S. Air Force. Swanson had heard a presentation by Air Force Major John Boyd about a concept called "energy management" and was immediately taken by it. In essence, energy management was a computer analysis of two opposing airplanes—let's say, a Russian MiG and an American F-4—to show the relative strengths and weaknesses of each. If a pilot knew, for example, at what speed and altitude a MiG performed worst, he could presumably engage in air combat with that in mind and emerge the winner. The doctrine eventually was accepted by the aviation industry.

Cal had gone to an experimental high school in Colorado, then to Swarthmore for two years, and had received a degree in chemistry from the University of Washington. He was at ease with scientific propositions, and applying energy management to the F-8 seemed the most natural thing in the world. But this was 1966 and *computer* was still an ominous word to many people. Three of the best pilots in the squadron—Dick Wyman, Black Mac, and Rick Adams—resisted Cal's doctrine. They saw themselves as stick-and-throttle pilots in the World War One tradition, white scarfs flowing in the wind. Rick Adams, who was something of a writer, composed romantic fantasies about air combat.

46

Black Mac was particularly skeptical. He had gone to a private school in North Carolina and to Georgia Tech for two years and was bright, in some ways even brilliant, but he had developed an aversion for anything that smacked of intellectualism. The main thing Black Mac had learned in college was a technique for blowing a fireball across a dark ready room or the officers' club bar at the most startling moments, making him famous throughout the fleet. It had started one night at Georgia Tech when he knocked on a student's door. The door opened and suddenly Black Mac found himself engulfed in a fireball that singed his eyebrows. After getting over the shock, he bought a fifty-cent can of lighter fluid, sprayed the contents under the student's door, and lit it. "You should have heard them trying to beat it out with scatter rugs," he said years later. After a truce was called, the student taught Black Mac how to make the fireball. The secret was to have more air in your mouth than lighter fluid, so you could spew it out cleanly. Otherwise, you would burn your mouth badly, as many who tried to duplicate Black Mac's trick were to discover.

When the time arrived for Cal Swanson to engage in his first dogfight, Rick Adams, who was considered the hottest of the combat veterans, was chosen as his opponent. Wanting to leave nothing to chance, Adams found the name of Swanson's old unit and telephoned his former squadron mates for a rundown on his weaknesses as a pilot. "We wanted to nail him to the wall," said Rick. "His old squadron mates told me everything about him. I decided the key, as with most senior officers, was his eyes. To start a dogfight, you usually break toward the other guy. But I broke away. He saw my profile and thought I was coming at him. When I pitched up and rolled he just lost the whole thing."

The anticomputer pilots were pleased to see Cal lose, and the word went around that he was a bookish pilot who couldn't fly out his theory in the airplane, which wasn't fair to Swanson. Charlie Tinker, a squadron pilot who doubled as an LSO, the man who stood on the carrier deck and directed landings, was in a position to know who were the best pilots, and Tinker considered Cal at the top. Bellinger ended the experiment with energy management by saying to Swanson, "It gets too hard to remember when you are in the middle of a dogfight."

Cal was disappointed. "The concept was so logical and clear to me," he said. "But when you started talking about trading off potential for kinetic energy to someone who'd majored in liberal arts you had a real problem."

The pace of getting ready to go to war was picking up, and Cal busied himself with other matters. Bellinger demanded punctuality. He encouraged Swanson to be more forceful in his ready room presentations. But the two of them got along remarkably well, considering Belly's volatile personality. Cal had learned as a child to approach his stern father obliquely if he wanted to get his way, and it was a technique he used to good advantage with his navy superiors.

"Cal and Belly were two different kinds of commanders," said Charlie Tinker. "Except on liberty. And then they were like peas in a pod. You talk about hell on wheels, those two were. Cal was more navy. Blue and Gold was showing through quite a bit of the time. But Bellinger, too, was extremely capable."

Bellinger and Swanson worked together to weld the squadron into a unit. There was a problem with what to do about Black Mac. Cal suggested he be given secondary duties as the safety officer. "My idea of safety," Black Mac told Cal, "is that if someone wants to go out and kill himself that's his business. I'll look out for my own ass. I'm not the type of guy to sneak around and look over somebody's shoulder, and then come report to you and the skipper about their dangerous tendencies."

Black Mac had never forgiven Bellinger for the way he treated the East Coast pilots when they arrived. And it didn't help matters that one night, while the squadron watched a movie in the ready room, Black Mac had launched a fireball over Bellinger's head, scaring everybody and most of all Belly, who jumped up and started cussing. In Cal's opinion, it wasn't so much a problem of personality differences as of similarities. Even Black Mac, trying to explain why he disliked Bellinger, said, "It got to the point where he would walk into the room and I would get up and leave. I guess I'm as gross an individual as there is, but Bellinger would gross me out."

Bellinger spoke to Swanson about getting rid of Black Mac. Swanson tried to mediate. Black Mac was presumptuous; he was loud; he could be obnoxious. But Swanson recognized his possibilities if not as a safety officer, then as a safety valve for the pressures that would build during the long months of combat. Black Mac was jovial and always horsing around. If he spotted a weakness in a pilot, he would tease it out of him and bring it to the surface, where it could be dealt with and conquered. The squadron needed a man—*one*—like that. Cal also recognized in Black Mac a natural pilot, someone as sensitive in the air as he was seemingly insensitive on the ground. Black Mac was proud of his flying ability and you could trust him to do a good job. Swanson believed the squadron needed top-notch fighter pilots who could adjust to new circumstances. He was beginning to realize that Vietnam was not to be a fighter pilot's war. Rather, it called for someone who could do dive bombing.

Hanoi had few MiGs, and against such heavy odds the North Vietnamese played a cagey game, choosing carefully when to challenge the Americans in air-to-air combat. Swanson figured out that a MiG was spotted once for every ninety-nine flights the Americans made. If Squadron 162 was to play a significant role in the war, it would have to become proficient at dive bombing.

During World War Two, American planes did mostly strategic bombing against fixed targets, the idea being to cover the whole target area with explosives. No one was very concerned about the civilians who might be caught in the wide bombing patterns. * But in Vietnam, because of the nature of the targets and because accuracy and preventing civilian casualties were demanded by Washington, U.S. warplanes engaged in dive bombing with few exceptions. The airplanes headed down toward the targets at thirty to sixty degree angles and released their bombs at about six thousand feet.

The kind of bombing usually associated in the public mind with World War Two was done in Vietnam by the huge B-52s of the Strategic Air Command, which, until the final period of the air war, were limited to carrying out strikes inside South Vietnam or just above the DMZ—not against fixed targets but most often against suspected enemy troop concentrations in the jungle. The eight-engined B-52s had a wing span of 195 feet (more than five times that of an F-8) and a length of 156 feet. The F-8s dove low with six five hundred–pound bombs

---

*The apartment building in the *proche banlieue* of Paris where I am writing this book was partially destroyed in 1943 by American bombers trying to hit a Hispano-Suiza motor factory a half-mile away. The then-occupants of my apartment were killed. Madame Langlois, our neighborhood historian, told me, "Ah, monsieur, your Americans were very fine. But they had the reputation around here for killing a lot of civilians with their bombs. The British were much more precise."

and exposed themselves to heavy antiaircraft fire; the B-52s carried eighty-five five hundred–pound bombs and dropped horizontally from a high altitude, unseen by anybody on the ground.

The dive bombing carried out in North Vietnam by the F-8 and by tactical bombers of the air force was called "precision" bombing. Dive bombing was unquestionably more accurate than the carpet bombing done by the B-52s inside South Vietnam. But the F-8 pilots had no illusions about hitting the target with absolute accuracy. Even under the best conditions, in practice, with no one shooting at him, and with the aim point perfectly visible, a tactical pilot was satisfied if his bombs fell within a radius of fifty feet of the target. Given a combat situation, with missiles in the air and the danger of colliding with another plane always present, dive bombing could be far from precise.

The A-4 Skyhawk was the primary bomber on the *Oriskany* and since bombers played the key role in the air war, there was some good-natured ribbing between the carrier's two A-4 attack squadrons, whose pilots considered themselves to be doing the most important work, and the two F-8 fighter squadrons, whose pilots thought of themselves as part-time bombers. The A-4 itself, however, did not measure up to the tactical bombers used by the air force. The A-4 was a single-seater, the last of the simple airplanes, so small and compact that pilots joked you didn't strap in but strapped it on. It was sometimes called Heinemann's Hotrod, after its designer. The A-4 was dwarfed by the F-105 Thunderchief, which, along with the F-4 Phantom, was the air force's primary bomber. The F-105 could carry twelve thousand pounds of bombs, compared to around three thousand pounds for the A-4. The Thud, as pilots called the F-105, was clumsy and couldn't turn well during air-to-air engagements. But the F-105, with the F-4, was the most effective bomber used in the war. Air Force pilots flying from bases in Thailand and South Vietnam were dropping more bombs than navy pilots.

The navy and air force struck in coordinated attacks during the first days of the air war. Each was given a time to arrive over the target. But having so many planes in the air led to confusion and danger. The air force, coming from far away, had to refuel from flying tankers, whereas the navy could make a short hop from carriers off the coast. A joint committee was formed to work on the problem, stirring up the old rivalry between the two services. A proposal was made to divide North

Vietnam along a north-south axis, with the navy responsible for attacks in the eastern half, the air force in the west. But the air force challenged it on the grounds that most of the important targets were in the eastern zone.

The solution adopted, after much haggling, was to divide the country into six geographic areas called route packages. The navy at first got Route Package 6, which contained Hanoi and Haiphong, North Vietnam's two major cities. But the air force argued once again that most of the key targets were located there. So the route package was subdivided into 6-A and 6-B, with a line drawn down the middle of Hanoi, following a railroad. The navy was assigned to bomb the eastern portion, 6-B, closest to the ocean, which also included Haiphong. Sometimes one service entered the other's route package to hit selected targets.

The American strategy, as much as it could be defined, centered on trying to stop the flow of war material to the South. North Vietnam's thirteen hundred–mile railway system, conceived by Paul Doumer, the Governor-General of French Indochina, and built between 1896 and 1902, became a major target. The Paul Doumer Bridge on the outskirts of Hanoi was the main entry point for supplies coming into Hanoi. The bridge was in an air force route package and Washington had not allowed it to be bombed. Farther south, seventy miles or so, at Thanh Hoa, was another vital link in the rail system. The Thanh Hoa bridge, which crossed the swift-flowing Song Ma River, had been destroyed in 1945 by the Viet Minh, who loaded two locomotives with explosives and ran them head on in the middle of the bridge. In 1957, with the help of Chinese engineers, the North Vietnamese began to respan the Song Ma. The new bridge, finished in 1964 and called the Ham Rung, or Dragon's Jaw, was five hundred and forty feet long, fifty-six feet wide, and stood fifty feet above the water. Its two steel spans rested in the center of a concrete pier and on concrete abutments at either end.

Navy pilots had hit the Dragon's Jaw time and again, but the iron bombs, tons and tons of them, seemed to bounce off. The Dragon's Jaw stood intact, a source of pride for the North Vietnamese, a symbol of frustration to the Americans. Navy pilots were left to try to knock out the smaller bridges like Co Trai between Hanoi and Thanh Hoa.

7

ON JULY 19, 1966, Frank Elkins, an A-4 pilot, was also thinking about the bridge at Co Trai. One of Elkins's friends on the *Oriskany* liked to say, "My courage diminishes in proportion to the distance inland." Co Trai was to the south of Hanoi, deep in the flatlands, which were densely populated, heavy with missile and flak sites. As Elkins saw it, there was a good chance of being hit, a high chance of hitting civilians, and no chance of escaping if he were shot down. He was worried about causing civilian casualties. He wondered if the barges he had recently bombed on a river were a legitimate military target, or a family's home. "I can say again and again that those were military targets," he wrote his wife, Marilyn, "but down deep inside I have to pray that I did right."

Elkins was twenty-seven, an honors graduate in literature from the University of North Carolina, and this was his first combat cruise. On the way to Vietnam the *Oriskany* had stopped in Hawaii. Elkins flew over Oahu, Pearl Harbor, down Waikiki Beach, and then to Molokai, where he sighted a leper colony. The colony was bounded on three sides by white shell beaches and on the fourth by a steep cliff overgrown with vines and bushes. "It was so lush and beautiful that it was difficult to picture the diseased inhabitants," he told Marilyn.

The skipper of Frank's A-4 squadron organized a palm tree–climbing contest while they were in Hawaii. He insisted that the previous year's champion was unbeatable. The contest was held in front of the Garden Bar, so that the manager would be sure to call the police when the beer-drinking pilots got rowdy, which was the skipper's idea of fun. Frank thought it all very juvenile. A friend of Frank's, Barry Jones, took the skipper's bet and made it sixty feet up the palm tree on Saturday, higher than anyone. The sheriff arrived and threatened to throw everybody in jail, because tourists at the Garden Bar were betting on the contest. Frank's skipper talked him out of making arrests and announced that everybody had until eight o'clock Sunday evening to top Barry's mark. Frank saw the cuts on Barry's arms and decided he wanted no part of it.

On Sunday morning Frank awoke feeling miserable. Never had he felt so lonely. He needed to share Hawaii with Marilyn; only by showing her the islands' beauty could he truly make it his own. An attractive redhead, bright and spunky, Marilyn had attended college on a debate scholarship. Three things in his life he loved more than anything, Frank decided: his mother, because she unselfishly wanted only what he wanted for himself; his flying, because it gave him joy and self-respect; and Marilyn, because he had never felt so close to another human being. Frank telephoned Marilyn long-distance, and their brief conversation made him feel warm, but it sharpened the edge of his loneliness when they hung up.

After making the call, Frank ran into his skipper, who chided him for not joining the palm tree–climbing contest. Frank took physical exercise seriously and liked to keep in shape. "All that PT talk of yours is just for sissies," the skipper said. "Palm trees are men's play."

"So I made an ass of myself and climbed the tree," Frank told Marilyn, "beating Barry's mark by ten feet. I climbed cold sober, cut my hands up, ruined my clothes, and gashed my left foot so badly that it needed a stitch or two. I gave it a bath in bourbon instead, and it hasn't turned blue yet."

Frank Elkins was always ready to take up a challenge. When he arrived on Yankee Station, he was anxious to know how he would react to flak and missiles, especially after seeing other pilots come back from their major strikes pale and shaken. Getting shot at, he thought, probably affected a man in different ways, perhaps depending on his wife's last letter, or even what he'd eaten for breakfast. He was convinced he was the best pilot in his A-4 squadron, but he wondered if he were unconsciously afraid. "I have to continue to prove myself to myself," he noted in his journal, "but as long as I succeed, I guess I'm okay."

Elkins believed the United States right in trying to prevent a communist takeover of South Vietnam. But he recognized that other factors besides a belief in the cause kept pilots like himself flying missions against the North. Naval aviators were volunteers. A pilot could say, "I've had enough," and be sent home the next day, unlike the GIs wading through South Vietnam's rice paddies, who were required to serve a year's tour. "At the same time," he noted, "it would be extremely difficult to turn in your wings and quit, even if you were afraid for your life, in the company of those with whom you've never been a quitter before." He understood how pilots had become obsessed with the idea of knocking out bridges during the Korean War, however insignificant the strikes may have proved to be. There was that sense of competition, that drive to do a good job, the urge to be respected by one's squadron mates, which pushed pilots to the edge.

On July 12, 1966, four days after the *Oriskany* arrived on Yankee Station, Frank wrote Marilyn to tell her he had been on his first big strike. He was ecstatic. ("I'm damned glad to be alive!") The *Oriskany*'s planes had attacked an oil storage dump between Hanoi and Haiphong at noon that day. Frank flew as the air wing commander's wingman, and though he lost sight of his leader at one point, he completed his run on the target and made it back to the ship without any problems. The question he had asked about himself was answered.

During the attack, an F-8 from Squadron 162 was shot down, and Elkins recorded the incident. The radio transmissions, he told Marilyn, went like this:

"Hey, Rick, you in 'burner'?"

"Negative."

"Then you're on fire. Now there's flames all over your bird! Get out!"

"Negative."

"You're going to explode. Eject! Eject!"

"Negs."

"Then the pilot, a lieutenant junior grade I didn't know, cool as ice says, 'Well, sorry about that . . . see ya next year!' and punched out."

The pilot Frank didn't know was Rick Adams. He had just been shot down for the second time.

8 · *Marilyn Elkins*

MY TROUBLES in school came from being too young emotionally and not liking hypocrisy. If the teachers had said, "Gee, I don't know," or "I've never thought of it that way," I would have never challenged them. It was people who pretended to know what they didn't know that I was against. Still am. I got suspended twice, once for throwing a book at a teacher, another time for playing hooky. Both incidents occurred my junior year when I was fourteen. I started school when I was five and skipped a grade. Our school principal was a religious type, totally intolerant of anything that wasn't of his church background. My hometown of Pikeville, Tennessee, had a population of only about a thousand, but it drew people from all over the Sequatchee Valley, which is the largest valley in the world caused by a limestone fault. And it was a stronghold of the Church of Christ. They didn't believe in lipstick, didn't allow organs in the church; and they had little lines they could quote from the Bible to justify all this. My mother, who was a schoolteacher, didn't much like the principal, either.

In 1959, not long after the Sputnik thing, they were giving tests all over the state to identify gifted students, and I won a chance to go to Tennessee Tech the summer between my high-school junior and senior years. I made good grades in high school in science and math because I had excellent teachers. But I almost failed English, which I've wound up teaching, because we got assignments where you had to write sentences and all they wanted was the correct verb. I'd been reading forever and I found that boring.

After high school I went to Tennessee Tech and started out majoring in chemistry, but then I hit calculus and discovered I couldn't coast through without studying, so I changed my major to English, because I was making A's and B's without working. My English and history teachers I liked my junior year, and I really studied in those classes. I was popular and dated a lot, which I hadn't done in high school. I was elected the senior class beauty, and I went out with a football player. Shirley was my second cousin and good friend. She and I made a trip to Florida during the Easter holidays. In 1964, when I finished school, I was twenty. I had a B.A. in English and couldn't type. I wasn't sure what I wanted to do. I knew I didn't want to be a secretary. And I knew I wanted to go someplace else.

I'd passed through Jacksonville on my Easter trip to Florida, and it looked like a nice place to live, so I said, okay, that's where I'll go. I didn't have a job, but my dad had given me a small amount of money as a graduation gift, and at one point I called him after I got there and he wired me some more. I made some friends not long after I arrived, and they invited me to a bar called The Happy Hour. That's where I met Frank. He was flying A-4s at Cecil Field outside Jacksonville. This was the time when people did the bop, the UT, that kind of thing, and Frank was a real good dancer.

My first impression was that he was short. He would hate me to say that! I was five-eight and he was about the same. Frank was very muscular, though, with huge shoulders, a weight lifter. He asked for my telephone number and later called to invite me to a squadron party. He showed up in Bermuda shorts carrying a guitar. He also brought along a book of poetry, something mundane, Robert Frost I believe it was. I thought, this is really weird, because all the people I'd gone out with before would not have let anyone know they read poetry, if in fact they did. Five minutes after we got to the party he had a crowd around him.

Frank was completely at ease with everybody. He played the guitar really well and had won all sorts of voice contests at his North Carolina high school, where he was the class valedictorian and captain of the football team. The only people I ever knew who didn't like him were men who were a little jealous because he was extremely handsome and so talented. He got up on the stage with the band at the party and sang a couple of numbers, including one he'd learned in New Orleans, *I wouldn't give a blind sow an acorn, I wouldn't give a cripple crab a crutch, because that woman I been lovin' ain't so mighty such a much.*

Frank's ship left on a training cruise. While he was gone, I walked into the place where I was staying and found my roommate in bed with a man. That upset me, so the next day I moved out, losing contact with Frank for a while, because he was writing me there and didn't know I'd left. I talked four of my girlfriends from Tennessee into moving to Jacksonville, including Shirley, and we took an apartment together. When Frank returned we started dating. I don't know whether *love* is the right word. I was infatuated, certainly. I was sort of overwhelmed by him. I was awfully young. And I wasn't about to go to bed with a man with the idea it might not mean something.

Frank thought navy pilots shouldn't get married, because they took so many risks. A significant number of them don't make it anyway, war or no. Just from night landings and so forth. That's what he told me later, but at the time, when we started dating, I didn't ask. I was seeing other people and so was he. We were living in a complex called Village Wood. It was really wild. The apartments were centered around the pool and the people who lived there were mostly single women—teachers, stewardesses, secretaries—and navy pilots. You'd open your drapes and within an hour friends would come over and the party would start. You didn't have to worry about whether you had a date. There was always someone to go to the movies or out to eat with. I loved to dance, though I didn't drink. This was such a happy time for all of us that several years ago we met in Atlanta and had a Village Wood reunion.

In October 1964, Frank was scheduled to make a six-month Mediterranean cruise. The steamship company I worked for sent me to Fort Lauderdale, and Shirley came down for a weekend. I introduced her to Jack Kilpatrick, who was later in Squadron 162, but warned her not to go out with him. I said, "You know, he's really not to be trusted." I had decided Jack was a corrupter of young women. He had dated one of the women I'd earlier roomed with who was sort of loose. We laugh about that now, they've been married so long, Shirley and Jack.

Anyway, one night I got a phone call from Frank. He told me not to get married while he was gone. We talked for a while. It sounded as though he had been drinking. I didn't respond. As it turned out, he had a girl in the other room while he was calling me. The question was, who is Frank going to write while he's gone, me or the other girls? I had a friend who would peek to see what mail the others were getting. I received a letter before anybody did, an incredibly long letter. He wrote beautifully. We began to write back and forth.

Practically everybody around was a single navy pilot. Three I knew shared a big rambling house we called the snakepit. I dated one of the pilots and introduced his two roommates to two of my roommates. Both couples got married and remain so to this day. The pilot I was seeing, Bill, was just determined that I should marry him. Frank was still on his Med cruise, and when Bill asked me to marry him in March 1965, I accepted. Somehow Frank heard I'd got engaged and wrote to wish me well. His tone was cool. He told me about the Italian girl, a ballet dancer, he was dating.

Bill was being assigned to California. I quit my job, sold my yellow Volkswagen convertible, and shipped most of my clothes to Bill's new duty station. I was supposed to fly to Tennessee, where friends of my mother had planned a bridal party for me, and then to California. Several days before I was to leave Jacksonville, I went out for a pizza with one of my roommates and when we got back there were balloons hanging everywhere, a case of champagne on the table, and the house was full of friends who had come to give me a going-away party. Around midnight, a pilot I'd once dated sat down beside me. "You are not in love," Norm said. "You are just getting married because everybody else is." Norm had a brotherly interest in me. He had met my mom and dad. One of my roommates was throwing up from too much champagne. Norm and I moved into the hallway and talked all night. At dawn he told me not to leave the apartment or do anything until he got back from work.

While he was gone I thought, yes, Norm is right. Frank's ship was due back soon and I looked forward to seeing him. I didn't really want to go to California and leave all my friends. I would be miserable married to Bill. He didn't read, he didn't—there were a hundred and one things we didn't have in common. That afternoon when Norm returned, I said, "But Norm, it's going to be so embarrassing." I'd already received wedding presents.

He said, "Wear my wings for a week. You can say that instead of getting married you got pinned to me."

I couldn't bear to tell Bill. Norm called him and I got on the line. There was silence on the other end. I later heard he drove his car into a telephone pole, drunk, not long after we talked. His mother called the next day. She said Bill had never had a girlfriend he liked, that I had broken his heart, and I should reconsider. She was a nice woman, but I refused to talk to her when she called again.

One day I had my hair up in curlers, no makeup on, and the phone rang. "I hear you're not engaged anymore," Frank said. "Can you come pick me up? My car is in storage and I don't have any transportation. I would love to see you." I tied a scarf around my hair and rushed out of the house, thinking how awful I must look. I was definitely in love. But I don't think I ever thought Frank would marry me. I knew he believed navy pilots shouldn't get married. And he seemed too, well, too perfect. I was popular with other men, but I was never as physically attractive as Frank, I don't think. I just thought it was too much like out of a book.

There was a dependent's day on Frank's ship, a time when pilots invited their wives and families to spend a half-day visiting the carrier. It was on Saturday and we got back at eight-thirty that evening. We were supposed to go to church the next morning. I knew Frank for six months before I realized he was seriously religious. He said he was tired and was going to his place to go to bed early. One of my roommates had a date that night. She saw Frank returning to his apartment after midnight with lipstick smeared on him. I got up next morning and went to the pool to wait for him. When he showed up, I said, "I'm not going to see you anymore. You lied to me. You told me you were going home, and Sue saw you and you had lipstick all over you."

"I did lie to you," he said, "and I'm sorry."

"Well, that's fine. I'm just not going to see you anymore."

"I need some time to think about this."

He asked to see me at dinner that night. I reluctantly accepted. Before we went to eat, he said, "You know, we didn't have an agreement not to see anybody else, so in a sense I haven't lied."

"Yes, you lied," I said. "You told me you were going home to go to bed, and you had a date. I'd call that a lie."

"But we hadn't made any real commitment. If you'll continue to see me, I'd like for us to agree not to see anybody else."

One of my girlfriends was getting married in the south of Florida, and Frank rode to the wedding with Sue and Leon, who were already married. On the way, he asked them questions about marriage, about what it was like, the problems and everything. Frank didn't mention the conversation to me, but of course Sue couldn't wait to tell me. Several weeks passed and Frank said nothing, so I decided to make him jealous. Frank could get jealous of other men, which was sort of alien, because he wasn't normally like that. I remember one night at a party a guy comes by and puts his arm around my waist and squeezes me, and next thing I know Frank wants to fight him. Anyway, I sent myself seven roses and had someone write a card, which said, "Seven roses. Today is the seventh of December. Do you remember us?" I had the roses delivered at a time I knew Frank would be at my apartment. Only Frank was late for our date and the roses got there before he did. Fortunately his good friend Dave, who was dating one of my roommates, was there, and he said, "God, you can't let Frank see those. This is terrible."

I put the flowers in a vase and sort of hid the card. Naturally, Dave told Frank about the roses when he walked in. Frank was furious. We went outside and had a big talk. He said, "Look, I'm going to get you an engagement ring for Christmas. What is this. Who's this guy?"

"I sent them to myself."

"Sure you did."

He refused to believe me. He went back to the apartment and threw the flowers in the trash can.

I flew home for Christmas. Frank went to North Carolina and then came to pick me up in Tennessee. We stopped on the way back to Florida and took a room. I slept in one bed and made him sleep in the other. Sounds fantastic considering what goes on today, but it's true. There was a time before we got engaged when he tried to get me to go to bed. But once we got engaged, he said, "If that's what you want, I'll respect it."

We reached Jacksonville and I learned what everybody else knew and wasn't telling me: Frank had orders to Vietnam. I was upset. I knew people already there. One pilot I knew had gotten shot down. I thought, this is terrible. And then Frank started driving me crazy.

One night he'd say, "We aren't going to get married till I get back." I'd say, "Let's go on and do it."

"No, that's unfair to you. If something should happen to me you are going to be more damaged emotionally if we are married than if we're not. We can wait."

Next day he would call, or I would call him, and he would reverse positions. "No, we've got to get married. I don't think I can go to Vietnam without getting married."

So we decided on a date. What happened then was really strange. A girl whom he'd dated off and on telephoned and said she was in the hospital and needed to see him badly. Before I knew what was going on, he flew to North Carolina to see her and stayed overnight. When he returned, I told him he was right, we shouldn't get married, and I threw the engagement ring across the room. He explained that the girl had tried to commit suicide and said they'd been friends for years. He persuaded me to take the ring back, and we decided to get married as soon as possible. I called my mom. Within a week the wedding was planned. We got married on January 22, 1966, at the Methodist church in my hometown of Pikeville. Then we left on a honeymoon of about three weeks, driving across country to California, where Frank was assigned to the *Oriskany*.

I'd already formed my impressions about being a navy wife. I said,

"I'm not having squadron cocktail parties and doing all that stuff. You've got to be good enough to make it on your own if you decide that's what you want to do." He was thinking of making the navy a career. I preferred he not, but it was his choice. A lot of things Frank didn't like about the navy and a lot he did. He liked to travel and so did I. Most of all, he liked flying.

We moved into an apartment. I worked as a substitute teacher. In the evenings we read, or Frank played his guitar and sang. Some of our Jacksonville friends had been transferred to California and we sometimes saw them. I was sitting by the pool one afternoon when Frank flew over and buzzed our house. Sometimes, when he was training on the *Oriskany*, I stayed with Shirley and Jack. In June 1966, a little more than four months after we were married, the *Oriskany* sailed for the Pacific, heading first to Hawaii. We had been up really late the night before. We went to a piano bar out on the island, in San Diego. Frank told me he wanted me to return to Pikeville while he was gone. He thought I would be happier there with something to do and with my parents. So I lined up a job teaching in the Head Start program, and after the *Oriskany* sailed, Shirley and I flew back to Tennessee together.

I'd given Frank a typewriter for his birthday. He was working on two novels, one about growing up in North Carolina, the other about a navy pilot. He decided to keep a journal while he was in the war and write a book about his experiences afterward. Frank felt that going to war was something you had to do, and if you didn't, you were chicken. But he also felt he was doing something for democracy, that we had to help the South Vietnamese. With Frank, there was none of that slant-eyed gook kind of thing I heard from some navy people. He believed in the cause.

9 · *Dick Wyman*

TALK ABOUT eating humble pie. I got my fill after I ran into those power lines. Lucky for me, it looked bad on a commanding officer's record to have an accident listed for his squadron. Belly decided his safety record was more important than punishing me, so he fudged on the report and said the engine of my plane was okay, that we'd just removed it for precautionary measures. It was listed as an incident rather than an accident, and I started flying again.

About that time, our operations officer started showing up late for work. I watched some of his night carrier approaches and listened to his voice. You could tell whether a pilot was scared by listening to his radio transmissions. The tenor of his voice would change, become nervous or excited, and you could detect almost a pleading tone, saying, "I need some help, who's gonna help me out?" His night carrier landings were terrible. Fear is not a bad thing; it keeps you alert. But if you can't control fear, it controls you. When you're not functioning normally, you make jerky stick movements or rapid throttle movements, and it shows up in your landing technique. He would come into the ready room after a night landing looking pale and sweating. He appeared to be losing weight. Then one morning he said, "That's it. I'm turning in my wings." He walked out the door and we never saw him again. I was his assistant and stuck with all the paperwork until John Hellman, the new ops officer, reported in. The idea of turning in my wings never entered my mind. I was excited by the whole thing, the war, and wanted to get on with it. The *Oriskany* finally sailed for the Pacific and we stopped off in Hawaii where the squadron took a beach cottage. Bellinger claimed the cottage was a morale factor, and it was, but Belly just liked to drink and raise hell.

We were scheduled to have an Operational Readiness Inspection in Hawaii, an important examination to be graded by an outside officer. At the briefing, with the grader looking on, Bellinger got up to give us our instructions. He smelled like a brewery and was obviously screwed up. He said, "You guys know how to do this. You've done it many times. I got the lead." And he walked out.

Rick Adams and I were going down the ramp, and we got Belly between us, bracing him so he wouldn't stagger. We took off and were supposed to go up and run a squirrel-cage pattern. Belly couldn't do it because he was nauseated. So he flew overhead and called in like he was running the pattern. I called in as his wingman acting like he was there. The grader never caught on because he was flying far behind us. When we came in to land Belly broke away and started flying away from the runway. I radioed, "Belly-One, this is Belly-Two. What's up? You got any problems?" "I got to go check something out," he said in a queasy voice, and away he flew. He was throwing up and couldn't land till he finished.

Bellinger was convinced we were ready for combat and didn't need any more of the navy's mickey mouse. When we reached the Philippines, three or four days before we were due on Yankee Station, we were told to take a two-day training course to learn how to survive in the jungle, in case we were shot down. Belly said, "We're not going to waste our time in the jungle running around getting dirty. We're going to have some fun." So we went to the club and stayed all day.

Another time, during the '66 cruise, we were back in the Philippines for a short break. By then Bellinger and I were inseparable. We'd been in combat together and I'd saved him a couple of times—he didn't have very good eyes. There were four of us and we met four nurses from Clark Air Base. We were drinking French 75s at the club, champagne and cognac, getting blown away. Everybody, of course, wanted to get laid. But we had to find a place. Belly said, "I've got it. We'll take them on board ship."

It was forbidden to bring guests aboard ship at night and I said, "You can't do that."

Belly said, "Wyman, you're coming with me."

Bellinger pulled under the prow of the ship, stopped the car, and marched up the gangway to the guard, bowling him over with a story about having "special guests." We went to Bellinger's room and the phone rang. The command duty officer. He knew Belly had women aboard ship and was looking for him. Belly said, "Quick, take the girls to your rooms and don't let them out." The nurses thought it was all neat—they were goosed up, anyhow. Bellinger somehow convinced the duty officer he'd taken them off the ship.

The nurse I took to my room asked for something to wear. She undressed, put on the T-shirt I handed her, and got into the bottom bunk, which belonged to my absent roommate. I crawled into the top bunk and immediately fell asleep from exhaustion and too much to drink. Belly phoned the next morning at nine. I didn't answer and the nurse was afraid to pick it up. Belly and his girlfriend came to my room. They saw that we were in different bunks. The nurse said I'd climbed into the top bunk and left her alone all night. Bellinger told everybody in the squadron. Somebody wrote on the side of my airplane, "Limpy Dick." That became my squadron nickname. "Limpy."

Belly marched the nurses down the gangway that morning and we got away. We heard at the club that the air wing commander was looking for us. We were in front of the club when we saw him coming. A van was parked nearby and we jumped behind it. The van drove off, leaving us exposed. The air wing commander said, "You're caught. I'm restricting you to the ship until we return to Yankee Station."

The day before we reached Yankee Station, on July 8, 1966, the executive officer of our sister F-8 squadron turned in his wings. Captain Iarrobino thought the presence of such a high-ranking quitter would be bad for morale, so he decided to get him off the ship as quickly as possible. The commander was put aboard a propeller-driven supply plane that was heading to the Philippines. By accident, his seat wasn't bolted down properly and during the catapult shot he was slung against the wall, cutting his head badly. The plane turned and landed, and he was taken to sick bay where a number of stitches and, afterward, I believe, a steel plate had to be put in his head.

Years later, in 1981, when I was executive officer at Pax River, we were having a big air show, and someone introduced me to an admiral who had arrived from Washington for the ceremonies. He had a scar down his forehead. I said, "Admiral, I'm sure I know you from somewhere, let me think."

His face turned red. After a minute he said, "Oh, you might have known me from the *Oriskany*," and then he changed the subject. It was the same guy who had turned in his wings because he couldn't hack it in combat, now an admiral.

I said to myself, "How could the system allow this to happen?" The thing that irritated me was the story going around Pax River that he had been a fighter pilot and had crashed, and that's how he got the scar. I never told anyone it wasn't true. It was the admiral's secret. If he wanted to keep it, that was fine with me. He was always friendly and courteous to me. But he knew, and I knew.

ON JULY 12, 1966, I flew my first strike over the beach. Jesus, what a day! There were twenty-four planes in the strike group. Four of us were from Squadron 162—Bellinger, me, Butch Verich, and Rick Adams. I was flying Bellinger's wing. We went north and cut back down to Haiphong. Like I say, this was my first hop and I got permanent wrinkles around my eyes from widening them so much. I was expecting and not seeing. My head was on a swivel. The theory was, in those days, that if they shot missiles, you got as low as possible, in order to defeat them. That was the theory. You tried to grab the dirt. Somebody called "SAMs!" and we all dove for the deck. There were twenty-four airplanes trying to fit into a small valley at five hundred knots apiece, fifty feet off the ground. Talk about wild—that was all the wildness a person could stand. You had the possibility of a midair collision, of hitting the ground, or of getting shot down.

When we got to the far side of the valley, Rick took a hit. That's why the following year the theory changed completely on how to fight the missiles. If you went down low to evade the SAMs, then the anti-aircraft fire got you. We had to start dueling with them at a high altitude. Anyway, Rick took a hit and Butch Verich, who was always polite, was saying, "You gotta jump, Rick, you gotta jump. Your whole wing's on fire."

Rick was saying, "Negative, I'm not getting out of this thing till it quits flying." And he didn't. I saw him as he cleared a ridge. His plane was a ball of flames. Suddenly out he went. We came along behind him, and I saw his parachute hanging on a tree. Bellinger didn't know where Rick was, and Butch Verich was having trouble directing the Spads that came to fly cover for the rescue helicopter.

"Belly-One," I said, "this is Belly-Two. I've got the lead." Then I told the Spads, "You are going the wrong way. I want you to turn one hundred and eighty degrees and head to the other side of the valley." I took them to where he was. "Dip your wing and Rick is right below you." I was so busy trying to help Rick that I forgot to check my gas gauge. I looked and saw I was about to run out. I called Belly and went up to plug into the tanker, then returned to the ship. The squadron crowded around Rick on the flight deck when he got back. It was like a family reunion. He was the first pilot to be shot down twice over the beach and rescued. *Time* did a story about it, and the navy ruled he couldn't fly over North Vietnam any more. He soon transferred back to the States.

We were flying an exhausting schedule. The heat was atrocious. My roommate Lloyd, the squadron flight surgeon, and I had a small room underneath the flight deck, between the two catapults. When the catapults fired, the room shook like an earthquake had hit it. We found an air conditioner and kept it running full-time, but the coolest the room got was ninety-two degrees Fahrenheit. Sitting in the airplane waiting to be launched, I and every bit of my clothing would be soaked. Guys got sick to their stomachs with the heat and the exhausts from the next plane ahead flaming back. Even though we weren't supposed to, I would take off my flight helmet after I was in the air and knock the sweat out of my eyes. You smelled so bad after a flight you had to bathe, but fresh water was so scarce we had to take salt-water showers, which left us sticky and itchy. I would shower and return to my room and fill my small sink with fresh water, and put a towel on the floor and sponge myself off.

Four days after Rick got shot down, Belly decided to set up a MiG trap. The North Vietnamese had been following the strike group back toward the sea after the target was hit, to give the folks on the ground the impression, I guess, that they were driving us away. Belly said, "Okay, we'll trail behind the strike group and catch the MiGs when they come out." There was Charlie Tinker, Bellinger, and me. A fourth plane was supposed to go, but it went down on the flight deck with a malfunction. So I was flying Belly's left wing and Tinker was on his right. As we were going through a layer of clouds, I looked down and saw a MiG pass through a hole in the cumulus.

"MiGs at nine o'clock!" I yelled.

I dropped down through the clouds but didn't see the MiG where I thought he should be. Then I looked and saw he was right in front of me. I was about to run into the guy. I put my speed brakes out, trying to slow down, so I wouldn't wind up in front of him. Although we didn't know it, when I called MiGs, Charlie Tinker jerked his head around to look and accidentally unplugged his headset, so we had no radio contact with him. Tinker flew right in front of the MiG. I screamed at him to break, but Tinker couldn't hear me and didn't see the plane. I was so shocked I forgot about shooting. I was just screaming on my radio for Tinker to break and get out of the way.

Another MiG came up on my left trying to get behind me. Tinker saw him and cut sharply. Bellinger was flying to my rear. Here we were, three Americans and two North Vietnamese, flying in a big circle, trying to get on each other's tail. As we came around the second time Belly yelled, "I'm hit! I'm hit!" I fired a missile at a MiG, but he was out of the envelope, not in range. Of my four guns, only one hadn't jammed. I hit the wing of the MiG in front of me maybe once or twice but didn't bring him down. Then I broke into the clouds and headed toward the sea.

I found Belly off the coast. Part of his tail was shot off and his wing was shaking like it was about to come off. He'd also lost his hydraulics, which meant he couldn't land aboard the ship and had to try to make it to Da Nang, the nearest land base in South Vietnam. The air controllers on the *Oriskany* gave Belly a distance to Da Nang. He computed it and figured he had enough fuel to make it. We were fifty miles down the road, when the ship came back on the air and said they'd made a mistake, Da Nang was farther than they'd told us.

"I'm not going to make it," Belly said. "I've not got that much gas."

"Let's stretch it out as far as we can," I said.

"I'm going to have to shuck out, and I think I'll do it while it's still running."

"I'll stay with you and keep track. I'll make sure we get some people out here to pick you up."

I radioed Da Nang and requested two rescue helicopters. I was nervous because Belly was going to jump, and I didn't think Da Nang was treating the matter with the same urgency as I was. You put a man down at sea and it's like looking for a needle in a haystack, and I didn't have much gas left to hang around very long.

"I'm going to jump," Belly said. "I'll see you later."

He had a perfect ejection. As he drifted to the sea I saw two Vietnamese junks sailing toward him. I got down on top of the water and came roaring across them. I would run one boat off and come back and the other guy would be trying to move in. I got their attention, though. Belly was picked up by a helicopter.

I landed at Da Nang. This was my first time in South Vietnam. I met Belly and we went to the Air Force officers' club. I told him, "I didn't see the guy who hit you."

He said, "I was watching you and not paying attention behind me." I felt bad. If I had shot instantly when I popped out of the clouds, it would have been a different ending to the story. My reaction was all wrong, to transmit on the radio to Tinker, rather than to shoot.

At the club, I met an air force pilot who said, "Stick with me tonight, I'll take care of you." The next morning I awoke in the bottom rack of a double bunk. I was naked and lying on my back. My head felt like it belonged elsewhere. I saw a pair of bare feet on the bar over the front of my bed. Down came the feet, and I saw a woman, the first Vietnamese I'd ever seen. She was a maid and had been making up the top bunk. I looked at her. She looked at me. I tried to speak to her in English. She just grinned. I said, "Jesus Christ, where am I? What's going on?"

I looked for my flight suit and it wasn't there. In its place was a towel and a clean air force suit. I got up and stumbled to the shower. While I was under the water, the Vietnamese maid came in and started washing down the shower walls. She acted like I wasn't there. I said, "They're supposed to be the enemy, for Chrissake, and here they are in my shower." I could hardly get out of Da Nang fast enough. Someone told me I had to call Monkey Mountain to make a flight plan, so I phoned and told them I wanted to go to Yankee Station. Then I ran into the air force guy I'd met the night before, and he thanked me for my flight suit. I said, "What do you mean?"

He said, "You remember—we exchanged flight suits during the night."

I came back aboard the *Oriskany* in an air force flight suit, with a wicked hangover, looking like all hell dragged over. I gave a talk to the guys in the ready room about the air encounter and told them I should have forgot about Tinker and just shot the MiG. One of the pilots said, "Wyman, you're bullshitting us." Bellinger hadn't got back and they had heard only Tinker's version. The pilot was accusing me of trying to wriggle out of what happened by claiming Tinker got in front of me.

This particular pilot had left me over the beach one time and I'd threatened to take action of a physical sort against him. The rule was, you never left your wingman or your flight leader, and I'd had the lead that day. We were going to take a shot at some barges. I made my pass and then couldn't find him. I started calling, "What's your position?" Finally he checked in. I said, "Are you out over the ocean?" Back on the ship I told him, "When you fly with me and we are over the beach, you don't leave till you know I'm with you."

"Well, goddamn," he said, "I wasn't going to hang around over the beach."

"We made our runs together," I said, "and we were supposed to exit together."

After that I felt I couldn't depend on him. There was an undercurrent of resentment. We partied together on liberty, but our relations were cool. I think he was trying to jump on the MiG encounter to even up the score. Belly got back and said, "Yeah, Tinker, there was a MiG right on your ass, ready to can you."

Tinker said, "I didn't know that." He admitted he'd accidentally unplugged and didn't hear any of our radio transmissions.

Bellinger got ragged about getting shot down. But he didn't hold it against Tinker and me. Whatever his flaws, Belly had no ego problems. He was open and didn't carry a grudge. I became very attached to him. I felt I had to protect him, that he needed me to keep him out of trouble. And he took care of me too. On my first fitness report, after I'd smashed up the airplane and he told me I ought to be a shoe salesman, he gave me an accelerated promotion recommendation and said I was the best pilot he'd ever known. That's the way Belly was.

Belly saw himself, I believe, as the last of the old fighter pilots, a cowboy being made obsolete by trains and trucks—in his case, by computers and rockets. He was a celebrity on the *Oriskany.* He did things people would never think an officer in his position would do, wild things, totally uninfluenced by questions of rank or protocol. Our squadron had a reputation for not caring about anything and that's the way Bellinger wanted it. The *Oriskany's* captain, John Iarrobino, liked Belly, I think, and realized that whatever his bad points, Bellinger had put together a squadron that would do the job without complaint and do it as well as could be done under the difficult circumstances of the kind of war we were fighting.

10

ON JULY 19, 1966, Captain John Iarrobino stood on the conning station just outside the bridge, to the right, where he directed the *Oriskany's* approach on the ammunition supply ship. "Steer one-four-one," he said into the intercom connecting him to the helmsman on the bridge. "Steer one-four-one," repeated the helmsman. Captain Iarrobino kept an eye out for the *Gidrofon,* the Russian trawler that was heading toward him in the distance. The salvage tug assigned by the Seventh Fleet to shadow the *Gidrofon* had, he was glad to see, reacted quickly and begun the chase. Just in case things got out of hand, Iarrobino ordered one of his two screening destroyers to act as a backup in blocking the *Gidrofon*'s approach.

"Steer one-four-zero," Captain Iarrobino said. After the helmsman repeated the command, the captain ordered: "All engines stop." As the *Oriskany* slid smoothly into position, he called, "All back two-thirds," to slow the carrier's momentum and to align her with the supply ship.

A sailor on the *Oriskany* fired a light line to the supply ship with a shotgun-type gun. Heavier lines were then attached to the light line and pulled between the two ships. One line held taut by a seaman had various colored flags fluttering from it, each flag indicating a different distance. Iarrobino liked to keep the *Oriskany* ranged between the yellow and white flags from a supply ship, leaving a hundred to one hundred and twenty feet separating the two vessels. He adjusted his forward speed to match that of the other ship.

The replenishment would take nearly an hour, enough time, he knew, for the *Gidrofon* to reach them. Like other American skippers on Yankee Station, Iarrobino did not believe the Russians would be so foolish as to ram a U.S. ship or put themselves in a position to be rammed. More likely, the *Gidrofon* was trying to spook the aircraft carrier into a collision with the supply ship. Iarrobino watched as his crew connected four heavy lines to stanchions between the two ships. The lines served as rails upon which pulley trolleys were towed back and forth between the ships with loads of bombs, missiles, and ammunition hanging in cargo nets or on prepackaged pallets. Food and fuel were transferred the same way from other supply ships operating on Yankee Station.

Once again, whether they were serious or not, the Soviets were thwarted in their attempt to get near the carrier. The American tug bore in close to the *Gidrofon*, shouldering the Russians away from the *Oriskany*. After a twelve-mile chase lasting seventy-three minutes, the *Gidrofon* gave two exasperated horn blasts, slowed her speed, and fell in behind the carrier, where she began to sift the *Oriskany*'s spumy wake for any trash thrown overboard that might be of intelligence value. Captain Iarrobino, dismissing the Soviet trawler from his mind, turned to the business of getting the carrier ready for flight operations.

Ideally, Captain Iarrobino liked to have thirty-five knots across the flight deck when the ship launched and recovered aircraft. He spent much of his time in the Tonkin Gulf doing what he called "scratchin' for wind." A peculiarity of the South China Sea was that it turned glassy calm at unexpected moments. The *Oriskany* could make thirty to thirty-one knots, so he needed at least a four-knot wind to make up the difference. The *Oriskany* zigged and zagged trying to find a breeze. Sometimes, when the ship was recovering aircraft after a strike, heading in the direction of North Vietnam's coast, Iarrobino feared he was going to run out of sea. But this morning he had only to make one course change—a turn of one hundred and sixty degrees—to find what he needed.

Below decks, in the weapons department, the young sailors could feel the ship turning into the wind, and they stepped up the pace of their work. The bomb most used was the Mark 82, a five hundred pounder. The olive green bombs were stored in fireproof magazines without their fins, to conserve space. The sailors moved the bombs from the magazines to an assembly area on the mess deck where the fins were bolted on and then up elevators to the flight deck. There, on the starboard side, forward of the island and away from the path an airplane might take in the event of a crash, the bombs were placed on a temporary holding spot called the bomb farm. They were loaded on the aircraft at the rear of the flight deck before the pilots manned their planes. The ship's ordnance officer personally inserted the fuses after the bombs were loaded, ensuring that they were the correct settings.

The bomb fuse contained a small propeller fastened to an arming wire. The arming wire was threaded through the bomb rack under a solenoid. When the pilot flipped a switch in his cockpit, the solenoid acted like a magnet and clamped the arming wire to the bomb rack. Then, on a mission, when he touched the button on his stick to release the bomb, the ejection cartridge exploded to push the bomb away from the bomb rack, which pulled the arming wire clamped by the solenoid from the fuse, which in turn set the small propeller to turning. After a predetermined number of revolutions of the propeller, the arming sequence was complete and the bomb was set to explode, say, at a certain altitude above the ground, on contact, or after a specified delay. If the pilot did not flip his arming switch before pushing the bomb pickle, the arming wire would not pull away from the fuse, the propeller would not turn, and the bomb would not explode. This gave the pilot the option of jettisoning his bombs on safety, if an emergency arose. To make sure the bombs did not accidentally fall off the rack while the plane was still on the ship a safety pin was inserted in the bomb rack. After the pilot taxied up the catapult to be launched, he held both hands in the air to indicate he had not flipped his arming switch to the "on" position and could not inadvertently touch the bomb pickle on the stick. Only then, at the last moment, was the safety pin removed from the bomb rack.

Piles of 20-mm ammunition and Sidewinder missiles were stacked not far from the bombs on the flight deck. To prevent the ammo and missiles from being ignited by stray electromagnetic energy, protective devices were placed around the area. The *Oriskany* was a fragile powder keg. Safety regulations were being bent in order to carry out the heavy mission load assigned by Washington. An accidental fire could be disastrous.

The air wing commander had designated himself as the overall leader of the Co Trai strike group. He had earlier gathered his assistants around a table, and surrounded by maps, charts, and glossy eight by ten photographs of the bridge, they had roughed out a strike plan. The position of the sun, the location of flak and missile sites, the number of planes and types of ordnance—all were considered as they plotted the direction and roll-in approach the *Oriskany*'s pilots would follow to bomb the bridge.

When Cal Swanson entered strike operations at 9:45 A.M., he felt a tension in the room that matched his own. There was little of the usual bantering among pilots from the various squadrons. Strike operations was a big, formal room filled with straight-back folding chairs. It had none of the comfort of a ready room and was not a place where pilots lingered. Photos of targets that had been hit or were scheduled to be hit were on the walls. There were pictures and silhouettes of enemy aircraft, and such things as the burst heights and lethal distances of the four main types of antiaircraft guns, plus a technical description of the SA-2 missile. Maps on the walls were marked with checkpoints, permitting a pilot to radio, "We have a plane down eight miles due west of checkpoint eleven," without giving away the position to North Vietnamese monitors on the ground.

At 10:00 A.M., the strike group leader stood and said, "Okay, everybody here?" He announced what the room already knew, that the strike would be against the bridge at Co Trai, which was just outside the town of Phu Ly; and then he turned the meeting over to the weather briefer, a birdlike man who held in his hands charts and last minute data gathered from satellites. Cloud cover was a point of interest to the pilots. The temperature was also important. An exceedingly hot day could affect the maximum launch weight and limit the number of bombs to be carried. If there was wind over the target, the pilots would have to throw a bias into their aim point and compensate for it. The pilots took notes that they would memorize and destroy before taking off. Near the end of his brief, the weatherman gave the A-4 pilots their D-value, a numerical conversion of the air's relative density, the temperature and the humidity, which had to be plugged into the A-4 computers to direct their bombing runs. He concluded by saying, "And for you F-Eight drivers, your NFT value is twenty-eight."

There was a brief silence. An F-8 pilot raised his hand and said, "Hey, what's the NFT value mean? Never heard of that before."

"Not a fucking thing," deadpanned the weatherman, walking off the podium. The room erupted into laughter at the unexpected joke, breaking the tension.

The intelligence briefing followed. Missile sites were numbered and displayed on a map overlay. "We expect number forty-seven to be hot today," said the briefer. His comments seemed to make no impression on the pilots. They were going to get shot at and what the intelligence briefer could not tell them, because he didn't know, was how many of the mobile SAM sites would be active. He noted targets the air force was scheduled to hit and what routes their planes would take. He gave them a rundown on the major battles being fought in South Vietnam. "And watch out for the I.C.C. plane," he warned. "Don't have a midair with it, and don't shoot it down." The International Control Commission plane, an anachronism left over from the 1954 Geneva Accords, made a milkrun to Hanoi from Cambodia and Laos, ferrying diplomats and, increasingly, antiwar activists from the United States. The warning caused wry smiles around the room. He ended by giving them the emergency word for the day. If they got shot down, the word would be used in radio transmissions to verify that it was in fact them on the radio and not a North Vietnamese using it to draw other planes into a trap. They had not figured out, however, a way to stop the Vietnamese from using the emergency radio's automatic beeper as a lure for a flak trap.

The intelligence briefer sat down and the strike group leader took over. There was a noticeable sharpening of attention in the room. He began to trace the flight, from the time airplanes were manned until they returned to the *Oriskany*.

"Fighters will rendezvous at twelve thousand feet for One-Six-Two and at fifteen thousand for One-Eleven," he said. "As soon as the A-Fours have finished refueling, the strike group will depart for shore. Once inbound we will climb to twenty thousand feet, so we can trade off that altitude to pick up a little more speed on the run in. As we cross the islands northeast of Haiphong, we'll hook in there to keep the North Vietnamese guessing till the last minute.

"We'll start down across the beach at fourteen thousand feet. Five minutes before crossing, I'll give the signal to get your electronic equipment up, select and on. Start jinking five miles off the beach, and everybody be heads up. Don't start diving or evading the SAMs, though, until you actually see them. Not long after crossing the coastline we should pick up the target. Whoever sights it first, make sure you identify yourself and call its location.

"As soon as I have the target in sight, I'll call for the flak suppressors to detach. At that time, I want the F-Eights to accelerate ahead of the strike group and hit the flak sites. I'll also give the final check to turn on master arming switches for the ordnance. We will roll in on the target in the sequence as I have displayed it here on the map.

"When we make our runs on the target, the fighters will pull off to the west to cover for any inbound MiGs. The A-Fours will pull directly off and head back to the beach. There will be no second runs on the target. As soon as your feet are wet, each section leader will radio me and I'll check you off to make sure everybody is back."

The strike group leader then told the pilots where the tanker and the search and rescue helicopter would be positioned after the target was hit. The tanker, with a full load of fuel, would be circling off the coast. If a pilot were downed, his squadron mates would try to mark his location, while others refueled from the tanker and returned to fly cover for the rescue chopper. The rescue effort would be coordinated by a U.S. destroyer steaming off the coast.

By 11:00 A.M. the main briefing was over. The pilots returned to their individual ready rooms, where each squadron flight leader conducted a less formal briefing for those flying under his command. Cal Swanson decided that of the six planes taking part in the strike from his squadron, two would fly MiG cover while the other four split up the flak sites around the bridge. They looked at the photos and identified the sites. Swanson assigned each plane a specific gun to take out. The information was detailed and technical. He read off the fuse settings to be used on the bombs, the amount of fuel to be taken on, the plane numbers, the emergency recovery time aboard ship in case of bad weather, and the ship's navigation data, her location after the strike.

Jim Nunn checked and rechecked his equipment. For the third time, he examined his .38 revolver to make sure there was an empty chamber under the firing pin. At twenty-three, Jim Nunn was the youngest pilot on the *Oriskany.* He stood six-four and weighed one hundred and ninety-five pounds. He was from Halls, Tennessee, fifty miles north of Memphis. His father was a banker. As a high school senior, Jim had applied to West Point, Annapolis, and the Air Force Academy—and won appointments to all three. He decided that Annapolis was academically the best, and he entered the Naval Academy, where he graduated 196 out of 952, class of '64. He was on the rowing team four years at Annapolis, at the top of his class in fighter-pilot school. That's the way life had been for Jim Nunn. Everything had fallen effortlessly into place. Now he was about to fly his first strike on North Vietnam, assigned as Cal Swanson's wingman, and he felt the gut fear of the unknown.

Cal Swanson began to put on his flight gear. First came the G-suit, which was designed to compensate for the pull of gravity. In level flight a pilot was exposed to one G, normal gravity. As he maneuvered—turning, diving, climbing—the pull of gravity increased, draining the blood downward from the head to the lower extremities, causing, if unchecked by a G-suit, the pilot to lose consciousness from oxygen deprivation. Rubber bladders were sewn into the G-suit across the abdomen, to the front and rear of the thighs, and the calves of the leg. The suit was connected by hose to a source of compressed air. As the number of Gs increased, the rubber bladders inflated and kept the pilot's blood from pooling and the flow of oxygen to the brain uninterrupted. The G-suit, a forest green color, was girdle tight. After the torso harness was put on over it, the pilot looked spindly-legged and walked with blocky steps. The torso harness, which connected the pilot to his ejection seat, was strapped on very tightly and contained the Mae West flotation gear, a collapsed rubber ring around the pilot's waist, which could be inflated with carbon dioxide cartridges. The survival vest went over the torso harness and included everything from Band-aids to water purification tablets, about twenty pounds in all. The beeper radio, which turned on automatically when the pilot ejected, was considered the most important piece of survival gear, and Cal Swanson checked to make sure the PRC-63's battery was still good.

In World War Two, pilots had been assigned their own airplanes, but the men of Squadron 162 flew whatever plane was available and ready to go. The squadron had twelve F-8s. Usually ten were aboard at any time, with the other two at Subic Bay undergoing corrosion control or routine maintenance. Only the plane captain, an enlisted man who saw to it that the jet was serviced and clean, stayed with a particular aircraft while it was on the ship. A few minutes before pilots manned aircraft, the plane captains sat in their F-8 cockpits like mother hens, watching the line maintenance crew scurry around checking all systems. After the flight, Cal would be expected to fill out a grading sheet indicating whether the plane captain had done his job well.

The call to man airplanes normally came thirty minutes before launch time. But today, because thirty-seven aircraft were involved, the announcement was made forty minutes in advance. Ready Room 4 was located next to an escalator that stopped just below the flight deck. Cal Swanson and Jim Nunn needed only three minutes to reach their planes. After strapping in, they went through a checklist, making sure all systems were operable. The flight deck was relatively calm.

At 11:40 A.M., the air boss from his tower called through the loud-speaker system: "Stand by to start aircraft. Check all wheel chocks and tiedowns. Stand clear of jet intakes and tail pipes." Giving the line crew time to follow his instructions, he then called: "Start engines!" The starter jeeps, small jet engines operating off batteries, were hooked to the airplanes and turned up until the energy transfer reached a certain rpm, at which point the airplanes, after ignition sparks and fuel were injected, began to idle, blasting out heat waves from their exhausts, creating an ear-splitting roar.

At 11:53 A.M.—seven minutes before launch time—an airplane tax-ied up to each of the catapults. The airplane was attached to the catapult shuttle, which ran in a groove along the flight deck, by a tow cable at the front and by a hold-back cable at the rear. Getting ready for the launch, the pilot pushed his throttle forward to full power and the airplane roared and quivered, straining like a wild beast to break loose its bonds. The hold-back cable was machined at the exact tensile strength necessary to restrain the airplane at full power but designed to break instantly when the catapult was fired. The tow cable, attached behind the nose wheel of the F-8, dropped off as the catapult shuttle reached the end of its track and the airplane left the ship.

Carrier landings were more dangerous than takeoffs, but at least there a pilot was master of his fate, whereas on the catapult shot he was in the hands of a number of people, some of them quite young and poorly educated, who had to operate with precision as a team. So many things could go wrong in two and a half seconds. The catapult pistons in the machinery below the deck might not have enough steam pressure to send the plane off at the correct speed. Or the tow cable could break during the shot. If the pilot hadn't attained flying speed when he reached the end of the deck, in no more than seventy-five yards, he plunged straight into the water. Hope, that's all he could do. When at full power and ready to go, the pilot signaled the catapult officer who stood to the side and front, by saluting him during the day, or by turning on the plane's exterior lights at night, and the cat officer suddenly, in a dramatic gesture, brought his arm down from over his head and touched the deck, whereupon his nearby assistant pushed the red button that fired the catapult. The shock of being hurled with such force was so abrupt, so unnatural, that a pilot, for the first several dozen shots, had little awareness of what was going on. He found himself in the air and had to start flying. Only later, after much experience, was he able to look at his instrument panel and the deck during the shot, and learn how to recognize a malfunction.

As Cal Swanson and Jim Nunn taxied to the catapults, the pilots of Squadron 162 who were not going on the strike settled down in the ready room to watch the launch on the TV monitor and to listen to radio transmissions as the attack began. The *Oriskany*'s tactical control center, its war room, was located next-door to Ready Room 4, which made it convenient for Commander Bellinger, Dick Wyman, Black Mac, Rick Adams, and the others to monitor the strike. The control center was a large room dimly lit so that its technicians could better see the radar scopes and electronic gear that occupied most of the space. Behind transparent plastic boards positioned around the room stood sailors who were writing backward with black grease pencils as fast as most persons wrote normally, so that the information they were recording—the fuel states, call signs, positions of each plane in the strike group—could be read instantly by officers standing in front of the boards. An officer was assigned to keep track of each plane's fuel state. In the event of a delay in landing, he could glance at the boards to determine which would need refueling by a tanker and give his orders accordingly.

Besides a brief transmission to see if their black-boxes were working, the pilots observed radio silence until they reached the coast. "Black-box" was the casual name for the top-secret electronics gear that helped them evade missiles. To maintain security in case they were shot down, the pilots knew the principles but not the mechanics of how the anti-SAM gear worked. When it was turned on, they heard various electronic sounds like a warble in their headsets, indicating the different stages the SAM site was going through as it prepared to fire the missile, whether it was tracking a plane with radar or was actually ready to fire. The Americans had ways to interfere electronically, to jam the missile site, forcing it off its computer-guided automatic mode. This required the North Vietnamese to aim the missile manually. The two Vietnamese technicians doing the aiming (one plotting azimuth, the other elevation) were not as fast or as accurate as the SAM's automatic tracking system, and this gave American pilots a crucial edge to outmaneuver the missiles, if they saw them coming in time.

It was a pretty day. The sun was shining, with visibility about ten miles. Jim Nunn was struck by the beauty of the islands to the northeast of Haiphong. It was, he thought, some of the loveliest scenery in the world. Sandstone cliffs rose from each small island and each had its own white crescent-shaped beach. He imagined himself owning one of the islands, a private vacation home perched on a cliff, overlooking a beach of incredible purity.

Nunn was jerked out of his reverie by a feeling that something was wrong. The strike group had crossed the shore and was turning toward the target. At the speed they were traveling—almost seven miles a minute—the strike group leader should have sighted the target by now and called it, but he had said nothing. There was a broken haze over the area, making it a little difficult to see the ground at an angle, and Nunn, like other pilots in the group, suspected that, besides not being the best pilot on the ship, the strike group leader's eyes were going bad. He was no Jim Stockdale.

The strike group leader called, "Anybody see the fucking target?" The profanity, rare in radio transmissions, which usually, as a matter of professionalism, were kept formal, calm, and to the point, was a measure of his frustration. Frank Elkins, who was flying his A-4 bomber to the left of the six F-8s from Squadron 162, responded, "I've got it at ten o'clock. Follow me and drop on my smoke."

"For twenty-three minutes there was flak, bullets, and everything that they could throw at us," Frank Elkins later told Marilyn. "I damn near blacked myself out dodging some of that garbage. At the target, our visibility was greatly reduced by flying steel."

Jim Nunn rolled in to hit a flak site. He got his bombs off and then tried to find Cal Swanson. He had lost him. Airplanes were all over the sky. It was mass confusion. Nunn told himself, "Careful, don't have a midair." He was worried about colliding with another plane, about the antiaircraft fire exploding around him, worried, too, about the thirteen missiles that looked like telephone poles trailing an orange flame that were heading toward the strike group. He decided to forget Swanson for the moment.

"After the run, the flak was walking a steady path up my exhaust trail and I looked out to the left, and there was an F-8 hauling home," said Frank Elkins. "I caught in my mirror the flash of a missile, called again, and went three hundred and sixty degrees to the right, behind the hills, or karst ridges. As I reversed at low altitude, I looked up to the left in time to see the missile hit the F-8, right up the intake, and the whole mess made one big ball of fire, disintegration."

On the *Oriskany*, in Ready Room 4, the remainder of 162's pilots were listening to the radio transmissions of the strike group. Suddenly through a soft curtain of static came the cry: "Missiles! Missiles!" The room tensed. Then the slightly nervous but controlled voice of Cal Swanson: "Has anyone seen Superheat-Three?" That was the code name for Terry Dennison. Rick Adams and the others shifted uneasily in their seats.

"Superheat-Three, this is Superheat-One." Cal Swanson tried again. No answer. He radioed Dennison's wingman. The wingman tersely replied that he had not seen Dennison's plane since they broke to evade the missiles. In the *Oriskany's* dim war room, Captain Iarrobino took out a small notebook and thumbed through it by the light of a radar set until he found the code name, Superheat-Three. Next to the code name was the pilot's real name and his squadron.

As the strike group reached the South China Sea, each plane radioed, "Feet wet." When the last "feet wet" was heard, the strike group leader made the final transmission of the attack: "One missing—Superheat-Three."

Jim Nunn still did not see Cal Swanson. He had almost reached the coast when he spotted another lone F-8. The plane was from 162's sister squadron. The pilot also had lost his flight leader. Nunn teamed up with the F-8, and they exited North Vietnam, weaving back and forth over each other to evade the flak.

When Swanson landed on the *Oriskany*, Nunn had already parked his plane. "What happened?" Cal asked.

"I rolled in and concentrated on the target, and looked up and you were gone," Nunn said. It was obvious that Nunn felt badly about his failure, and Swanson, concerned by the loss of Terry Dennison, hurried on to the ready room.

Rick Adams said it first. "I'm sure I heard Terry trying to call in. They just didn't hear him. There was too much confusion. His radio probably malfunctioned after that, just like mine did. He's coming in. Just wait."

Another pilot picked it up: "Yeah, I heard him trying to radio. Sure, he's coming in."

And another, his face cupped in his hands: "Yes, I heard it too."

Captain Iarrobino walked into the ready room. Everybody stood without speaking and, military courtesy extended, sat back down. Iarrobino moved to the coffee urn where Commander Bellinger was standing, with both hands wrapped around a cup. Cal Swanson entered before they had a chance to exchange words. "They were really popping today," Swanson said. "I saw three whiz by me. There were so many I lost count." He reached into a sleeve pocket of his flight suit and fumbled out a pack of Luckies. His hands shook. Bellinger quickly extracted a lighter from his own pocket and lit the cigarette for him.

"You lost one?" asked Captain Iarrobino.

"Yes, sir. He took a missile." Swanson looked at the floor. "After a while, all everyone was doing was dumping their bombs and getting out of there as fast as possible. We didn't score the bridge." His voice tightened. "We had too many planes for that kind of game, too many in the air."

Bellinger stepped in quickly. "What we ought to do," he said loudly, smiling, "is send them five million bucks and ask them to blow the goddamn bridge themselves."

Swanson and Captain Iarrobino left for the debriefing in the strike operations room. Rick Adams was at Bellinger's side before the two men got out the door. "Skipper," he said, "I'm sure I heard Terry call in. Some of the others did too."

"No, Rick. They got him," Bellinger said, putting his arm around the younger pilot.

---

11 · *Marilyn Elkins*

FRANK THOUGHT he was going to leave the war early. He had orders to report to test pilot school. I was looking forward to seeing him at home in a couple of months. But there was a mixup in his orders, and it turned out he had to stay for the whole cruise. On July 19, 1966, after he returned from the Co Trai strike, he wrote in his journal:

"I still haven't written Marilyn about having to stay for the whole cruise. I'm planning to ask her to fly to Manila in early September. The ship will be in port for ten days. I'll ask for leave, and I'll be able to be with her for the period when the ship is in Hong Kong as well— a grand total of three weeks. It'll be a great trip for her, and one we may never get the chance to take again, at least not for a while.

"I almost wish for her sake that I had never received the original orders. I'm really torn up inside. I belong here, and the fact that I don't like it and would rather be somewhere else shouldn't matter as much as it does. The skipper's right, the XO's right, but I had dared to hold the idea of wrapping my arms about Marilyn in September, knowing that I wouldn't have to say goodbye for years, and now I have to let that idea go. Having her over here will be expensive, but it will be worth it. Why not? Might be our only chance."

Frank waited a few days to write after he learned he wasn't coming home. He asked his brother to call and tell me the bad news. I was terribly disappointed. But I began to plan my trip to Manila and Hong Kong. I had to get a passport and tons of shots. My grandfather really liked Frank and was afraid we couldn't afford the trip. He pulled two one-thousand-dollar bills out of his wallet, and said, "Here's the money. You've got to go."

"Thank you," I said, "but put the money back in the bank. I'm going, don't worry."

My plane was delayed in San Francisco and we didn't take off until four in the morning. Then we reached Guam and circled and circled, trying to land. I said, "Suppose the plane crashes and I don't get to see Frank. What irony." But we finally arrived in Manila and I went to the hotel. I was a day late. It was hot and humid, and I was suffering from jet lag. I opened the telegram waiting for me. The *Oriskany* had been held up on Yankee Station two more days. I fell into bed. Next day there was a knock on the door. He was wearing his flight suit. It seemed forever since we'd seen each other; we stayed in the room a day or two without leaving.

Five other wives had also come to meet their husbands, and we decided to take a trip to the mountains together. There was millionaire's row in Manila and just outside nothing but destitution. I was appalled by the poverty. One of the wives said, "Well, I don't think there's anything to feel sorry about. They can always eat bananas and coconuts off the trees."

And I said to myself, "Oh, God, what am I doing? Who are these people I'm with?"

Frank was upset, too, by the navy wife's comments. We decided to spend the rest of the time by ourselves. After a week in Manila the *Oriskany* sailed for Hong Kong. The other pilots had to go with the ship, but Frank and I took a commercial flight. His skipper thought that since we had been married only a short time Frank should have more time off. In Hong Kong, we were walking out of our hotel, when a tour bus pulled up and a couple got off. It was an officer Frank knew, a flight surgeon from the *Oriskany*, Lloyd, I believe his name was, and Frank said, "There's the guy whose wife you like so much. Let's go say hello." He pulled me with him before I could say anything. We had a brief conversation with the couple, then continued on our way.

Frank said, "My God, I've never seen him act so cold."

I said, "That's not his wife."

Frank said, "Oh shit, I'm sorry. I didn't know that."

I did not believe in double standards. I liked the officer's wife. She was a beautiful woman. I knew she wasn't playing around back in the States. I was outraged. I didn't see Shirley's husband, Jack, doing anything, but if I had, I probably would have picked something up and thrown it at him. In the basement of the President Hotel, in Kowloon, where we were staying, was a disco place called the Firecracker Lounge, which had one of those fake American bands that sang rock 'n' roll. When Frank and I went there to dance, we ran into other married pilots who had girlfriends with them. I wasn't shocked anymore, just disgusted and sick of it.

I said to Frank on the dance floor, "I don't know whether I want to stay."

He said, "I'm sorry you're bothered, but there is nothing I can do about it."

We went to the biggest floating restaurant in the world and did a lot of shopping. He had a gorgeous camel's hair blazer and a couple of suits made. I purchased a wool dress and coat, a couple of silk dresses, and some handmade shoes. I found my mother a piece of silk and bought ashtrays and things like that to ship home, to use as Christmas gifts. Time passed like a blur. The night before Frank had to leave we dressed up as though we were going out and had dinner in the room. Room service wheeled in this really elegant setting with candlelight and roses. Frank called the hotel photographer and asked him to come up to take our picture. After finishing the chateaubriand, we talked all night.

Frank was not sure about the war. He had a friend who had turned in his wings. Frank respected him. "It's not that he's a coward. He just doesn't believe this war is right. And I keep wondering, too, what we're really dropping our bombs on." He talked about getting out of the navy. But he didn't know for certain what he wanted to do.

The pilot with whom he had arranged to ride back to the *Oriskany* phoned three times, telling him they had to go if they were to make it on time. Frank didn't want to leave. I was in bed, crying, my face turned away. I didn't want to see it happen. He closed the door quietly. I stayed in bed most of the day. Then I got on a plane to Hawaii by myself, instead of going with the other wives. I was writing Frank a letter while I was on the plane, crying and writing. I spent a week in Hawaii and then returned home to Pikeville.

At 8:30 A.M., on October 13, 1966, I was in my bedroom when I heard the doorbell ring. I put on a housecoat and went to see who it was. Two navy men in blue uniforms, an officer and an enlisted man, stood on the doorstep. When I opened the door, the officer said, "Mrs. Elkins, are you alone?"

I said, "Yes, why?"

He said, "We have something to tell you, but we don't think you should be alone."

Obviously, it had something to do with Frank—his plane must have been shot down. I said, "This is ridiculous. Why do I have to have somebody here? My mother is teaching school and I don't want to interrupt her. Tell me why you have come."

They would not say anything. I telephoned my mom. Shirley was working as a secretary at the high school where my mother taught. It turns out she had called Mom earlier that morning, because she'd heard on TV that Robert McNamara had been aboard the *Oriskany* the day before, and a plane had been shot down. Shirley called to see if we'd heard anything. She was terrified every minute something would happen to Jack, while I was never afraid anything would happen to Frank. I knew he would come out all right.

The officer was in his thirties. He was straight navy, with a crewcut, a nice man, actually, in a difficult position. I was insistent. Before Mother and Shirley arrived, he said, "Your husband has been shot down, and he's dead. I'm sorry." The two of them sat on the couch in the den, staring at their hands. Mother and Shirley came. They told Mother Frank was dead. They asked if they could use the telephone, to report to their headquarters that they'd advised us Frank was dead.

After making the call, the officer returned and said, "We've made a mistake. Our telegram is in error. Actually, all we know is that his plane has been shot down."

That gave me something called hope. I didn't cry. I was calm and cold. I tried to reach my mother-in-law, to make sure they didn't give her the wrong telegram first. I called Frank's older brother, an attorney in Wilmington, North Carolina. He decided to drive up to tell his mother himself. We received the correct telegram, which said:

> *I deeply regret to confirm on behalf of the United States Navy that your husband, Lt. Frank Callihan Elkins, 658100 / 1310, USN, is missing in action. This occurred on 13 October 1966 while on a combat mission over North Vietnam. It is believed your husband was maneuvering his aircraft to avoid hostile fire when radio contact was lost. An explosion was observed but it could not be determined whether this was hostile fire exploding or your husband's aircraft. No parachute or visual signals were received. You may be assured that every effort is being made with personnel and facilities available to locate your husband. Your great anxiety in this situation is understood and when further information is available concerning the results of the search now in progress you will be promptly notified. I join you in fervent hope for his eventual recovery alive. I wish to assure you of every possible assistance together with the heartfelt sympathy of myself and your husband's shipmates at this time of heartache and uncertainty.*
>
> *The area in which your husband is missing presents the possibility that he could be held by hostile forces against his will. Accordingly, for his safety in this event, it is suggested that in replying to inquiries from sources outside your immediate family you reveal only his name, rank, file number, and date of birth.*
>
> Vice Admiral B. J. Semmes, Jr.
Chief of Naval Personnel

Within an hour, the news was all over town. The Methodist minister arrived. He was a nice young man, very polite, but I told him I was not religious and asked him to leave. I sat talking to Shirley and Mother. I'd never seen my mother cry, but, suddenly, she started taking short intakes of breath, hyperventilating. My father was the assistant manager of the local telephone company. I asked him to install another phone in our house. I had teenage brothers who were on the phone all the time, and I wanted a private line so when they found Frank, I could be reached right away. The phone was put in that afternoon. People were coming around to the house. They thought I shouldn't be left alone. I thanked them for the food they brought and talked for a while, but I tried to explain as best I could that Frank wasn't dead.

Having gotten in touch with Frank's mother, to make sure she didn't get the wrong telegram, I didn't care about anything else. I was focusing only on myself. I did not call anybody to tell what had happened. The husband of one of my closest friends from high school had cancer. My friend asked me to go with them to a North Carolina hospital. I said, "I can't. Frank's plane has been shot down, and I need to be here in case he calls."

She said, "Why didn't you let me know, Marilyn?" I did not call to tell her, of course, because—I don't know, I just didn't.

My dad had a friend in the community who had been a POW in World War Two. Everybody had thought he was dead, until he returned home after the war. To me, he became empirical evidence that some people did return. Other people, I knew, had been believed dead but weren't. Frank would not be home soon; I realized that. Probably he would be gone four or five years. He was listed as missing in action. But I knew, deeply believed, he was a prisoner of war.

II

October 26, 1966

The Fire

1

ON OCTOBER 26, 1966, when the fire alarm sounded, Cal Swanson was sleeping more soundly than he had on the morning of the Co Trai strike three months earlier. The *Oriskany* was due to leave soon for San Diego, her combat tour nearly over, and Co Trai stood out in Swanson's mind as the worst strike he had taken part in, the only one during which a pilot of the squadron was killed. Butch Verich had been shot down in August—slow, polite Butch—but was recovered by helicopter without any trouble. And then a few weeks ago, on October 9, Commander Bellinger had brought down a MiG. It was a classic dogfight. Belly did everything right. He was, of course, euphoric— deservedly so, thought everyone, although Bellinger's conduct after the shootdown, when he walked around the flight deck drinking one brandy after another, in plain view of the crew, disturbed some of his subordinates. Alcohol was forbidden on American ships, except on special occasions, after a rescue from enemy territory or an important triumph, and then only one ceremonial brandy was served. There was plenty of drinking aboard ship, but it was kept undercover, never flaunted as Bellinger had done. Captain Iarrobino ignored Belly's indiscretion and sent him to describe his victory to reporters in Saigon at the daily press briefing, the Five O'Clock Follies; and stories appeared in newspapers back home about the *Oriskany* and Squadron 162, which pumped up the squadron's morale, already high, and made everybody feel they were an important part of the fight to keep South Vietnam free of communist domination.

Captain John Iarrobino, who was sitting in his sea cabin doing paperwork when the fire alarm sounded, also had reason to be pleased with the *Oriskany*'s tour on Yankee Station. The pilots and men of the carrier had performed wonderfully. No air wing had carried out its assignments over the beach with more courage and determination; no

ship's crew had worked longer hours under more difficult and dangerous conditions. Iarrobino was too modest to suggest that his shiphan-
dling had been a factor in the *Oriskany's* success, but it was true that
the ship had set an ordnance replenishment record, untopped by anyone on Yankee Station, when an average of 435.5 tons an hour were
transferred at sea from the ammunition ship USS *Mt. Katmai*. Iarrobino was gratified to see the way his men had reacted when he told
them that the *Franklin D. Roosevelt,* the aircraft carrier assigned to
replace the *Oriskany,* had thrown a screw and returned to Japan for
repairs, which meant they would have to stay longer. The *Oriskany*
was already two weeks overdue to go home, and a planned stopover in
Hong Kong was out, a big disappointment to everyone, but the crew
had taken the bad news in stride. Morale remained high.

Besides the loss of pilots to enemy fire, there were only two incidents during the tour that he recalled with less than satisfaction. The
first occurred the night the wire broke as a refueling tanker touched
down on the carrier. An airplane landed by catching with its tail hook
one of four cables stretched across the flight deck. The tail hook engaged
the arresting wire and the wire jerked the plane to a teeth-rattling halt
in a very few feet. When accidents happened and the wire broke, as it
occasionally did, it whiplashed across the deck like a scythe, mowing
down anything in front of it. On this particular night, an enlisted man
and a junior officer were in the wire's path. A pilot from Squadron
162 who had just climbed down from his cockpit suddenly felt something wet and sticky hit him full force in the chest. It was a leg of the
junior officer who was lying on the flight deck trying to stand up,
puzzled as to why he could not, in shock, not realizing both his legs
had just been lopped off. The enlisted man was also badly injured.

The rescue crew, trying to find if anybody else was hurt, stumbled
in the darkness upon two young seamen sitting in the safety net at the
edge of the flight deck, giggling, their eyes strangely lit. It took Iarrobino and his staff some time to work out what was wrong with the two
sailors, for this was the first instance of drug use aboard the *Oriskany.*
Iarrobino became as angry as he ever got, outraged by the combination
of the accident and the dope. He was usually lenient with first-time
offenders, but this time he threw the book at them, and then got on
the public address system to let everybody know there would be no
more drugs brought aboard ship. Throughout the navy, skippers of

American ships were saying the same thing, although, as time would prove, to little effect.

The second incident Iarrobino remembered as unpleasant had occurred two weeks before, on the evening of October 12–13, when a party of high-ranking officials, headed by Secretary of Defense Robert S. McNamara, visited the ship as part of their tour of Southeast Asia. Also included were Arthur Sylvester, the Pentagon's chief spokesman; General Earle G. Wheeler, chairman of the Joint Chiefs of Staff; and Admiral U. S. Grant Sharp, Jr., Commander-in-Chief, Pacific.

After showing them around the ship, Iarrobino escorted the officials to the wardroom, where a special dinner and ceremony was planned. Commander Bellinger had been put in for a Silver Star for downing the North Vietnamese MiG three days earlier, and it was decided that McNamara would pin the medal on him. Captain Iarrobino made an introductory speech, remarking with a straight face that, as everyone knew, Commander Bellinger was noted on the *Oriskany* for his sense of humility—a comment that drew laughter from the ship's officers and puzzled the official party; and then McNamara made some remarks, which were perfunctory. Maybe it was because McNamara was tired, Iarrobino thought, that they got off on the wrong foot. The secretary looked pale and fatigued, obviously suffering from jet lag. The first question McNamara asked concerned the number of missions over North Vietnam that each of the *Oriskany*'s pilots averaged per day.

"Two," Iarrobino replied. McNamara was brusquely critical. Why weren't they averaging only one and a half, as he had laid down in his guidelines?

"Because we have too few pilots and too many missions," Iarrobino said.

Iarrobino could have told McNamara that he was also suffering from a loss of key personnel among the enlisted men, especially in the petty officer ranks. When a sailor's enlistment period in the navy was over, he was flown off the ship, unless, of course, he reenlisted, and few were reupping. Washington was trying to fight the war on the cheap, without an all-out national effort, and it was showing up in the staffing of the ship. But Iarrobino decided not to push the matter with McNamara. Instead, sitting next to him at dinner, he tried to make cheerful small talk, only to be turned away by the secretary's lack of interest. When McNamara made his speech before pinning the Silver

Star on Bellinger, Iarrobino was surprised to see how ill at ease he seemed. He clutched the microphone with white knuckles, evidently very nervous. Maybe Secretary McNamara did not like the navy, or pilots, or the air war—maybe all three. Iarrobino couldn't figure it out. To top it off, one of the A-4 pilots, Frank Elkins, was shot down while the official party was aboard. All in all, it had not been a good night.

But that was over and done. At 7:21 A.M., on October 26, 1966, when the fire alarm sounded, Captain John Iarrobino had no reason to be worried and every reason to be pleased. He had turned forty-six on October 9, the day Bellinger got his MiG, and his future in the navy seemed assured. The promotion board to select new admirals would meet in several months. Skippering an aircraft carrier in combat was a sure ticket to two stars.

Captain Iarrobino picked up his phone and received a report from the bridge about the fire. It was in hangar bay one, said the duty officer, which was all the information available at the moment. Damage Control Central had a panel with scores of small amber lights, each one connected to a heat sensor somewhere on the ship. When a fire broke out, an identifying light on the panel blinked red. The *Oriskany* averaged anywhere from one to fifteen fire alarms each day. Usually they were caused by small electrical fires, something minor and easily contained. The standard response to each alarm, no matter how inconsequential, was the same. The sailor on duty in Damage Control picked up his phone, dialed 222, and told the bridge, "I have a fire alarm indication," specifying its location. The bosun's mate then clanged the chrome-plated fire bell and his voice rang out over loudspeakers throughout the ship: "Fire, fire, fire. This is no drill! This is no drill!"

Iarrobino decided to find out what this one was about. He pushed his paperwork aside and walked to the bridge, where he would have a clear view of the ship. As he reached the bridge, he could see clouds of dirty gray smoke roiling toward him. He knew it was not a small one.

CAL SWANSON had learned to sleep through the unceasing noise of an aircraft carrier—the banging of the catapult, the whirring of machinery, the rush of air, the clanging of bells, the announcements over the loudspeaker—relying on his subconscious to recognize anything out of the ordinary. The voice of the bosun's mate contained more excitement than usual, and Swanson awoke with a start. Swanson was sure he heard the bosun's mate say, "This is a drill!" and then, "This is no drill!" That sort of confusion was rare and suggested real danger. He popped out of his bunk, pulled on a pair of khaki trousers, stepped into his shoes without socks, and left his room.

The passageway outside was dense with smoke. It had the acrid smell of a freshly extinguished kitchen match, only hundreds of times stronger, infinitely more choking. A whiff of the smoke left one gasping for breath. Swanson started up a ladder, then stopped when he saw a fireball rolling overhead. He realized it was a magnesium fire, the worst possible kind, and guessed it must have started with the flares.

Swanson was right. The launch scheduled for the night before had been canceled due to bad weather. The crew, preparing for the first strike of the morning, was removing the flares from the planes and returning them to their storage locker when the accident happened: a dropped flare ignited. Released from an airplane by parachute, the flares, six feet long and eight inches in diameter, created a light of two million candlepower, turning night into day for two or three minutes.

Magnesium did not need oxygen to burn, and it was a question of whether the firefighters could drench the flares with enough salt water to cool the magnesium oxide below its burning point. While the hoses were being reeled out, an explosion occurred in the flare locker, igniting all eight hundred flares stored there, sending a huge ball of fire rolling through the hangar bay, knocking firefighters off their feet. The intensity of the fire was so great it began eating through the bulkhead of the hangar bay, heading toward the fuel supplies and bomb storage areas.

Captain Iarrobino still did not know what had happened. He thought an airplane had caught fire. With all the smoke, though, he knew the ship had a very serious problem on its hands, and he ordered the quartermaster, who stood next to the helmsman, to sound general quarters. The quartermaster jumped to the loudspeaker. Banging for attention, he cried: "General quarters! General quarters! Man your battle stations!" Heavy clouds of smoke billowed over the flight deck. Iarrobino gave a series of commands to turn the ship to the starboard, so the wind would blow across the deck, helping clear the smoke away. The ship's executive officer made his way to the hangar bay, where he could telephone Iarrobino an account of what was happening.

The internal geography of the *Oriskany*, like that of any aircraft carrier, was extremely complicated—a maze of compartments, hatches, ladders, storerooms, passageways, and dead ends. Even under ordinary circumstances it took a long time to learn one's way about the ship. Some sailors knew nothing other than the route through the maze that allowed them to reach their work, to eat, and sleep. Now smoke from the burning magnesium was being sucked through the ship's ventilating system, blinding and choking the men as they stumbled through the darkness trying desperately to find a pathway to safety.

Cal Swanson had a keen sense of direction and knew his way about the ship better than most. But every route Swanson tried he found blocked by fire. A knot of men, many of them young sailors, gathered behind him. He was the ranking officer. The smoke was getting thicker. He would have to do something before they all died.

Through the gloom an officer, a commander, groped his way toward them. Blood poured from a gash on his head. His skin was charred and blackened. He saw Swanson's group and turned and started running away. He was in shock. A young seaman grabbed his arm to restrain him. Skin sloughed off in the sailor's hand. "I'm dying," the commander said. Swanson gently brought him into the group.

A sailor moved forward in the passageway. He climbed a ladder and opened a hatch that led to the hangar deck. A fireball rolled overhead, burning his neck. He turned and said, "Sir, the only place we can go now is down."

Cal tried to think. It was hard to believe this was really happening, that suddenly it was a matter of life or death, no kidding. He recognized it as a state of mind, a refusal to face reality, that went along with a disaster, and he forced himself to concentrate, to try to remember everything he could about this part of the ship.

Supplies. A few days before, Swanson had seen sailors loading supplies by hand through a nearby hatch. He knew the ship had a few blind shafts about six feet square that dropped straight down to the ship's hole, from the second deck to the seventh, a function of the ship's design. A ladder ran down one side of the shaft and tiny platforms stuck out at each level, where there were small storerooms used to keep casual supplies. Were the sailors loading the supplies in a blind shaft? Swanson moved forward and checked the hatch. It was open. Yes, it led to a shaft.

He had a decision to make. If the ship was in danger of sinking and he led the men into the shaft, they could die by drowning. But if they didn't get away from the smoke, they were likely to die anyway. Swanson looked at the faces of the thirteen men following him. Then he gave the order to climb into the shaft and seal the hatch behind them.

The hangar bay was a mass of flames. Hoses strung from the forecastle burned through. Others had to be brought from aft. The fire spread to two helicopters. An ejection seat in a jet cooked off and shot skyward. Ammunition, unseen in the heavy smoke, began exploding as men removed bombs from an A-4. Ordnance on the forward starboard posed an immediate danger. Firefighters led two hoses down from the flight deck, to play water on the bombs to keep them cool.

No one had to say it. Every man understood. The *Oriskany* was fighting for her life. Reports began flowing to the bridge. The ship's senior medical officer was dead, as was the chaplain. Casualties were mounting. Men were trapped in their rooms, sure to die if not rescued soon. Captain Iarrobino radioed the USS *Constellation* to ask the carrier to send all available doctors. Martha Raye, the entertainer, was visiting the *Connie* and volunteered to go to the *Oriskany* as a nurse but was turned down. The fire continued to spread.

Captain Iarrobino looked from the conning station and saw bombs being thrown over the side. He watched, hypnotized. If one bomb exploded it would set off the rest. That would be the end. He looked closely and realized that two sailors, small guys, were heaving thousand- and even two thousand-pound bombs over the sides. Two men!

Jim Nunn was in his skivvies when the fire broke out. He put on his flight suit and boots, and left his room. Hearing two sailors call for help from the wardroom, he yelled for them to come his way and took them to his room. He gave them water-soaked towels to cover their faces, then led them to safety. He heard that a seaman was trapped in the bowels of the ship, in pumproom number one, and would die soon if no one got to him. Nunn joined with two other men who had found some scuba gear; they began to make their way through the water-filled compartments to the bottom of the ship.

Down in the shaft, Cal Swanson was trying to stanch the flow of blood from the badly burned commander's head with the wet handkerchief he had been using to breathe through. The men with him had distributed themselves at different levels, to equalize demands on the available oxygen. Two sailors found a heavy wrench and were working their way down the shaft, knocking off the padlocks on the storerooms, opening the doors to free the extra air. Other survivors joined the group. One of them, like a man before him, slipped off the ladder and wound up wedged between the ladder and the bulkhead at the bottom of the shaft. The burned officer was moaning, "Nobody touch me, please."

Time passed and Swanson began to get the tingly feeling he knew came from a lack of oxygen. They would have to leave the shaft soon. It was after 9:00 A.M., nearly two hours since the fire began. If progress hadn't been made toward bringing it under control, the ship was doomed. A sailor climbed to the top of the ladder, opened the hatch, and climbed out. He returned in a few minutes leading two men from a rescue party. They said the worst of the fire was over. Now was the time to get the men out of the shaft.

"You've got to help," Swanson told the burned commander.

"Okay, Cal, I'll do it," he said.

The officer put one foot on the ladder and passed out. Swanson grabbed him and then looked with horror at the charred skin that came off in his hand. They finally got him up the ladder and lashed him to a basket litter. Once in the passageway, they reached a sharp turn, which took precious minutes to get around. Then Swanson went back to the shaft, telling the others to follow him. He stumbled through the smoky darkness, leading them forward until, at last, he spotted a dim light ahead, and then a moment later, the safety of clean air.

Or so Swanson thought. He turned around. Nobody was following. They had lost him in the smoke and returned to the shaft. He found two stretcher bearers and started back. One of the men had passed out. Swanson could see that all of them were about ready to start dropping. He organized them into a human chain. The stretcher bearers could not make the sharp corner in the passageway. A lieutenant behind Swanson was getting faint. Swanson held him, trying to help the stretcher bearers at the same time. They negotiated the corner and Swanson made it out on the deck for the second time. Once again he looked around to find that, except for the lieutenant he was helping, nobody was following him.

Swanson returned for the third time. He got the human chain moving and pulled it forward. At the sharp corner in the passageway, he ran into rescue men carrying a dead body. "Get out of the way!" he yelled. "I've got people here who can walk." This time everyone made it to safety. It was 10:00 A.M.

Jim Nunn and his two partners made their way through the ship, trying to save the young sailor in the pumproom. Many of the compartments were flooded by the washdown from the firefighters' hoses. Nunn popped the hatches and drained the water, then climbed down to the next level. It was dark in the public affairs office, but Nunn could see the outlines of twenty-eight men, dressed and ready for work, dead in their seats. He surmised that the fire had sucked all the oxygen out before they realized what was happening. Nunn and his partners took turns using the scuba gear. They thought the water pouring downward in their path might drown the sailor. But in the next ten minutes they found him, groggy and nauseated. The scuba gear they were using belonged to the rescued man.

The fire was extinguished after three hours and seven minutes. A number of pilots were among the forty-three killed. Many more were injured. The burned commander whom Cal Swanson had saved later died, bringing the toll to forty-four. As the smoke cleared, the men began to exchange tales of heroism and narrow escape. There was the story of the two roommates, one of whom left immediately when the fire alarm sounded, the other who said, "Wait a minute, I'm going to comb my hair." The second did not make it. The same with two more pilots, one of whom stopped to put on his shoes. The tale that had everybody shaking their heads was Commander Bellinger's incredible escape through a porthole that some said was only eighteen inches in diameter and that even the most skeptical conceded to be no more than twenty-two inches across. Trapped by the fire, the porthole his only possible escape route, Bellinger took off his clothes and popped like a cork to safety. Captain Iarrobino, years later, still marveled at how Bellinger, with his barrel chest and tremendous belly, had managed to save himself. Dick Wyman, who was manning a hose on the flight deck, saw Belly walking around naked after his escape and found him some clothes to put on.

Dick Wyman's roommate, Lloyd, the squadron flight surgeon, and Ensign Boggs, the squadron intelligence officer, hadn't been so lucky. Both died in the fire. Wyman had grown to love his roommate. Doc had told Wyman his life had been one long struggle, to get through college, to get through medical school, his internship. The first money he had ever made, and not much then, came when he joined the navy to do his military service as a flight surgeon. Wyman knew Doc was having an affair with a bomber pilot's wife. The pilot was assigned to another aircraft carrier on a different cycle on Yankee Station. He did not think it his right to judge Doc. Sometimes he gave up his room to the couple when the *Oriskany* was in port. It was Doc and his friend whom Marilyn Elkins had seen in Hong Kong. Wyman went through Doc's personal effects and found a Polaroid of the woman, with an inscription on the back: "I hope this will remind you of when we were together. We were truly one." Wyman burned the picture and a box of love letters.

Later, after he got back to the States, he took the rest of Doc's effects to his wife's home, where she awaited him with her sister. The two women greeted him coldly. The sister started questioning him. Where did they go when they were in port? Did Doc have any friends? "Oh, we used to go to museums," Wyman said. "And to church." They looked at him, faces set in cold fury. He realized that Doc, before he died, had confessed to his wife about the affair. Doc felt terribly guilty about it. Now that Doc was no longer around, their pride required they call Wyman to account. He left as quickly as possible.

Barry Jones had handled Frank Elkins's personal effects after he was shot down. Jones also died in the fire. He had been charged by the navy to act as a censor, but he had sent Frank's papers to Marilyn intact, telling her, "Reading Frank's diary I became upset by my own lack of sensitivity and have decided that I will not be responsible for changing one word of this diary." He added, "I think Frank is one of the most skillful and daring pilots I know. Until I read his diary, I never understood the cost of his apparent lack of fear."

The *Oriskany* remained seaworthy. Most of the damage was confined to the hangar bay areas and forward officers' quarters. The electrical circuits were out; an elevator was damaged; the launching catapults had been warped. Extensive repairs were needed before air operations could continue. Wrapped in gloom, the ship limped to Subic Bay, where the crew stood mustered in silence as the fire's victims were carried in flag-draped coffins to an airplane returning to the States.

2 · *Marilyn Elkins*

A DART BOARD, one that I'd given Frank along with the typewriter, was included in the box of his personal effects. I went through the stuff, and when I returned, my younger brother, who was about twelve then, was playing darts. "How dare you take Frank's dart board!" I screamed. "Frank isn't dead. He might want that dart board." I was furious, upset that my brother could be so callous when, underneath, I knew he was very sensitive. He looked at me, stunned.

It was shortly before the 1966 congressional elections. I was going to the dentist and I saw William Brock, who was known in Tennessee as the heir to a candy fortune. He stopped me and said, "Hi, I'm Bill Brock. I'm running for Congress on the Republican ticket and I hope you'll vote for me."

I said, "My husband is missing. What is being done to help the missing in Southeast Asia?" I was not emotional. I was matter-of-fact and proud of myself for being in control.

My grandmother was president of the local Republican women. That night Bill Brock spoke to her group. He talked about campaigning on the street and meeting a beautiful girl with long blond hair (my hair was red) who, with tears streaming down her cheeks, begged him to do something about her missing husband. If reelected to Congress, he said, he was going to do something. My grandmother and the other ladies, of course, said, "That's our dear little Marilyn. Let's go vote for this nice man."

Oh, the hypocrisy of it! How could he use and misquote me for his narrow political purposes! God, I hated him after that. Later, I would go to Washington on some of those POW-wives things and he would send an aide over to ask me to have my picture taken with him. And I'd say, "I have no intention of ever having my photograph made with Bill Brock." This was the beginning of the political use some people tried to make of the POW and MIA issue. I thought Brock was dishonest for doing that, but, of course, I'm sure he did not perceive himself

99

that way. I hated politicians who tried to appeal on an emotional rather than a rational level.

By December I had lost twenty-five pounds. I was down to a hundred and must have looked horrible, but I never glanced at a mirror. It made people uncomfortable to be around me. I was young, my husband was missing, and if they told you they were sorry, you were liable to cry, and they didn't want to see you cry. But if they ignored it and didn't say anything, they knew they would come across as callous. Shirley's husband, Jack, who was in Squadron 162, returned home after the fire. She was afraid for me to see him, afraid it would make things worse, Jack coming back, Frank not with him. He finally came around to the house but didn't know what to say or do. I was in a period of suspended disbelief, a time capsule. You talk yourself into believing what you want to believe and ignore any fact that doesn't fit in. It didn't register on me that Jack failed to go on and on about how I mustn't give up hope.

I had diarrhea, terrible diarrhea. I continued to lose weight. At Christmas, my doctor sent me to a hospital in Chattanooga, where the navy would pay the bills. I'd had my appendix out as a child, but didn't remember much about it, except the ether and having the stitches removed, the people who brought gifts. I wasn't prepared for the hospital. There's something very dehumanizing about having diarrhea and having to undergo examinations of the very intimate parts of the body with a proctoscope. And I didn't like the doctor. My family doctor, whom I'd known since I was two, always teased me. But this doctor was detached. He talked to me about my husband without looking at all sad.

The hospital told me I had a disease. Ulcerative colitis. "Oh, God," I said, "that's wonderful!" I was so pleased. Even though it was connected to my nerves, at least it was a real disease. All this time I had thought I was going crazy.

3

A RUMOR SPREAD that the two sailors who were downloading the flares when the accident occurred had been fooling around, throwing them like footballs. Iarrobino discounted the story as a dramatic embroidery of a partial truth. After making a quick investigation, he believed that the two young seamen had wheeled the flares to the locker door and were stacking them like cordwood. Probably they were passing the flares to each other, tossing them a short distance as you would in stacking wood, when the accident happened. But the flares were supposed to be perfectly safe, ordnance that could be handled a bit roughly, and so he was puzzled to hear that the legal officer sent by the navy to conduct an investigation was acting like a prosecutor, badgering the crew to confess their culpable negligence in causing the fire.

The legal officer, a young lieutenant, short and overweight, came aboard the *Oriskany* in the Philippines, along with an admiral who was officially in charge of the investigation. The legal officer was a nonaviator, a black shoe, in itself hardly a recommendation to Iarrobino's staff, and his self-important attitude quickly made him unpopular with the crew. When assigned his room, he objected and demanded a larger one, even though the ship, already overcrowded before the fire, had much less space since the forward officers' quarters had been burned out. Members of the crew complained to Iarrobino that the legal officer was trying to force them to say what he wanted to hear. Iarrobino in turn complained to the admiral, a genial man, who made consoling noises and said he didn't agree with the young officer's tactics, either. But nothing changed as the investigation continued during the ship's transit back to San Diego.

Captain Iarrobino was not worried, though. Maybe the young legal officer was out to make a name for himself, but he had come up with nothing that Iarrobino could not answer properly. As he charged, there should have been a rated ordnanceman supervising the flare downloading, and there wasn't. The level of supervision had deteriorated throughout the ship because of a personnel shortage. This was a growing problem in every unit of the armed forces. The ship's key personnel were supervising the launch of strike aircraft that was supposed to go off at seven-thirty that morning.

There was also a matter of whether the flares were being stored in the proper locker. The locker was in a nonfloodable space, unlike ammunition magazines, where water could be let in quickly to stifle a fire. But the *Oriskany*, in order to fulfill her mission, carried so much ordnance that pilots literally had to walk over bombs to reach their planes, and the flare locker, while not strictly regulation, had been authorized by BuShips at U.S. Navy headquarters in Washington. What it came down to was that a small, aging, overcrowded aircraft carrier was being asked to do too much.

Despite the warning signs in the wind, Captain Iarrobino was stunned by the investigation report that the legal officer wrote and the admiral signed. Essentially, it recommended that the two sailors downloading the flares be charged with forty-four counts of murder, that the hangar deck and weapons officers be court-martialed, and that Iarrobino and his executive officer be given letters of reprimand. What struck Iarrobino was that they were all being blamed for a fire caused by a flare, but there was no investigation of the flare itself.

A navy board in San Diego rewrote the report, putting the charges in less apocalyptic terms. Iarrobino was required to file a response before a final disposition was made. A captain was ultimately responsible for anything that happened to his ship, such was naval tradition, and Iarrobino was perfectly ready to go down with the *Oriskany* in combat, but he thought he was being railroaded by a one-sided investigation, being made a scapegoat by a young legal officer who understood nothing of the war and its demands, and he decided he would not take it lying down. After all, Iarrobino knew people throughout the navy, high-ranking officers, and they knew him, knew that John Iarrobino's career was impeccable, that his devotion to duty was unquestioned.

Captain Iarrobino conducted his own investigation of the flare, which, for some unexplained reason, had not been touched on by the legal officer, or anyone else. Friends at the naval ammunition depot in Crane, Indiana, where the flares were made, gave him a computer analysis of the tolerances of the flare's fuse. The computer printout indicated that given the flare's design, as many as ten out of every ten thousand could ignite accidentally. This was a scandalously high rate for ordnance; the flare should have had a zero potential accident rate. Yet nothing had been done to change the flare's design. Investigating further, Iarrobino discovered that other ships on Yankee Station had had flares go off accidentally. Lucky for them, the accidents had occurred on their flight decks and were easily contained.

Armed with this new information, Iarrobino tried to get an appointment with the admiral who commanded all the navy's aircraft carriers in the Pacific. "I had worked for the admiral three times during my career," Iarrobino said. "He was the skipper of the *Forrestal* when I was the operations officer. We knew each other well, were good friends, even. I'd helped make him an admiral by working my tail off for him. But now he refused to see me, because he thought I was investigating a matter that might reflect back on him in a negative way."

The admiral sent his ordnance officer to talk to Iarrobino. The captain had put together a prototype of the flare's fuse, with the ledge for the striker pin constructed just a hair off the width called for by the flare's specifications. His demonstration was simple enough for a schoolkid to understand. He dropped the fuse on the table. The striker pin slipped off the ledge. A small jar could have set off a flare with such a fuse and started a fire that killed forty-four men.

The next day an order went out to all aircraft carriers instructing them to dump forty thousand flares into the ocean. The admiral refused, however, to change the report putting the blame for the fire on Iarrobino and his crew. "Did it shock me the way the navy was treating me?" said Iarrobino. "Yes, it really did. I expected more people to go to bat for me than did, considering the circumstances of wartime. Later they changed the flares and also stabilized the crews on ships, so that if you went to Yankee Station with a crew, you returned with the crew intact. But too late for me."

The affair dragged on. The board to select new admirals met while the letter of reprimand for Iarrobino was pending and he was passed over. Five *Oriskany* crew members were court-martialed but acquitted. Eventually, Iarrobino received a letter of nonpunitive caution, which, unlike a letter of reprimand, was not added to one's permanent record. In theory, such a punishment was not supposed to affect an officer's career. But that, of course, was just theory and Iarrobino, now assigned to Washington, was passed over the second and final time for admiral.

Three other aircraft carriers suffered accidental fires at sea. One of them was worse than the *Oriskany*'s, with more men lost. But all three skippers were promoted to the rank of admiral. It didn't escape the notice of Captain Iarrobino, or anyone else familiar with the workings of the navy, that they were graduates of the U.S. Naval Academy. John Iarrobino was not.

Captain Iarrobino retired to work as a defense consultant and to play golf. Twenty years later the *Oriskany* remained a large part of his life. He tried not to be bitter about it. Still, there was a feeling that he had been wronged; and he very much wanted to write a book to tell what had happened. The friends he talked to who knew the story, retired admirals and the like, said, "Yes, you were treated shabbily. But, John, be careful. Don't say or do anything that might hurt the navy."

4

ON DECEMBER 19, 1966, Cal Swanson assumed command of Squadron 162 in a ceremony held in San Diego. For Swanson, it was the moment he had been waiting for since he stood in the fields of his family's farm and watched a DC-3 make its first run between Denver and Cheyenne, a silver twin-engined airplane flying over a backdrop of blue sky and snow-tipped mountains, a sight Cal would always remember. Both of his older brothers had been World War Two pilots; his three sisters had married aviators; and with a name like Charles A. Lindbergh Swanson it seemed inevitable he would put aside early ambitions of becoming a veterinarian for the more exciting prospects of being a fighter pilot. He had not regretted the decision.

After the ceremony the squadron pilots and their wives went to the Chart House Restaurant in San Diego, making a noisy entrance that heralded a party that would be at all times on the verge of breaking out of control. The headwaiter, making a quick assessment of the situation, seated them as far from the other diners as he could. When Black Mac's wife, jammed near the wall, climbed on the table and threaded her way with great dignity around the glasses and plates, the headwaiter decided to make a stand and ordered her down, only to be informed that she was heading to the ladies' room and would do what she had to do right there, on the table, if he didn't act more like a gentleman. The headwaiter retreated, leaving the party to follow its natural course.

When it was over, Bellinger, or rather his wife, decided he had had too much to drink, and he asked another couple to drive his blue Thunderbird. The police pulled the car over and took the driver, Bellinger's friend, to jail. They warned Belly not to drive home. He waited a few minutes and climbed behind the wheel. He was stopped before he got a block. Cal and Nell passed by as the police were taking him to jail. Nell told Cal not to stop, to go straight home, and Cal knew by the tone of her voice she meant it. Richard Bellinger could destroy himself, but Nell wasn't going to let him spoil the night for which they had worked so long and hard.

Indeed, given what was to follow, it was somehow fitting that Bellinger spend the night in jail. For the end of his command of the squadron signaled the beginning of the end of Bellinger himself. There was nothing sadder to see than an aging fighter pilot trying to hang on to a young man's game. You either went up or out, and Bellinger, to no one's surprise, had not been selected as an air wing commander. He was assigned as the *Ticonderoga*'s operations officer. Bellinger acted as though it didn't bother him, but the squadron noticed that his drinking became heavier, his actions more frantic. "Everything was closing in," Dick Wyman said, "and Belly was running—running hard." He made his mark on the *Tico* by slugging the ship's air wing commander. Later, in Washington, he threatened the admiral who was deputy chief of naval operations for air in his own office. The United States Navy then gave Commander Richard M. Bellinger his final assignment. He was committed to the psychiatric ward of a navy hospital.

CAL SWANSON had a lot of plans for the squadron. But first he wanted to make sure the best pilots returned for the '67 cruise. Dick Wyman would be coming back, of course, and Butch Verich, Jim Nunn, and John Hellman. Cal asked Black Mac if he could handle another combat tour. Black Mac, secretly pleased to be wanted, replied in an offended tone, "What do you mean? Did you think I was chicken?"

Swanson planned to convert the squadron as much as possible into a bomber unit. That's where the action lay. Washington seemed to be loosening up on the targets. Admiral Sharp, just a few weeks earlier, had asked Washington for permission to strike close within the restricted zone encircling Hanoi, and he was given the go-ahead.

Of course, after the strikes were carried out on military targets near Hanoi's city limits, on December 13 and 14, the North Vietnamese started yelling that U.S. planes were bombing civilian areas and that America was embarked on a policy of genocide. But Swanson thought their response was to be expected. The North Vietnamese were, after all, waging a propaganda war as well as military war.

5

As SQUADRON 162 celebrated with champagne in San Diego, Harrison E. Salisbury of the New York *Times* was getting ready to board an airplane at Kennedy Airport on the first leg of a trip that would take him, among other places, to the area of the Co Trai bridge. Salisbury would describe the effects of the bombing, some of it carried out by the *Oriskany's* pilots, in dispatches that would appear with a shock on the front pages of the world's major newspapers.

Harrison Salisbury had received an invitation to visit North Vietnam forty-eight hours after U.S. planes hit Hanoi for the first time. Seymour Topping, foreign editor of the *Times*, put the slightly garbled cablegram on Salisbury's desk, asking, "Does this say what I think it does?" Salisbury agreed that it did but decided to ask Hanoi to reconfirm that his visa would be waiting in Paris. The reply quickly came back affirmative. Like other reporters, Salisbury had applied for a visa many months before but had heard not a word. Now, suddenly, the North Vietnamese were anxious to see him. Also on the way to Hanoi via Moscow were four American women, in a trip organized by Dave Dellinger of *Liberation* magazine; and invitations were being sent to Wilfred Burchett, the Australian journalist, and to a team of investigators for the Bertrand Russell International War Crimes Tribunal.

Until this point the American public had to rely on the North Vietnamese and their announced sympathizers, or official spokesmen in Washington and Saigon, for information concerning the air war. Most of that news, by far, emanated from the auditorium of the Joint U.S. Public Affairs Office in Saigon. There, each afternoon at five o'clock, a spokesman for the air war, usually an air force major or lieutenant colonel, took to the podium and briskly pointed out with maps and slides where U.S. planes had struck that day in North Vietnam. He was followed by an army officer who described the ground battles taking place inside South Vietnam.

The air briefing was seldom contentious. Reporters usually had covered some of the military operations being described by the army briefer and they were ready, not to say eager, to challenge him on factual or interpretive grounds, and as a result the army briefing often grew quite heated. But no one had flown with pilots on their missions over the North—that was forbidden—and so the air briefing passed in a routine manner.

Unchallenged, the air briefer was able to present the air war in terms of the Pentagon's choosing. Thus the bridge at Co Trai became part of the "Phu Ly-Co Trai military complex"; a fishing junk was a "waterborne logistics craft"; targets were hit with "surgical precision." Not once did he say, "Today U.S. planes ran into such heavy antiaircraft fire that they dumped their bombs which landed God knows where and got out of there as fast as possible." Instead, he intoned: "Today U.S. warplanes cratered the approaches to the Co Trai bridge." There were frequent announcements of "cratered approaches," which journalists duly reported.

In reality the air briefing was a bore. Occasionally, when someone like Commander Bellinger shot down a MiG or an extraordinary rescue occurred, pilots were sent to Saigon for a show-and-tell, which enlivened the session. But normally reporters yawned and wrote their stories from the blue mimeographed press release, often quoting it word for word. What gave the air war its startling impact, from a journalistic standpoint, was the way targets were parceled out by Washington, providing reporters with a fresh news hook several times a week, a headline grabber for papers back home, an opener for the TV news. *Today U.S. warplanes struck for the first time . . .* Described in the Pentagon's swollen terms, it sounded as though the United States were bombing not an underdeveloped country with mainly a peasant economy, but something akin to the Ruhr Valley, the industrial heartland of Germany during World War Two. On this point at least, Harrison Salisbury's reports would set the record straight.

As the New York *Times* reporter began his trip to Hanoi, the debate within the Johnson administration about the air war was growing intense. The McNamara strategy of using the bombing as a credible threat to force concessions from the North Vietnamese had not worked, and there were signs that McNamara and his adherents were beginning to question its value. Lyndon Johnson, faced with critics who wanted to end the air war and others who wanted to expand it, slid into a role of making decisions on the bombing that seemed capricious to the outsider but allowed Johnson to portray himself, at least in his own eyes, as a moderate on the question, a beleaguered president holding a sensible middle ground between the hardliners whose recommendations might escalate the conflict into a war with Russia or China and the weak-willed who would have America lose its honor by giving up in Vietnam. Oddly, American pilots were not permitted to hit such seemingly legitimate targets as Phuc Yen, a MiG airbase, with Johnson being overheard to say, "And I told them they couldn't hit that damn Fuck-Yen either"—although he didn't explain why not.

Admiral Grant Sharp waged a discreet but unceasing battle over the question of targeting. When it became clear that Lyndon Johnson had no intention of approving the all-out twelve-week effort recommended by the Joint Chiefs fifteen days after the air war began, Sharp shifted gears and came up with a plan that provided for bridge and ferry destruction and the blockage of road and rail routes. Sharp's staff picked the targets with the idea that they would be difficult to bypass. He thought that cutting the roads would create a series of new targets such as backed-up convoys, off-loaded material, dumps, and staging areas. The Pentagon revised its assessment that the country had only ninety-four significant military targets. By the end of 1965 the target list numbered two hundred and thirty-six and was growing.

The restrictions placed on the bombings were, by any measure of warfare, remarkably specific. From December 1966, the areas within a circle of ten miles from the center of Hanoi and, after June 1967, four miles from the center of Haiphong were designated as prohibited zones. No target could be struck in these zones without Washington's express approval, which was hard to come by. In addition, the areas within a thirty-mile radius of Hanoi and ten miles of Haiphong (excluding the prohibited zones) were marked as restricted areas, with tough limitations imposed on attacks therein. Most of the country's key targets were located in these two zones.

There was, moreover, Washington's persistent concern about civilian casualties. Before Sharp was given permission to hit a target in the Hanoi-Haiphong area, he was asked to estimate the number of civilian casualties and to explain how he intended to keep them to a minimum. Many targets were hit once and then permission was withdrawn to restrike them, giving the North Vietnamese plenty of time to repair the damage.

The way strikes on North Vietnam's petroleum supplies had come about was the best example of the targeting controversy. It didn't strain logic to suggest that a country's gasoline and oil reserves might appear automatically near the top of any strike list. But the debate about whether or not to hit North Vietnam's petroleum storage facilities had become a major issue in early 1966. The military and political risks were carefully gone over, hashed and rehashed, with some officials saying that a strike might bring Russia and China into the war, others warning that domestic political repercussions would be severe. The debate spilled over into the press, which did nothing, of course, to slow North Vietnam's program of dispersal.

Finally, after Defense Secretary McNamara gave his backing to the attack, President Johnson followed with his approval. Sharp was ordered to use only the most experienced pilots, to select an axis of attack that would avoid populated areas, to use weapons of high precision delivery. So great were Washington's apprehensions that Sharp's men were instructed to radio minute-by-minute news of how the strikes were going.

The Pentagon let out whoops and cries after the strikes began the last of June 1966, claiming that 70 percent of the North's oil storage capacity was destroyed, numerous secondary explosions were sighted, flames reached high into the heavens, etcetera. Admiral Sharp had told the Joint Chiefs six months earlier that the destruction of the petrol sites would either bring about peace negotiations or cause the insurgency in the South to wither from a lack of support. Yet as time went on, North Vietnam's war effort appeared not to be noticeably slowed by the strikes. For all intents and purposes, the strikes had failed, and this failure was sure to be used to justify the disenchantment of civilian officials who already questioned the air war's value. Why had they failed? Was it because, as McNamara and certain of his aides were beginning to believe, the air war would never be able to accomplish its goals and therefore should be de-escalated? Or was it because, as the military believed, Washington's hesitancy in ordering the strikes had given the North Vietnamese plenty of time to disperse their gasoline supplies? The lines were drawn. Few bothered to suggest that the answer might lie in a combination of the two.

If Admiral Sharp was embarrassed that his predictions had proved vastly overoptimistic, he did not show it. He contended that the enemy had been forewarned and the element of surprise lost. At the end of 1966, Sharp was preparing another proposal for the bombing. He divided North Vietnam's targets into six basic systems—ports, airfields, military complexes, transportation networks, electricity supplies, and war-supporting industries—and asked Washington to approve targets to be hit within each system as a package, instead of on a piecemeal basis, which he believed would bring more effective pressure on Hanoi.

Whatever the merits of Sharp's position on targeting, the controversy tended to obscure the fact that the air war was not being conducted with the greatest competency either by the Pentagon or by Sharp himself. For starters, the military had set up a command and control system mind-boggling in its complexity and inefficiency. When the air force and navy had met to settle their squabble about who got which targets to hit in North Vietnam, General Westmoreland's headquarters in Saigon, MACV, had jumped in and also demanded a piece of the action. MACV argued that air operations in Route Package 1, just across the border, adjacent to South Vietnam, were an extension of the ground battle inside South Vietnam. The argument was accepted, and MACV was given operational control of the route package.

Not only was there a three-way split in operational control of the strikes on North Vietnam but the naval task force in the Tonkin Gulf reported to Admiral Sharp in Hawaii through the Seventh Fleet, while the air force went through a different channel. Later, when B-52s became involved in the bombing, the Strategic Air Command set up its own control system. This did not take into account the control of the bombing exercised by U.S. ambassadors in Laos and Cambodia. There was .a hodgepodge of five or six separate command and control systems. Rationality called for an Indochina-wide allocation of resources under a single commander, so that airplanes could be employed in an efficient manner.

The system caused tension between Admiral Sharp and General Westmoreland. Westmoreland controlled air strikes within South Vietnam and continually lobbied the Pentagon for more resources, to the detriment, Sharp thought, of the air war in North Vietnam. Westmoreland's staff believed they should control the entire war. Admiral Sharp, drawing a complicated chart to show how the system worked, conceded that it was criticized but, "Usually," he said, "by people who did not understand it, and occasionally by people who had a parochial axe to grind." Sharp and Westmoreland were too politically aware to let the debate become public. They had enough on their hands trying to contain the basic controversies of the war, of search-and-destroy operations in the South and targeting in the North. Even top civilian leaders remained ignorant of the mechanics of the air war. In 1972, Richard Nixon politely inquired of the newly appointed air force commander in Saigon, General John Vogt, if he needed anything. Vogt startled Nixon by asking him to simplify the command and control system, to put the general in charge of the air war as a single commander. Nixon thought he was trying to make a power grab to take command of the entire war, and he described the encounter this way in the first draft of his memoirs written after he left the White House. A skeptical aide got in touch with Vogt and under the general's protest the incident was dropped from Nixon's book.

On a daily level, there was the competition between the air force and navy, which sometimes led to the misuse of men and equipment, and, if not to outright lying, then to exaggerated claims about the damage inflicted during air strikes. One manifestation of the competition was in the sortie rate—a sortie being one round-trip combat flight by one airplane—which was used as a measuring stick to show how hard each service was working to win the war. When a bomb shortage occurred in early 1966, both the air force and the navy sent their planes up with only one or two bombs per plane, to keep their sortie rate high and prevent their competitor from getting ahead in the statistics game. There was constant pressure to show results in the numbers of targets hit, so that anyone listening to the Saigon briefing might have concluded that North Vietnam possessed more trucks per capita than any country in the world.

6 · Dick Wyman

I WOULD come back from a strike and get debriefed by the air intelligence officer, who prepared a damage report that would go up the chain of command and ultimately be made public to show the effect

we were having on North Vietnam. One day, for example, I told him
I had seen ten trucks.

"How many did you get?" he asked.

"I don't know," I said. "There was a lot of smoke down there after
the bombs hit and I couldn't see very well. I'm pretty sure I got three
of them."

"You must've hit more than that."

"Maybe I damaged a couple; I don't know."

"You probably got five or six."

"I can't say that."

"Look, the admiral's staff is not going to accept anything as vague
as that. Let's say you destroyed five trucks, damaged three."

"Say what you want, but that's not what I'm telling you."

There was a constant tug by the staff to show results that would
reflect well on the air wing, the ship, the navy. You couldn't avoid it.
After a while, your attitude became, ah, what the hell, I'm just a pilot,
let them worry about the score. On the other hand, there was little to
no indiscriminate bombing that I saw.

A flak site sat at the entrance to the Haiphong harbor on a deserted
island. We would hit the guns and they would come right back and
put them up again. Just below the site was a cluster of five houses. It
seemed obvious to me that the people manning the site lived in those
houses; there was nothing else on the island. One day my bombs happened to land smack in the middle of the houses, and they just disappeared. We got back to the ready room and Black Mac laughed and
said, "Wyman, you s.o.b., did you see where your bombs landed?"

I said, "Yeah, right where I wanted them to, Mac."

That's the only time I did anything like that during two years and
nearly two hundred missions. I didn't see or hear of anyone else who
went out to drop bombs on a populated area. And we were never briefed
to hit a village or houses—much to the contrary. But, you know, if
you are flying at a speed of five hundred knots, and you've got a couple
of missiles chasing you and flak exploding all around, you are just
liable to miss the target. And you don't have to miss it far to hit something. The North Vietnamese often put their antiaircraft sites near
schools and other civilian facilities. They did this in a coldblooded
manner to try to keep us from hitting the flak sites.

I was making a run on a SAM site one day. Tracers were coming up as I rolled in. One got bigger and bigger, I swear I could've reached out and touched it. It startled me so that I hit the bomb pickle. Two of my six bombs went off and landed four hundred yards short of the target. Luckily, it wasn't a populated area.

There was a widespread misperception about precision bombing. Precision compared to what? To B-52s? Yes, in that sense, we did have precision. You could get pretty good and do a respectable job once you got the feel and technique. That took time, though. The fact was, if you dropped early or high, you were going to miss the target by a big margin.

7

WITH THE BUILDUP of the American nuclear arsenal after World War Two, theories on how to wage a war took on an increasingly abstract coloration. Nuclear strategy was based almost entirely on psychological considerations. No one wanted an atomic war—that was madness. But America's enemies had to know that it possessed the means of annihilation, a credible retaliatory threat, to protect the country's security. It was not surprising, then, that McNamara's theory on how to wage a conventional war against North Vietnam was a modification of the nuclear strategy. America would give the North Vietnamese an example of what it could do to them and they would be cowed by the possibilities of such overwhelming power.

But the difference between an iron bomb and a nuclear weapon was the difference between extensive destruction and total annihilation, and a threat was only credible if the threatened believed they could not survive the consequences with acceptable losses. The North Vietnamese based their strategy not on abstract theory but on past experience. They had not the slightest doubt that America was the most powerful country in the world. But the French, too, had been powerful, and the Vietnamese had won by pursuing a military strategy based on nothing more complicated than endurance. They had outlasted the French.

Two days before the air war began on March 2, 1965, the North Vietnamese leadership began methodically to prepare the country for the bombing. They had three factors to consider. First, the safety of the population must be given priority and, to the degree possible, the security of the industrial base; second, the transportation network had to be kept open so that the war could be supported in the South; and third, an antiaircraft system should be developed not only for protection but also to make it costly for the Americans to wage the air war. A decision was made to evacuate nonessential personnel from Hanoi and Haiphong. Foreign observers who were persuaded America was fighting a war narrow in scope thought the evacuation order was an overreaction on the part of the North Vietnamese, or perhaps was being used as a psychological step to prepare the population for war, but the Central Committee of the Communist Party acted as though the destruction of the cities was a foregone conclusion and told the people to get ready for a long war. *The bomb shelter is your second home* became a national slogan. A goal was set to provide three shelter spaces per person. The North Vietnamese claimed later to have dug twenty-one million bomb shelters. Whether the figure was correct or not, Hanoi and Haiphong quickly took on the look of a concrete beehive. Hundreds of thousands of circular one-man shelters were spaced at six- to thirty-two-feet intervals along almost every road. Two and a half feet in diameter, about five feet deep, the shelters were made of pre-stressed concrete, with two-inch-thick lids that were left ajar for quick occupancy. Half-buried communal shelters, made of cement and brick with roofs of tin and earth, were scattered throughout the country. Shelter upkeep was added to other Sunday housekeeping chores. The manholes filled with rain during the monsoon season and had to be drained. Larger shelters had to be swept and cleaned, and repaired after near misses.

The population's reaction to the air-raid sirens varied with time and the changing bombing patterns. At first, loudspeakers placed on street corners gave a running commentary about the attack, and air-raid wardens were there to make sure each person was in his proper shelter. But as months passed and the bombing became routine, few bothered to run to the shelters until the antiaircraft guns started booming and bombs were whistling down. The wardens urged people not to mill around or sit on the ground to watch the fireworks, but without much success until the heavy bombing of the cities began in 1967, and then the alerts were taken seriously.

If North Vietnam's long-war strategy were to succeed, it was imperative to keep the traffic flowing to the South. Needed was a massive repair system. Youth brigades were established for the day-to-day repair of roads and the building of alternate routes to be used as detours. Teenagers, boys and girls, worked at night, filling in bomb craters with dirt carried in bamboo-woven baskets, painting white posts along the sides of roads to guide truck drivers who moved without lights, being careful to defuse the delayed-action bombs that had been dropped to interrupt their work.

The kids could handle filling in craters, but bombed-out bridges presented a more serious matter. North Korea had faced the same problem fifteen years earlier in its war with the Americans; and North Korean advisers soon arrived to teach the Vietnamese six ways to move a truck across a river after a bombing attack. The simplest bridge was constructed of bundles of bamboo and stalks tied together to float on water, with wooden planks laid across and lashed to the stalks, something that cost practically nothing and could be replaced with little effort. A more sophisticated version was built by bringing together flat-bottomed canal boats, about three feet wide and sixteen feet long, and laying a roadway of bamboo and boards across them. These pontoon-type bridges were hidden along riverbanks by day to prevent their being bombed and brought out at night. Rivers that were wide and fast-flowing were often crossed by ferry boats operating from a system of piers and heavy cables. Materials to repair bridges and ferries were stockpiled nearby. Seldom did traffic stop longer than a day or two after an attack.

This did not mean the bombing was not exacting a heavy toll. By 1966, it took about five hours to drive the crater-filled obstacle course that the sixty-five miles of road between Hanoi and Haiphong had become, as opposed to two hours before the bombing began. A Western reporter estimated that four days were needed, driving only at night, traveling at a speed of ten miles an hour, to traverse the four hundred and fifty miles from one end of North Vietnam to the other. With delays caused by fresh craters and recently destroyed bridges, the trip could take much longer.

Repairing a railroad was harder than fixing a highway. The North

Vietnamese decided to concentrate on keeping the railway that ran from Hanoi to China in good working order. With the help of Chinese laborers, they built a third rail into China, so that rail cars adapted to the Chinese standard gauge could move directly onto the narrow North Vietnamese tracks. To compensate for the damage inflicted on the railroad, they expanded their already elaborate inland waterway system. Farmers were told to clear rivers to a depth of five feet, so that shallow barges could use them, and later the call went out for a fourteen-foot dredging of certain rivers. Barges became a frequent target for bombing. From 1965 to 1968, U.S. pilots reported they destroyed or damaged 23,978 "water vehicles;" and in early 1967 they began seeding the country's rivers with mines.

With so many planes daily flying overhead on armed reconnaissance missions, as the Americans called them, camouflage became an art form. Drivers attached branches, palm fronds, and banana leaves to the roofs of their buses and trucks. Jeeps were covered with a fishnet in which leaves were inserted. Saplings were pulled over and tied to conceal pontoon bridges. Few jobs were as dangerous as that of truck driver. Trucks traveled alone or in small groups to avoid being spotted from the air. Besides having mechanical breakdowns, they frequently got lost because of detours and the lack of signs on bombed roads. But the material continued to reach the South. If it couldn't be moved by truck, barge, or by train, then a bicycle with a bamboo frame attached to carry six hundred pounds could be pushed a distance of one hundred and seventy-five miles in eighteen days.

North Vietnam's limited industrial base was made up of about a thousand enterprises. Of these, nearly two hundred were large, relatively modern plants controlled by the central government. A machinery factory, for example, built in 1958 with fifteen million dollars in Soviet aid, was one of the most important of Hanoi's plants. Spare parts, lathes, tools, electric motors, and so forth were made there. After the bombing began, much of the plant's equipment was scattered around Hanoi, broken up into fifty separate workshops. To a Cuban writer, the gutted machinery factory had an air of emptiness and desolation, yet some workers continued to operate around-the-clock on the bulky machinery left in place.

A similar evacuation of other factories was carried out. While most of them continued to operate, production steadily declined. Exports of coal dropped by half; the country, once an exporter of cement, became an importer. Prewar gains in the textile industry were halted; both the quality and quantity of cloth fell, with the army demanding vast supplies of new uniforms, leaving the civilian population with small amounts of the worst possible material for their personal use.

Although an iron bomb could do little damage to an unmechanized farm, food production declined because the communist party transferred farmers to other war-related activities. The pig was the country's most important meat supply, and the pork ration remained the same as before the bombing—ten ounces per person each month—but even this low amount was rarely available. A sugar ration of about one pound a month was issued only to mothers of newborn babies. Fish, *nuoc mam* (the national condiment), and flour were seldom seen. Two boxes of matches and a bar of soap were distributed every three months. To try to offset the deficiencies, the government ordered pharmaceutical factories to increase their production of vitamin pills.

The personal hardships caused by the bombing were many. Still, it did not denigrate the tenacity of the North Vietnamese, which even their opponents grudgingly respected, to point out that theirs was already a culture of deprivation and hardship. To describe the difference in attitudes toward daily life separating Hanoi from New York, for example, where a power failure lasting a few hours in 1965 rated a *Time* cover story, was difficult indeed. The North Vietnamese were tightening their belt, as the saying went, but it was a belt that originally came with few notches, and this could not be minimized in searching for an explanation of their resilience.

They tried, as much as possible, to protect their industries by putting defensive weapons nearby. The surface-to-air missiles, however, had not proved very effective in the usual sense. By early 1967, a total of fifteen hundred SAMs had been fired, bringing down only thirty-one planes. The reason could be partly laid to successful American jamming techniques and evasive aerial maneuvers. But also at blame was the incompetence of Vietnamese technicians, many of whom were barely out of their teens and were assigned to the sites with little training. A Russian adviser complained that they fired the missiles like machines guns.

Nevertheless the missiles inadvertently proved their worth in another way. They drove American pilots down into the range of antiaircraft weapons that the North Vietnamese could fire to good effect like the machine guns to which they were accustomed. The explosions of the thirty-seven- and fifty-seven-mm flak looked to pilots like smudged popcorn outside their Plexiglas cockpits, with the heavier eighty-five- and one hundred-mm fire taking on a darker, more ominous color. The North Vietnamese discovered that positioning their guns in formations of triangles, diamonds, and pentagons concentrated their fire and gave them a better chance of catching a dive-bombing airplane in a deadly cone of exploding shrapnel.

Early on the North Vietnamese also recognized the value of another weapon. The spectacle of the richest country in the world bombing one of the poorest, whatever the political ramifications of the conflict, left many people, including friends and supporters of America, uneasy. After the war, North Vietnam's leaders boasted that they had manipulated the antiwar movement to their own ends. Propaganda was a legitimate weapon of war and since the North Vietnamese were, as they saw it, fighting to win over a much stronger power, one could hardly blame them for taking whatever steps they could to influence world opinion. If a movie star or a college professor, spurred by conscience or ideology, or any combination or the two, wanted to help publicize what she or he considered the essential injustice, if not the criminality of American policy, then Hanoi was often ready to issue a visa. Western journalists who proclaimed an allegiance to objective reporting were another matter. In North Vietnam's opinion, one objective view existed: America was wrong. Hanoi did not consider it helpful for a reporter to suggest otherwise, even if he included the on-the-other-hand qualifications in his story, which generally served as a basis for his claim to objectivity. The Agence France-Presse was allowed a reporter in Hanoi but his dispatches, whether from self-imposed or official censorship, carried none of the probing bite of his AFP colleagues in Saigon. British journalist James Cameron was permitted to tour the country in 1965, and he wrote a series of articles sympathetic to North Vietnam. No American reporter, however, had been invited until Christmas, 1966.

8

IT WAS NOT in the nature of any newsman to question the motives of his sources, so long as the information provided was accurate and newsworthy, and Harrison E. Salisbury of the New York *Times* could not be faulted for barely touching on the implications of why the North Vietnamese suddenly invited him to Hanoi and could be indulged for making it sound as though he alone, out of all the reporters who'd applied for visas, had cracked the story simply by journalistic enterprise. It was truly one of the war's biggest scoops. Yet Salisbury, taken even in the context of the times, when nobody really knew what the North Vietnamese were up to, occasionally displayed an ingenuousness about his trip to Hanoi that some of his colleagues found hard to credit to the author of numerous books and a veteran reporter who had largely made his reputation by reporting from Russia and other communist countries, where news was a synonym for propaganda, with no bones made about it.

As he sat on the terrace of the Phnom Penh airport, in Cambodia, drinking a Coca-Cola and waiting for the delayed I.C.C. plane that would take him to Hanoi, Salisbury talked to several East European diplomats who said they hoped his visit would prove to be a positive step toward peace. They told him a young African journalist, a communist, had recently visited Phnom Penh and applied for a visa to Hanoi but was turned down. Salisbury was impressed by the story and saw it as "a small straw in the wind. But not an insignificant one. When a Communist country begins to admit enemy nationals and excludes some of its close friends and sympathizers," Salisbury wrote, "something important is afoot. The instinct of the East European diplomats seemed correct to me. My visit clearly had important implications."

What was afoot, as the North Vietnamese quickly made plain, was their desire to inform the world through the New York *Times* that

American planes were aiming not only at military targets but also at civilian areas. After getting his first look at the damage to Hanoi, Salisbury was not at all sure the North Vietnamese were right. While it seemed unlikely the damage was caused by a misfired SAM missile, and thus the fault of the North Vietnamese themselves, as the Pentagon was claiming, neither did it look like U.S. planes intentionally had bombed civilian areas. It could have easily been an accident. That was what diplomats in Hanoi, who had observed the attack, believed. Moreover, Salisbury, whose ideas about bombing had been formed by his World War Two experiences, was surprised by the flimsiness of the houses that had been hit along the banks of the nearby Red River. Many of them were huts made of grass thatching. And the number of casualties—four killed and ten injured—seemed light considering the swath of destruction.

Outside Hanoi in the small village of Phuc Xa, Salisbury talked to villagers who told him that on August 13, 1966, at 12:17 P.M., a bomb had exploded over their village, destroying twenty-four houses, killing twenty-four persons, wounding twenty-three. They said the plane first dropped a bomb on a nearby dike and then on them. Phuc Xa had been rebuilt in a month with help from other communities. Fragments of the bomb were placed in a building at the village's center, which became a sort of museum. The fragments bore the date July 1966. The villagers were amazed that the Americans could make a bomb and rush it a half-world away, to drop on them only four weeks later.

They believed the plane had bombed them deliberately. Salisbury considered it unlikely. "But who really could know what he intended to hit?" Salisbury wrote. "Possibly he had been attacking the dikes. He might have been trying to knock out shipping in the Red River or an antiaircraft gun along the shore. Or he might have been dropping his bombs in evasive action to get away rapidly from a very hot corner." Whatever the explanation, Salisbury's doubts about the precision of American bombing were growing.

He was also surprised by the seemingly inconsequential nature of the targets. A truck depot on Hanoi's outskirts, a supposed major target of the December 13 attack, did not look to him very formidable—just a half-dozen loading sheds. Somebody told him there were only twelve or fourteen broken-down buses and trucks in the sheds when they were bombed. "For this kind of target was it worth jeopardizing $2 million planes and the precious lives of American pilots?" he wondered. Not only that, the Polish Friendship School, a half-mile away from the sheds, had been hit accidentally at the same time.

On Christmas morning, as he drove south from Hanoi to the area of the Co Trai bridge, Salisbury's questioning of the bombing continued to increase. Co Trai was just outside Phu Ly, which lay along Route One, next to the main railroad line to the South. At Phu Ly was a railroad siding, a few strips of track where boxcars were shunted and reordered. Salisbury could see that planes had come to bomb the railroad siding, and in doing so they also had wiped out the town, which once held ten thousand but was now home to only a handful, though actual casualties appeared to be light. As he walked among the ruins, a train chugged by on the already repaired railway.

Later on Christmas day, when he reached Nam Dinh, about sixty-five miles south of Hanoi, Salisbury found the material for a story that would encompass his growing doubts. Approaching Nam Dinh in the Soviet-made black Volga the government had assigned him, along with a guide and interpreter, he could see that almost all the streets bore signs of bomb damage. He stopped in town and two local officials briefed him over cups of tea. Nam Dinh, they said, had been a textile center of about ninety thousand inhabitants, before most of them had been evacuated in the face of fifty attacks by U.S. planes.

The city's textile plant had employed thirteen thousand workers and was listed as one of the twelve most important factories in the country. The town also had a silk mill, a fruit-canning factory, a farm tool plant, a rice mill, and a thread-making cooperative. All in all, Salisbury thought, it didn't amount to much. "Nam Dinh might be North Vietnam's third largest city," he reported, "but if this was all it produced, it hardly sounded like a prime target. The officials, including the mayor, a petite woman named Tran Thi Doan, who had been a textile worker herself, insisted that so far as they were aware the city possessed no military objectives whatever."

The actual civilian casualties after fifty attacks—eighty-nine killed and four hundred and five wounded—were low, perhaps due, he thought, to the evacuation that had left Nam Dinh a relative ghost town. But Salisbury was told that 13 percent of the city's housing had been reduced to rubble. The textile plant had been crippled after nineteen attacks, the silk mill wiped out. "The whole story of Nam Dinh had a quality of unreality, like some terrible dream in a Dada painting," Salisbury recorded. "One could almost imagine our bombers coming again and again and again, attacking and attacking, trying to hit some phantom which ever eluded them because it never had existed."

Was Nam Dinh's textile factory, which was large enough to qualify as a major industry in any country and capable of producing uniforms for soldiers, a legitimate military target? The Pentagon believed it was and believed the city possessed other important targets. * That was a matter of opinion between a journalist and military specialists. Less easy to deal with were his eyewitness accounts of damage to civilian areas. The Pentagon opened a publicity campaign to discredit Salisbury's reporting, with Defense Department spokesman Arthur Sylvester charging that his articles were "grossly exaggerated." Other government officials questioned his patriotism. A U.S. senator said that the New York *Times* had always been against the war.

Yet it was clear that the military, encouraged by civilian leaders who were under pressure from the antiwar movement, had created a myth that was to prove costly to them. The figures provided Salisbury by the North Vietnamese themselves—eighty-nine killed out of fifteen thousand inhabitants left in Nam Dinh during fifty U.S. attacks—did not suggest a campaign of indiscriminate bombing, given the haphazard nature of air warfare. But the American public had been led to believe U.S. planes were striking with such precision as not to incur a single civilian casualty, and so Salisbury's revelations hit with the effect of another kind of bomb. Not long after his articles appeared, touching off a fierce public debate about the air war, a poll conducted at fourteen colleges in the Washington, D.C., area showed 66 percent of the students opposed to the bombing of North Vietnam, with 80 percent of them having no idea who the Viet Cong were.

If anyone had reason to be sensitive to signs of indiscriminate bombing, it was John Gerassi, sent to Hanoi as one of five investigators for the Bertrand Russell International War Crimes Tribunal, a commitee operating on what it considered to be moral rather than legal grounds. French writer Jean-Paul Sartre was chairman of the tribunal, with Dave Dellinger, a pacifist, and Stokely Carmichael, a civil rights leader, its

---

* Nam Dinh's textile factory, however, was not included on the official target list, and thus the Pentagon wasn't obliged to announce publicly that it had been hit. But its destruction hardly could be blamed on collateral damage. A little military duplicity seemed to be at work here.

American members. To the tribunal, it was not a question of American guilt or innocence but the degree of criminality. Yet, as Gerassi admitted, he did not see the kind of systematic bombing of Hanoi he expected to find. Another tribunal investigator, a Scottish professor, told Harrison Salisbury that after several days spent inspecting bomb damage in many parts of North Vietnam, he was deeply troubled by "the factor of intent." The damage to civilian areas, he said, could well have been accidental.

What puzzled John Gerassi, as he traced Harrison Salisbury's steps to the area of the Co Trai bridge and then to Nam Dinh, was the matter of targeting. He apparently failed to see the railroad siding at Phu Ly that Salisbury had noted as an obvious military target. Gerassi told his driver to circle the town, and he spotted the small Co Trai bridge, about a half-mile outside the city limits. The bridge had been downed and repaired. It seemed hardly significant to him. At Nam Dinh, the railroad siding that the Pentagon claimed was a major target appeared to be no larger than a station in the New York suburbs. Much of the civilian damage to Nam Dinh had occurred around the textile factory, but, Gerassi wrote, "I kept asking myself, 'What is so goddamn militarily important about a textile mill?' "

Accidental or not, the fact remained that civilian areas were being hit. And for what kind of targets? "Like most of the 'military objectives' I was to see in North Vietnam," Harrison Salisbury said, "Nam Dinh seemed much more imposing in the language of a Pentagon spokesman than when viewed with the naked eye." Yet there were undeniably imposing targets in North Vietnam that to Salisbury's astonishment were not being hit. The Paul Doumer Bridge, for example, now called the Long Bien. "Not only was the Long Bien Bridge visible for miles," Salisbury noted, "it was in all probability the single most important military objective in North Vietnam. Without the bridge the movement of traffic from north to south would be radically impeded. Loss of the bridge would not knock North Vietnam out of the war. But it would make Hanoi's war effort infinitely more difficult. . . . The Long Bien Bridge was not the only important military objective in Hanoi. There were others—for example, there was the city's main power plant. This, too, presumably was heavily defended. But, like the bridge, it had not been attacked. It was situated in a region some distance from areas of heavy population."

Targeting. After waging an air war for nearly two years, the U.S. still had not bombed the most obvious military targets in North Vietnam. To Harrison Salisbury, it made no sense. On that point, and probably on that point alone, the New York *Times* reporter and the admiral in charge of the air war completely agreed.

9

WHILE HARRISON Salisbury was en route to Hanoi, Admiral Grant Sharp requested permission to bomb ship-repair yards and a naval base at Haiphong. Hanoi's charges that the U.S. was hitting civilian areas, however, had turned Washington gun-shy. Sharp was told he could not conduct air operations involving any targets in the Hanoi prohibited zone and, if possible, planes should not even fly over the area. That was too much for Sharp. He fired off an angry message to the Pentagon that he knew would be read by Robert McNamara.

"We are just starting to put some real pressure on Hanoi," said Sharp. "Our air strikes on the rail yard and the vehicle depot were hitting the enemy where it was beginning to hurt. Then, Hanoi complains that we have killed a few civilians, hoping that they would get a favorable reaction. And they did, more than they could have hoped for. Not only do we say we regretted that any civilians were killed, but we also stop our pilots from striking within 10 miles of Hanoi. Hanoi has been successful once again in getting the pressure removed. They will be encouraged to continue their aggression, hoping to outlast us."

Aiming at McNamara, Sharp said, "This war is a dirty business, like all wars. We need to get hardheaded about it." Instead of apologizing in the face of Hanoi's propaganda assaults, Sharp wondered if Washington couldn't take a different approach. "When Hanoi complains about civilians being killed, is it not possible to say, 'Perhaps some were killed, we tried to avoid that, but this is a war and some civilians are bound to get killed. Hanoi can prevent it by calling off the aggression in South Vietnam.' "

There was also an implicit threat buried in Sharp's message. He had taken his own sounding of public opinion, he said, and talked to "quite a few members of Congress." He believed time was running out. "The American people can become aroused either for or against this war. At the moment, with no end in sight, they are more apt to become aroused against it. It's up to us to convince our people and Hanoi that there is an end in sight and that it is clearly defeat for Hanoi." Without saying so directly, Sharp was suggesting that political action might be taken to force the targeting issue.

Eight months later, in August 1967, Admiral Sharp and other military leaders successfully encouraged U.S. Senate hawks to launch a widely publicized probe into the bombing policy, putting Robert McNamara on the defensive. Senator John Stennis of Mississippi and members of his armed forces investigating subcommittee called for an intensification of the air war. Lyndon Johnson, trying to defuse the political controversy, gave the military permission to hit a number of new targets, including—for the first time after two and a half years of bombing—the Long Bien Bridge, which Harrison Salisbury, no supporter of the air war, had considered probably the single most important military objective in North Vietnam.

10 · Dick Wyman

I READ Harrison Salisbury's book. I had been to Nam Dinh many times. There was a photograph showing a street almost destroyed. That surprised me. I hadn't intentionally dropped any bombs on the city, and I hadn't seen anyone else do it. There was another photo showing a kid with a leg missing. I love kids; I have three of my own and to see a child with a leg torn off for any reason—Christ, he hasn't had a shot at life and look what has been done to him. That bothered me, it really did. I had not thought of what I was doing as killing people. If we hit a flak site, we were stopping a flak site. You didn't even think of someone being in an enemy airplane. That's a machine. This is me.

It sounds terrible, I know. But the air war differed in this respect from the ground war. You go up and do it. Then you come back and sleep on clean sheets. Someone gets shot down, he just disappears.

You don't have a guy lying beside you bleeding and all bashed up. You don't have to look somebody in the eye and shoot them. So you think you aren't killing anyone. But when I saw those pictures, I said, "Goddamn, Wyman, that little kid hasn't even had a chance at life."

Of course, many of the guys didn't read books. The ones who saw Salisbury's reports got furious because they did not look at some of the things he was saying. They thought he was simply acting as a propagandist for the North Vietnamese. Another thing, nobody really had time to think about the war except in a programmed way. We were caught up in the day-to-day happenings, doing the job assigned us, and we were kept so busy that we never had time to get enough sleep. It must have taken me two months to read Bernard Fall's *Hell in a Very Small Place*.

III

July 19, 1967

Attack on Co Trai

1

AT 4:33 A.M., on July 19, 1967, the USS *Oriskany* launched her first strike of the day. The carrier had arrived on Yankee Station a week earlier for her third combat tour. Herb Hunter, Squadron 162's new executive officer, was awakened by the jarring thump of the one-ton catapult pistons being brought from one hundred and fifty mph to zero in nine feet, as the catapult shuttle reached the end of its firing stroke and an airplane was hurled into the air. Fifteen minutes later, the launch completed, Hunter tried to get back to sleep. He lay in his bunk thinking about the bridge at Co Trai. The attack on Co Trai was scheduled for noon. He would be leading his first strike on North Vietnam. Exactly one year before, Cal Swanson had flown his first strike against the same target when he was the squadron's new executive officer. Jim Nunn had been Swanson's wingman. Today, Leabert Fernandez, Nunn's Annapolis classmate, would fly as Hunter's wingman.

Herb Hunter was as unlike Cal Swanson as Swanson had been from Richard Bellinger. Swanson was intense, concerned about details. Hunter was easygoing. Swanson believed in the war and thought America was right. Hunter, in his low-key way, questioned U.S. involvement in Vietnam, but believed it his duty to follow orders. Swanson brought an engineering approach to flying. Hunter, as a former member of the Blue Angels, the navy's elite acrobatic flying team, made piloting a jet plane look effortless. In a short time, Herb Hunter had become the most popular senior officer of Squadron 162.

Jim Nunn and Leabert Fernandez were in the same company at the Naval Academy for four years, which was like being fraternity brothers. Both of them won letters on the rowing team. Each did well academically and was considered by his classmates to be earnest, hardworking, and serious-minded. Lee Fernandez, however, unlike Jim Nunn, had begun to turn against the war, and the attack on Co Trai would change his life. Years later, when members of Squadron

162 were asked to describe Fernandez, the adjective invariably used was "quiet." Lee was quiet. It was said as one might say, "He had one arm," or, "He was an albino." Fighter pilots were not normally quiet, and the fact that Lee spent a lot of time in his room reading—Gandhi, Camus, Fromm, history books on Southeast Asia and the war—set him apart from the squadron. But Lee, who was courteous and soft-spoken, was a good pilot, even though he was having increasing problems landing aboard ship, and his courage was unquestioned, which assured his acceptance by the others.

The son of a plastic surgeon in Honolulu, Lee Fernandez was from an old-line Hawaiian family and was born the day before the Japanese attacked Pearl Harbor. The U.S. Navy, after years of taking the islands as one big liberty port, did not enjoy the unqualified esteem of certain segments of Hawaiian society, but Lee was encouraged by his parents to attend the Naval Academy, despite his second thoughts about accepting the appointment from Congressman Daniel K. Inouye. During his third year at Annapolis, he became disenchanted with what he considered the rigidity of the school's curriculum and thought about resigning but found he was obligated by law to serve in the navy as an enlisted man if he left the academy. His interest turned to naval aviation, which, he discovered, was more than satisfying, especially after he was picked to fly F-8s.

He arrived on the *Oriskany* a month before the fire. His apprehensions about being assigned directly to Yankee Station without the usual training period with the squadron at Miramar turned out to be unfounded. Cal Swanson made sure he was broken in slowly and carefully, taking Fernandez on hops over the less dangerous parts of North Vietnam. He learned the country on those flights by comparing what he saw to the small map he carried in his cockpit.

"One evening at dusk," Fernandez said, "the land seemed to mesh into the western horizon in varying hues of blue, purple, violet, and green. What appeared to be thousands of streams and rivers were lit up in bright ribbons of silver blue, as they caught and reflected the remaining light from a darkening sky. It was difficult for me to believe a war could be going on amid all that tranquil beauty."

The questions had begun almost immediately. A flak suppression mission did not bother him, because it involved a duel between two armed parties. "But too often," he said, "the civilian on the ground was the loser, since in the heat of battle bombs were not dropped with quite the precision they should have been. This bothered me, especially on the smaller strikes, when you could make several passes and see exactly where your bombs hit. Another kind of mission I hated was armed reconnaissance, where two airplanes flew over territory that for the most part was undefended, searching for anything that looked suspicious. Bombing bridges and railroad cars was no problem. But boats, trucks, and buildings disturbed me, because a hit would certainly mean a loss of unarmed life."

Two days after Cal Swanson took command of the squadron, Lee Fernandez married Dorothy, a nurse in San Diego. Swanson did not yet sense the depth of Fernandez's disaffection with the war. "Lee," he said, "was so quiet I don't think I would have recognized whether his questions were designed to enlarge his knowledge about the war, or whether he was questioning its validity." Swanson believed, though, that Dorothy was not the ideal wife for a fighter pilot. She seemed reserved and standoffish, the type who'd rather read a book than take part in social functions with the squadron wives. Dorothy wanted to move to the Philippines to be closer to Lee while the *Oriskany* was on Yankee Station for the '67 cruise. Swanson persuaded her such a move would be bad for the morale of the other pilots whose wives would be in the States.

Swanson believed that Herb Hunter would have a salutary influence on Lee Fernandez. He assigned Fernandez to fly as Hunter's wingman. The two of them got on even better than he had hoped. Lee thought Herb Hunter was one of the finest naval officers he had ever met. That Hunter and Fernandez would be flying against Co Trai, as Swanson and Nunn had done the year before, was a coincidence of scheduling. Had he known how the attack on Co Trai was going to turn out, Swanson said later, he would have changed the schedule and taken it himself.

2

CAL SWANSON was not having an easy time of it as the new commanding officer of Squadron 162. A naval air squadron was unique in the armed forces. It was composed of a small group of highly competitive officers chosen for their intelligence, self-assuredness, and technical ability, who spent most of their time at sea constantly on top of one another in a room no bigger than a suburban living room, a pressure-cooker environment that was the ultimate test of unflappability. Flying from an aircraft carrier was so demanding that a pilot was encouraged to believe he was the best in the squadron—indeed, in the navy—for a drop in a pilot's self-confidence could result in an accident or death. Needless to say such men were not easily led.

It was hard to list exactly what made a good leader. On the *Oriskany,* Bryan Compton, the commander of an A-4 squadron, was admired for his leadership qualities. Compton was nicknamed "Magnolia" not only because he hailed from Georgia but also—according to fellow pilots—because his flight suit smelled to high heaven. You could always find a vacant seat next to Magnolia at the briefing before a strike. "I would have followed Bryan Compton anywhere," Dick Wyman said. "I think everybody felt this way. He was the kind of guy, the worse things got, the better he was. He was the ugliest s.o.b. you ever saw. But he was our shining star."

Black Mac agreed. "The first time you talked to Magnolia, you'd say, 'Here's the dumbest goddamn farmer in the world.' But he was smart as hell—and gutsy."

The Naval Aviator's Guide listed the traits it considered crucial to good leadership. There were the obvious things: courage, integrity, tact, industry, honesty, devotion to duty, and self-sacrifice. Less expected was the *Guide's* emphasis on the importance of humor. "One of the personality traits conspicuous in navy aviators is a sense of humor," the *Guide* said. "Humor and good spirit can soften the tough moments which come to those who fly, making the unpleasantness seem less, while 'staying loose' in the process."

Though strict in a military sense, Magnolia was noted for "staying loose," for making it all seem not very serious, while exhibiting a high level of competence and courage. "You'd almost be downtown Hanoi," said Wyman, "and he'd say something funny on the air. Some people tried to be funny when they were scared and it dropped like a ton of lead. But he had the kind of humor that made you tuck in together." When you got down to it, that was probably the essence of good leadership. Being a good pilot. Staying loose. Herb Hunter and Cal Swanson were both outstanding aviators. Herb Hunter was loose. Cal Swanson was not.

Moreover, Cal faced a peculiar problem in staffing. If the *Oriskany* suffered overall from a lack of qualified personnel, Squadron 162 had the opposite problem. "There were literally hundreds of lieutenant commanders in the service who had no combat experience," said Black Mac. "The navy pumped them into squadrons left and right. Usually you have three lieutenant commanders as department heads—admin, operations, and maintenance—and two commanders as the commanding and executive officers; then the rest of the squadron is made up of young lieutenants and ensigns. But in our squadron we had six lieutenant commanders, senior guys who'd been around a long time, who were set in their ways and didn't want to yield to Swanson's ideas."

The most outspoken of the lieutenant commanders was Pat Crahan, an Irish Catholic from Ohio, at five-six the shortest pilot in the squadron. Crahan, who was thirty-two, had a handsome face that was settling into lines of bitterness. He had entered the navy as a pilot, then decided to get out and work as a salesman for the National Cash Register Company, where his father had been a manager. "I have trouble with people saying no straight at me," Pat said. "I'd go in and say I was from National Cash Register, and then someone would just rudely walk away from me without a word. I couldn't stand it. I really had trouble with on-site rejection from sales, and cash registers are the kind of equipment you aren't selling every time you talk to someone."

Pat visited Jim Stockdale at his home to see if Stockdale, who was once executive officer of his old unit, could help smooth the way for his return to the navy as a fighter pilot. Stockdale gave it a try but Crahan wound up in the training command as an instructor. He was the *Constellation*'s catapult officer when Ev Alvarez, flying from the *Connie,* became the first pilot of the war to be downed and captured, during the 1964 Tonkin Gulf crisis. The navy beat selling cash registers, but Crahan was not satisfied. He learned that United Airlines was hiring flight instructors. He had five kids and his navy pay exceeded what United was offering. Still, he was tempted. Not long afterward, he was passed over for lieutenant commander. He saw no apparent reason for his failure to be promoted, and neither did the *Connie*'s air boss, who checked into the matter. Crahan was angry. He filed a letter announcing his intention to resign from the navy, then flew to Seattle and applied for a job with United.

Near the end of 1965 the war was gaining momentum and the navy decided to freeze requests for resignation. A regular officer could resign but would have to serve another twelve months before getting out and that year would begin when he was assigned to a squadron or a ship. Crahan complained to Senator Everett M. Dirksen, asking him to intercede. Dirksen's office was told by the Pentagon that Crahan had orders to Squadron 162. After a year's tour, he would be allowed out.

Pat finished his training course in the F-8 ahead of Herb Hunter and received travel orders to Japan. He had been promoted to lieutenant commander the second time around. "When I got to Japan," Pat said, "the chief petty officer handling transportation asked when I wanted to go to the Philippines and from there to Yankee Station. I said, 'Oh, about two months from next Wednesday.' He said, 'Sorry sir. Can't give you but a week.' " Pat met Herb Hunter in Japan and they flew to the Philippines together. Herb was anxious to get to the *Oriskany* and he tried to line them up a flight but was greeted by an air of mystery about the whereabouts of the ship. It was that morning, October 26, 1966, that the *Oriskany* caught fire. Crahan and Hunter waited for the ship to reach the Philippines. The rest of the squadron took a commercial flight back to San Diego, while Pat and Herb returned on the *Oriskany,* which stank of charred flesh. On the trip back, Pat noted that the ship was not overflown by Soviet airplanes, as was usually the case, either as a courtesy or because the Russians knew Air Wing 16 had no capability to come up and meet them, to play the usual games.

Pat did not meet his new commanding officer until shortly after the change of command ceremony. In the meantime, he completed a course at the naval safety school in Washington, which meant he would be the squadron's new safety officer. When the meeting between Crahan and Swanson finally took place, it did not go well. "Sir, I've been assigned to your squadron," Pat began, "but I really would like to get out of here. If there's any way you can pull it off, I certainly would appreciate it. I'll do what I have to do, but you have to understand I'm a short-timer. In any case, I'll be out of the navy within a year."

Cal Swanson was startled by Crahan's declaration. Pat could tell he was offended, though Swanson managed to keep his composure. It was not until they were training in Arizona that Cal revealed what he really thought. "It happened at the bar in Yuma," Pat said. "We all drank too much, always. We were somewhere at an edge and would say what we wanted to say when we got to the bar. I was telling somebody about getting out of the navy, and Swanson blew up. It surprised everybody there. When we got back to Miramar, he called me into his office and read me the riot act. I repeated to him, 'If there's any way you can get me out of here, it would really be good for both of us.' "

Cal was caught in a bind. "Pat Crahan came in with a chip on his shoulder," he said. "I thought his influence was detrimental to the squadron's morale. He was vocal about how he hated the navy, how the navy was screwing him over. I told him to keep it to himself." Swanson could not get Crahan transferred out of the squadron because Senator Dirksen had been told Pat would be serving a year with 162, and neither Swanson nor the Pentagon wanted to risk stirring up trouble with that powerful politician. Besides, the way the navy looked at it, Crahan was Cal's problem. It was a test of leadership. That's what he got paid for, as Cal knew.

What made the problem doubly worse was that Pat Crahan was actually a sharp naval officer, competent and well turned-out ("Pat was a good pilot," Cal said, "no question about that"), and even had an engaging personality when he wasn't complaining about one thing or another. He was sociable and ready to take part in macho games such as drinking "flaming hookers," a late-night favorite of Dick Wyman and Black Mac, whereby a cordial glass was filled with brandy and then lit and tossed down while flaming, the goal being to empty the glass and leave the sides still burning, a bit of nonsense that sometimes left the drinker with a stinging redness. Crahan's competence and likeableness gave his complaints about the navy in general and Swanson in particular greater force than had he been, in navy slang, a dud.

Swanson tried to ignore Crahan. He set about converting the squadron into a bomber unit. They had dropped bombs the year before against such targets as Co Trai, but most of their missions had involved the traditional fighter pilot role of flying air combat patrols. Swanson's plan did not stem from a desire to wreak destruction on North Vietnam but from a practical consideration that the squadron frequently wasted its time flying MiG cover. If you were going to get shot at anyhow, he thought, better to reply in kind and help the war along. The other F-8 squadron on the *Oriskany* also wanted to assume a primary bombing role, and Swanson fought hard to win the assignment for 162. The decision was finally made by a toss of the coin. Cal called it right. His squadron, however, did not immediately applaud.

"At first everybody was dead set against bombing like Swanson wanted," Black Mac said, "We had a million reasons why it was impossible to hang enough bombs on the F-8. But, of course, Swanson turned out to be absolutely right, and later everybody agreed his plan was a good one."

The pilots against Swanson's plan got a chance to engage in some private smirking when he led a strike group on a training mission in Arizona, to drop bombs filled with sand and water on a fake airfield. "I wanted to make it as realistic and close to combat as possible," Cal said. "So I turned off all my navigation equipment and was doing it strictly by sight. It's not difficult to mistake one road for another when you're doing visual navigation at a low altitude over a desert at four hundred knots—and I made a mistake."

Black Mac: "Swanson picked out a field and said, 'Is that it?' I said, 'Looks good to me.' He rolled in to drop. As I rolled in, I saw a huge X laid out across the field, panels of international orange. I said to myself, 'Damn, they aren't going to mark a target like that.' I pulled off and dropped my bombs on some nearby woods. At that moment, I heard somebody, an A-Four pilot, I think, scream: 'You're on the wrong target!' Swanson had led us to an Atomic Energy Commission complex sitting out there in the middle of the desert. The AEC people had no way of knowing he was dropping dummy bombs and they probably said, 'Hey, there goes Arizona and half of California.' Were they pissed! The air wing commander chewed Swanson out, and he never got to lead a major strike group after we reached Yankee Station. I think that sort of got to him, because leading the big strikes was the way you won a Silver Star."

"I was extremely embarrassed," Swanson said.

The problem with Pat Crahan came to a head as the *Oriskany* prepared to leave for Yankee Station. Lee Prost, one of the original East Coast pilots and Dick Wyman's close friend, was taking target practice on a spar towed by the ship. It was a routine training flight, the kind pilots made without much sweat, but for some reason Prost didn't pull out of his run on the target and went straight into the sea. As safety officer, Pat Crahan was assigned to investigate the accident and write a report.

The plane was unrecoverable. No recorded transmissions were available. The best anyone could figure out was that Prost had fallen prey to the always present danger of target fixation. Pilots occasionally suffered a kind of hypnosis on bombing runs and instead of releasing their bombs and pulling up, they flew straight into the bull's-eye. It was something they were warned against in flight training. Pat Crahan had nothing more to work with than that. He turned his report into a broadside against Swanson's leadership. "Looking back," he said, "I was probably trying to get a dig in at Swanson. But at the time I really had it in my mind to get facts out I was sure wouldn't otherwise come out." The usual procedure was to give the accident report to the commanding officer, who sent it up the chain of command with his endorsement. Pat decided to try to bypass Swanson. He mailed the report directly to Washington. Accompanied by Burt Shepherd, the new air wing commander, Swanson retrieved it from the mailroom before it left the ship.

"The accident report was the crowning blow," Cal said. "That's when I called him in and really chewed ass. He blamed Prost's accident on operational deficiencies and said there was insufficient supervision. I said, 'You know the report is wrong. You've turned this into a vendetta against the navy and me. Go back and write it like you know what really happened. And if you keep acting this way, I'll make sure you never get out of the navy.' I drafted what I thought was a more appropriate report, and he went along with it. But he was still resentful and thought I was using command influence to water down the investigation."

"We spoke very little after that," Pat said. "He fired me as safety officer. I did my job as a pilot. I never presented a confrontation; I didn't want one. I hung a model of a United Airlines DC-8 over my ready room chair. That really irritated him, but he never told me to take it down. I think he figured if he did, he would be playing into my hands. It was that kind of relationship."

Whatever Crahan personally thought of Cal, he had to agree with everybody else that Swanson knew his stuff when it came to understanding airplanes. Cal could walk to the blackboard and illustrate what he was talking about with advanced mathematics, easy as pie. It was the kind of stuff the others had memorized to get through flight school and then largely forgotten. You had to listen to what he was saying. Swanson was one of the first to figure out how to beat the SAMs. Getting down low was all wrong, he said. You might confuse the missile's guidance system by putting a hill or some other terrain feature between you and it. But at that low altitude even a kid could fire a slug through your cockpit.

Swanson advocated dueling with the missiles at a high altitude. It was risky business and took ice-cold nerves, but the tactic was almost foolproof if done right. First you had to decide whether the missile had your name on it by trying to establish relative motion. If, for example, you were walking in the desert and saw someone in the distance, you could sight the figure with your thumb, to tell where he was headed. If he was coming directly at you, he would seem not to be moving at all but would just grow larger. If he were not coming at you, he would move to the left or right in relation to your thumb. When a pilot saw a missile, which was traveling at a speed of eighteen hundred mph, he was supposed to drop the nose of his plane and use it as he would his thumb. If there was no relative motion, if the missile did not seem to be moving off to either side, then he knew it was coming at him. At the last moment, he was supposed to dive into it and do a barrel roll— a maneuver where he pulled up hard and turned left or right contin- uously while going over the top. Three-dimensionally, the barrel roll resembled one segment of a corkscrew. The pilot came out of the maneuver roughly on the course he was flying when he began it, headed in the same direction. The corkscrewlike maneuver, since it involved simultaneously changing the airplane's vertical and horizontal aspects, plus its speed, complicated the intercept solution for a missile. The missile's guidance system could not react quickly enough to the barrel roll—its radius of turn was not small enough—and it would pass by to explode harmlessly.

The better pilots in the squadron immediately recognized the value of the tactic. It took split-second timing, but that was what Dick Wyman and Black Mac were noted for, and, moreover, the black-box had been improved, giving pilots access to more sophisticated electronic coun- termeasures to use against the missiles. In addition, each plane was equipped with a supply of aluminum foil that the pilot could release to act as metallic chaff to spoof the missile site's radar system, a tactic that had been developed and used in World War Two.

"On the first cruise the closest I came to dying was when I almost hit the ground trying to evade a missile," Dick Wyman said. "So in 'sixty-seven I said to hell with it, I'll stay up here high and take a look at them, wait to see if I can detect any relative motion. The metallic chaff we had was psychologically helpful. There was a button on the side of the cockpit and you hit it to kick out a bundle of chaff. I would sit there banging on the button. It was sort of my pacifier."

As the *Oriskany* approached Yankee Station, Cal Swanson felt confident the squadron was well prepared for combat. The war was becoming increasingly unpopular at home, though, and he hoped no poison would seep in from that direction to hurt his pilots' morale. In order to do a good job, not to mention stay alive, a pilot needed to be psychologically up at all times. He decided to write a letter to all the squadron wives, to tell them how they could help.

"On the eve of our entering the combat zone," Swanson wrote, "I'm sure you've all asked yourselves, 'Why is my husband doing this when he could have a nice, safe civilian job?' Frankly, we do it because we're doing what we like best. We all know the risks involved, yet we accept these risks because we feel the gratification and satisfaction associated with military flying far exceed the hazards involved. The challenge, when met and mastered, gives one a feeling of accomplishment—a job well done. There are few men in the world today who have the opportunity to accept such a challenge, and fewer still who have the ability to overcome all the obstacles en route to becoming a carrier pilot and successful Naval Officer. Your husbands are outstanding members of this elite fraternity, which is composed of only a minute percentage of the nation's top men.

"Whether you admit it or not," Swanson told them, "you all know that you have a great deal of influence on how your husband performs." For this reason, he asked them to be understanding when their husbands didn't write as frequently as they wished and to try to keep their own letters cheery and free of problems. His wife, Nell, he said, "will always be available for any assistance or guidance you may want to seek. Though she's not very tall, she has a great big shoulder and a tight lip.

"This leads me to the last subject I want to discuss—patriotism. It's not a very popular word today and there is usually an embarrassed silence if someone is labeled as being patriotic. Perhaps it's the word itself, because each and every one of us, in addition to having the satisfaction of being members of an exclusive brotherhood, feels as though he is also protecting our country. We serve this cause because we want to leave a heritage of freedom and better living for our chil-

139

dren. Military life has always been fraught with danger, but the price of freedom has always been high. Our forefathers faced many unknown dangers in conquering the wilderness and settling our country. Though we know more about the dangers we face, we cannot turn our backs to the threat of aggression. We must have courageous men who are willing to serve their country in the cause of protecting the freedom that our ancestors fought so hard to gain for us. Your husbands are these same courageous men. They're proud of the job they do, and they do it well. You should be proud of knowing that they are serving God and country in a manner few men can claim."

The letter was dated July 12, 1967, the day the *Oriskany* arrived on Yankee Station. Swanson showed it to Herb Hunter. He was going to send a mimeographed copy to Diane, Herb's wife. She would receive it about the time Herb was leading his first strike on North Vietnam. Cal and Herb had hit it off immediately. Herb Hunter was an easy guy to like, completely loyal. He would be taking over the squadron the following year and he knew that although some of the pilots weren't particularly enamored of Swanson, these were personnel problems that practically any commanding officer was liable to face. Fighter pilots had large egos. Swanson, in turn, realized that his direction of the squadron was made a lot easier by Hunter's amiable presence. Thank God for Herb, he told Nell.

3

TWO DAYS LATER Swanson commanded the squadron's first strike on North Vietnam of 1967. It went off without a hitch. The commanding and executive officers never flew together and by military protocol Herb Hunter should have led the second strike. But Herb had no combat experience and Swanson wanted to make sure he got his sea legs before he took any pilots over the beach. So it was decided that Butch Verich would lead the second raid. Butch was a senior lieutenant commander, the squadron's operations officer. Dick Wyman could fly as Hunter's wingman on the flight Butch led, giving Herb the benefit of his experience. The date set for the second strike was

July 16, 1967. Swanson believed that after this flight Herb would be ready to lead his own strike against Co Trai three days later.

Butch had gotten shot down the year before. There was some question about his agility over the beach, though not about his courage. Demetrio Verich, forty, was from Wisconsin, a first-generation American whose parents came from Yugoslavia and Italy. The Slavic genes of his father had clearly won out over the Latin ones of his mother, for Butch was stolid and ponderous. He was courteous almost to a fault. It was a squadron joke, exaggerated of course, about the way he'd chosen to tell Rich Adams his plane was on fire the year before. Hating to be a bearer of bad news, Butch had said, "Hey, Rick, you in 'burner'?" Afterburner provided an instant increase in speed, was a way to kick the airplane into overdrive and caused more flames to pour from the exhaust pipe, but didn't make the plane look as though it was completely on fire, as Rick's was. "Negative," Rick said, puzzled. Butch, sadly: "Then you're on fire."

The year before Butch had been the squadron's maintenance officer, a good one. The jet planes were susceptible to frequent malfunctions, especially in the tropical climate, and keeping the availability rate high was a problem. Verich told Bellinger and Swanson they were going to see all twelve of the squadron's planes in the air at the same time. They said it couldn't be done. But Butch did it. "Butch was the type of guy if you gave him long enough to sit down and figure out the problem, he would invariably come up with the right answer," Black Mac said. "Everything about him would focus on that one thing."

Such single-mindedness was an excellent attribute for a maintenance officer to have. But it could prove a handicap when split-second decisions had to be made while flying through flak and missiles. His tendency to concentrate on one thing got Butch into trouble in August 1966. He and his wingman were flying an armed reconnaissance mission. They found nothing suspicious and Butch decided to drop his bombs on a bridge. As he was pulling off, he noticed five barges in the river. His bombs were gone but he had some rockets left, so he made a run on the barges. A rocket failed to fire. He reached down to reset the switch, giving the problem his total attention. As Butch later admitted, he let his plane get too low while he was doing this. He was hit by small-arms fire. He made it out to sea and was picked up by a helicopter.

The press treated pilots who were shot down with respect, almost as heroes, like an injured football player carried off the field. But their squadron mates, who knew what was involved, tended to divide shoot-downs into two categories, the ones that could have been prevented and those that could not. Many in the squadron believed Butch's shootdown fell in the first category.

After Swanson took over the squadron, he gave Butch his choice of whether he wanted to remain as the maintenance officer or take over as operations officer. Swanson suggested he would be happy to see him stay with maintenance, but the choice was Butch's by virtue of his rank. Verich decided it would be a better career move to take the operations job. There, too, he proved himself a conscientious staff officer, and was well liked by everybody in the squadron.

The strike on July 16, 1967, was against Phu Ly. Herb Hunter would be taking the one against Co Trai, just outside Phu Ly, three days later, but on this mission Herb and Dick Wyman were flying under Butch's lead. Butch's wingman went down on the flight deck with a malfunction as they were taking off.

"The three of us were going to kick on our afterburners and go ahead of the strike group, to take out the flak sites," Butch said. "The idea was to go to burner, climb, get our speed up, and roll in. I called, 'Burner now!' As we went up, I could hear the electronic countermeasures in my headset, which was pretty standard. Then suddenly I got the warble, the electronic sound that meant a missile had been fired, so I rocked my wings and looked down. Two SAMs were coming up at eleven o'clock. I started to dive. I picked up relative motion and could see they were going to pass by my tail.

"I came back up to finish my roll in on the target. I looked down and saw another missile headed for my wingtip, this time with no relative motion. I was going to do a barrel roll into it as Swanson had been preaching so. But I started to pull up and noticed I'd lost speed. My airplane was heavy with bombs. I couldn't maneuver very well. I looked again at the missile. It was doing nothing but coming straight at me. All this was happening within a five- to ten-second time frame. Instead of completing the barrel roll, I did a split-S maneuver. When my nose was down, the missile tagged me.

"The plane was rattled by the explosion. White-hot shrapnel flew by the cockpit. I didn't have any control, was headed straight down. I punched out at a low altitude. Seeing that chute open above me was a nice feeling. There was a horrendous *boom!* Another missile had gone off not far away, leaving a big cloud of orange smoke hanging in the air.

"I heard flak guns going *rat-tat-tat* below. I saw two F-8s that had to be Wyman and Hunter. They were laying down suppressive fire and I knew they must have seen me get hit. As I drifted down an airplane exploded, my own. A gentle breeze began pushing me toward the burning wreckage. I said, 'This is ridiculous, I'm going to get burned up by my own airplane.' I pulled on the risers with all my might. It was a stroke of luck, because I started going toward a small hill and not only avoided the burning wreck but landed on the high ground above an antiaircraft site.

"I could smell the gunpowder from the flak guns and see paper wadding—it looked like blown-up firecracker paper—floating down. I felt a shower of hot bits of expended shrapnel hitting around me. I had landed two hundred feet from the guns. The North Vietnamese starting spraying the trees around me with small arms and automatic weapons. I think they were trying to scare me, and they succeeded. I ran like hell in the opposite direction, ran till I couldn't run any more. I got shot down at 5:52 P.M. I knew it would be dark soon.

"I called on my beeper radio and said I was okay, transmitting in the blind. Nobody answered. I left the beeper on for a while, then turned it off, I didn't want to burn up the battery. I saw a small hole that had a stone in front. I found some tree branches and used them to cover the hole after I got behind the stone. I could hear the North Vietnamese moving through the brush, yelling to one another. My flight boots, I noticed, had a bright shine. I was sure they would get me captured. I started scraping away at them with a rock."

---

4 · *Dick Wyman*

I SAW the missile and screamed, "Superheats break!" I broke to the left and Herb to the right. Butch was left sitting in the middle. After you've been around jet engines for a while, your hearing starts to deteriorate, and Butch had a problem. My hearing is bad, but he'd once been a catapult officer, and they were exposed to more noise than anybody. You had to stand on his right side to talk to him. As I rolled back, I saw a SAM go right up his tail pipe. His airplane disappeared in a huge ball of orange. "Holy Shit!" Then suddenly a chute popped out of the fireball. "That's impossible," I said.

"Mayday! Mayday! We've got a guy down!"

I circled round and laid down fire to keep the North Vietnamese low until Butch landed. As I turned the corner, I felt something thumping my plane. We later found sixteen holes in my fuselage. I radioed Herb Hunter and said, "I've taken some hits and I'm getting out of here." I went into afterburner and headed toward the water. "If the engine quits," I said, "I'll just glide out." When I got over the water, it was obvious the engine wasn't damaged, but I discovered I was almost out of gas. I called up and said I needed to tank.

The tanker said, "I'm heading south. I'm in an emergency fuel state myself."

I said, "Say again."

He said, "I haven't got enough fuel."

I said, "Jesus Christ!"

I zoomed up and started calling for help. "I need some gas. I'm not going to make it."

Red Crown, the U.S. destroyer coordinating our attack, said, "There's a tanker headed your way. It's at one-thirty." I looked up and saw the tanker at fifteen thousand feet going in the opposite direction. I didn't have enough fuel to climb and get him.

I called the *Oriskany* and said, "I'm in an emergency low state. I don't have time to make any turns. I'm just going to put it on idle and come straight in to land." I was telling this to the air boss. The pilot in front of me had had his tail pipe shot off, and the LSO told him to shut down his engine immediately when he landed as a precaution against fire. This would've put him in my way as I came down. The air boss and I screamed, "Negative! Negative! Emergency low state in the groove!"

I said, "Oh, my God, I'll never make it." I leveled off and squeezed the throttle just enough to keep flying. No fuel was showing on the gauge. I nearly wet my pants. I could hardly believe it when I felt myself being slammed forward in my torso harness, as the airplane caught a wire. It flamed out when the crew put the chains on to tie it down.

My knees were shaking uncontrollably. I got out of the cockpit, and a crewman came over to help me. I said, "Chief, you can forget about Commander Verich. He got shot down."

He said, "Sir, the admiral wants to see you as soon as possible in the war room." The admiral commanding the carrier group was using the *Oriskany* as his headquarters. I went to the war room and they asked me to pinpoint on a map where Butch was downed. He had landed about thirty miles south of Hanoi. Nobody had been rescued that deep in North Vietnam. Two members of the admiral's staff, both captains, argued that it was too dangerous to attempt a rescue. Other planes might be lost in the operation. It was already getting dark and nothing could be done till the next morning anyway. By then, Butch probably would be in North Vietnamese hands, if not dead.

Burt Shepherd, the air wing commander, CAG, as we still called him in old navy terminology, was there. "Negative," he said. "We've got to try to get him out. It's early in the game. We've got to let our pilots know we are willing to take risks to rescue them. If we don't, it is going to cost us in terms of morale in the long run."

"No, it's not worth it," the two staff captains said.

The admiral let them argue it out. I was sitting there keeping quiet, shaking and listening. My mouth was still dry. I was just getting back to where I could blink my eyes. The admiral said, "CAG, I like your idea. We're going in to get him at first light."

5

THE NORTH VIETNAMESE turned searchlights on the trees. They fired automatic weapons and made noise, trying to drive Butch out of hiding. He had given up hopes of being rescued, but he intended to put as much distance between himself and his pursuers as he could. By 11:00 P.M. the noise had died away, with only an occasional shot fired in his direction.

"If I was one of those troopers out there and an officer told me to look all night for an American pilot, I'd say, 'Screw you,' and light up a cigarette," Butch said. "I figured that's what they were probably doing, and I decided to make my move."

Butch took out his compass to orient himself. He had changed his survival pack the day before, and now he discovered he'd forgotten to replace the maps. It was the first flight he'd ever made without his survival maps. He started moving. He got only a few feet before he decided he had made a mistake. He could see nothing in the darkness and frequently lost his footing. Nor could he find his way back to his hiding place. He settled in another spot, not as good as the first, and tried to sleep.

"I felt the warmth of the valley start to rise early next morning. I smelled manure. I knew there were farms close by. Soon the search for me resumed. There was more talking, more noise; the Vietnamese were back in the woods. About that time an airplane flew over. I clicked on my radio and said, 'This is Green-One. How do you read me?'

"It was Marvin Reynolds. He said, 'This is Old Salt-One. Butch is that you?'

"I said, 'Hi, Marv. Be advised there are many enemy around here.'

"Antiaircraft guns started firing at him. He said, 'Roger, Butch. Just sit tight and we'll be back in a short while.'

"It was an hour before they returned. It seemed like a long time. First the A-4s came and made runs on the flak guns. Then the propeller-driven Spads arrived, flying low over me, trying to establish my exact position. I started coaching them. One of them said, 'I think I've got you, but let me make one more pass. Okay, that's it, the helo will be here shortly. Good luck.'

"There was another wait. Then I saw the helicopter coming *whump-whump-whump* in the distance. I radioed him directions. After he made a couple of turns I said, 'You're flying toward me and I'm going to fire a flare to mark my position.' I got out two pencil flares. I fumbled the first one. The helicopter was making a turn to avoid running into the hill and didn't see it. I turned him around and fired another. This time he spotted me. I could see the pilot and the copilot in the cockpit.

"The North Vietnamese were firing. The helo was firing back. It sounded like the end of the world. Bullets were whistling around me. I saw an opening in the trees. I ran to it and waved my arms. The helicopter hovered over me and dropped a jungle penetrator, a hoist attached to a thin cable. It landed ten feet away. I scrambled down a rockside to grab it. As I got my hands on it, the helicopter moved and jerked it away. I scrambled after it again—and missed. This happened three times. I was desperate.

"Once again I lunged for the hoist. This time I got my arms around it and hung on while the crew pulled me up, sure I was going to get shot, my back tensed for the bullet. I hugged the crewman who pulled me aboard and said, 'Am I glad to see you guys!'

"He said, 'Great. Hand me that gun.' He pointed to an M-60 on a tripod. His own had jammed. The two crewmen continued to exchange fire with the North Vietnamese.

"I saw we were headed toward an antiaircraft site. I barged into the cockpit and yelled, 'Don't fly there. You're going to get hit!' The pilot looked at me, startled. 'Turn right!' I screamed. 'Turn right!' He hauled it around.

"The helicopter took numerous hits. The pilot, Lieutenant Neil Anderson, later told me he had made up his mind to drop the hoist one more time and if I didn't catch it, that was it, he intended to leave me. He knew he was about to get shot down. He was awarded the Navy Cross, the second highest U.S. medal, for making the rescue. It was the deepest anyone had been picked out of North Vietnam and the first time anyone had been rescued after staying on the ground overnight.

"The first thing I did when I got to the *Oriskany* was have a bit of brandy. Then the flight surgeon checked me over. The admiral wanted to talk to me. Swanson told me I was going to Saigon for press interviews. I was like a puppet. As I started to leave, I saw I didn't have as much money in my suit as I thought I had. The day before I'd had over a hundred dollars.

"My roommate was a good friend of mine from years back on the *Kitty Hawk*. I saw him on the flight deck and said, 'How about lending me some money till I get back from Saigon?'

"He said, 'Sure, how much you need?'

" 'Oh, a hundred bucks should do it.'

"He handed me the money and said, 'By the way, fifty of that is yours.'

"I'd owed him fifty dollars and when I got shot down he was certain he would never see me again, so he reached in my suit pocket and took the money. He admitted that.

"I said, 'You rotten prick.'

"He grinned and said, 'Yeah, that's war, isn't it?' "

6 · *Marilyn Elkins*

IN JANUARY 1967, I entered graduate school at the University of Tennessee. I'd planned to enter the previous fall and that's why Frank had been a little nervous about my going to Asia to meet him when the *Oriskany* was in port. "You can always take the courses some other time," he said. "I promise. We'll be stationed near a college where you can go to school." I'd always wanted to have braces on my teeth. I had them as a child but they didn't turn out as I liked. So I went and had all my wisdom teeth removed and braces put on. I didn't worry about how I looked. I didn't buy a new dress for six months after Frank was shot down. I love clothes and for me not to buy anything new meant I was really depressed. Going to graduate school would be accomplishing something. I wouldn't just be sitting around waiting for news of Frank. I studied for a master's in teaching. You took education and literature courses on the graduate level and had to practice teaching, which I did that summer at a practically all black school called Central High. I wound up with a 3.7 average out of 4.0, the first time I'd really studied.

When I met people I wouldn't tell them Frank was missing. I'd say, "My husband is in Vietnam." If we got to be friends, I might tell them later, but I felt it was nobody's business, and I didn't like all that pity stuff. After a while, though, I began to resent the way the navy acted about his being missing. The Pentagon sent me frequent telegrams, each time advising me to keep everything confidential. Please don't tell anybody you've committed the sin of having your husband missing. I mean, the telegrams didn't say that exactly. But you were almost made to feel you were an inconvenience, an embarrassment.

The North Vietnamese would, of course, know about Frank. So

what was the Pentagon talking about? Why didn't they want me to speak about my husband or tell anyone he was missing? I thought it was paranoid. On the other hand, I didn't want to do anything that would endanger Frank's career. He might come back and want to stay in the navy. By the fall, though, I was beginning to get angry. My father was just having a fit. He thought I was being horribly unpatriotic. He was World War Two, very happily, and couldn't imagine why I thought we shouldn't be in Vietnam, or how I could be upset with anything the government did.

7

THE SAIGON PRESS CORPS was pleased to have a story that was truly heroic in every sense, and Butch Verich's rescue received wide play, with accounts appearing in papers across America, on TV, and in the New York *Times*. Few pilots had shown greater fortitude. Cal Swanson recorded an interview with Verich and passed the tape around the *Oriskany,* where it was listened to avidly. Special note was taken of Squadron 162, which now had two pilots—Butch and Rick Adams—to be shot down twice over North Vietnam and rescued, a record for the war.

Yet Swanson, who was ready to give Butch his due in public, expressed other thoughts about the shootdown in private. He wrote Nell to say he suspected that Butch was downed because of an error. From talking to Butch, Cal believed he had turned and tried to outrun the missile, instead of doing a barrel roll into it. That might be an understandable reaction on the part of someone new to the game, but Butch was a combat veteran on his second tour. How many times had they gone over the best way to evade a missile? To Swanson, that meant Butch had lost two planes, several million dollars worth of the taxpayers' money, because he wasn't doing what he was supposed to do. Others in the squadron also believed Verich had made a mistake.

Dick Wyman was an exception. In this case, he believed Butch's downing was unavoidable. "Butch wasn't afraid, he didn't lack courage," Wyman said. "He was a good performer over the beach in the sense that he went, did his job, and was coherent. I told everybody when I got back that Butch didn't break, that he must not have heard me call the missile. But I think Swanson thought he screwed up and got himself shot down."

When Rick Adams, who was flying as Butch's wingman, was downed and rescued for the second time, the navy decided that two times was enough to ask of any man, and Adams was transferred out of the combat zone. This time, a year later, after many pilots had been killed or captured and the navy was beginning to experience a shortage, no one rushed to urge Butch to give up flying combat. He and Swanson talked it over but reached no conclusion.

Butch wanted to take a few days leave in Australia before deciding what he was going to do. He was anxious to see his fiancée. She was an Australian, a secretary for Qantas Airlines, whom Swanson and Bellinger had first met in a restaurant when the *Oriskany* was in Hong Kong. "Belly saw me," Butch said, "and says, 'There's a gal who is dying to meet you.' I said, 'I don't believe you, but who's the girl?' I took her out to dinner. She was younger than I. She was a lady, and I treated her like one. I think she probably appreciated that."

After Butch returned from Australia, Cal Swanson said, "You've got your choice. You can go back to the States. Or you can stay with us."

"I thought it might be good for the morale of the junior officers if I stayed," Butch said. "I'd been twice rescued. That showed what was possible. And I felt a loyalty toward the navy. I didn't want to bug out. So I told them I would stay. The air wing commander said, 'Well, Butch, if it gets too hot for you, don't press it.' "

It was the consensus of the squadron that it did get too hot for Butch after he returned and that he should have never been allowed to stay on Yankee Station. An American soldier serving in South Vietnam could go for days, weeks, or even months without getting shot at. That was the nature of the ground war. The majority of American casualties were suffered in ambushes lasting no more than a few minutes. But a pilot knew every time he crossed North Vietnam's coast that somebody down there was shooting at him, whether or not he could see the tracers. A jet engine was a fragile piece of machinery. A bullet fired from a rifle held by a teenager of either sex could, and sometimes did, help bring down a plane. After two shootdowns, that knowledge would have worked on the mind of anyone but the most insensitive, and Butch was not insensitive.

"Butch Verich was never the same after he got shot down the second time," Ron Coalson said. "He was afraid, no doubt in my mind. And he had damn good reason to be afraid. We were at Haiphong and they fired two missiles at us. You put the nose of the airplane down and the missiles go down, and you pick the nose up and the missiles go up, following your every movement, and you say, 'Holy Shit! They've got my name written on them!' And Verich was gone; he was out of there. I didn't want to fly with him after that."

"There was a pilot shortage and this was one reason I gave him the choice of whether he wanted to stay," Cal Swanson said. "He was a competent pilot and well organized. Until that point he had followed orders precisely. I assumed he would continue in that manner. But I was wrong. When it came time to write his fitness report, I spent a lot of time trying to decide how I should evaluate Butch. I knew the fitness report would be a key factor in deciding whether he would be selected to command a fighter squadron. As much as I liked Butch and sympathized with the fact that he had been shot down twice, I felt I owed it to the navy to say that he should not have a fighter squadron."

Several years later the Navy Department wrote Swanson to ask if, in retrospect, the fitness report was valid, or whether he would like to revise it, to improve Verich's chances for command. Swanson replied and sent a copy of his letter to Verich. "Butch," he wrote, "I'm very sorry and I never really wanted to put this in words, but, yes, the fitness report represented a conscious decision on my part. I thought it was better for you and better for the navy that you not have command of a fighter squadron."

Butch retired from the navy and did well in civilian life. Over the years, he occasionally bumped into Cal during chance encounters. He was always unfailingly polite.

8

ON JULY 19, 1967, as Herb Hunter and Lee Fernandez were catapulted off the *Oriskany* for the strike on Co Trai, Ron Coalson walked to the LSO platform on the landing area, to the rear of the flight deck. Coalson, who was Lee's roommate, was in training to become an LSO. He would be there to help Lee get back aboard ship after the attack was over. Pilots called landing on a carrier "a controlled crash." That was when it was done right. Lee seemed to be losing some of his control, and Coalson was worried about him.

The Landing Signal Officer had changed since the days of World War Two or Korea, when he stood on the carrier deck and waved planes in with two semaphore flags or two luminous paddles. A good LSO was still called "Paddles" as a mark of respect, but the only thing he held now was a pickle switch that controlled a panel of lights and a radio headset for communication. A lens box, with six horizontal green lights on either side, was positioned at the edge of the flight deck on the port side. Put simply, the lens box acted as a window that the pilot watched as he came in to land. If he was on a correct glide slope, a yellowish-orange light in the window would be perfectly aligned with the twelve horizontal green lights outside. If he were too high, the yellow light would appear above the green lights; too low, below. Pilots referred to the yellow light as the "meatball," or simply the "ball," and they were supposed to call it when they first saw it. The LSO talked them down, trying to help them get on a glide slope that would align the ball with the green lights. If he saw that the pilot could not make a safe approach that would permit him to land and catch one of the four wires stretched across the flight deck, the LSO quickly punched the pickle switch, causing a vertical column of five red waveoff lights on either side of the lens box to start flashing, which told the pilot to start over, to make another pass at the ship.

Landing on a carrier was tricky under the best of conditions. A pilot had about ten feet to play with in putting the tail hook down from the edge of the *Oriskany's* back ramp. At night landing could be positively testicle-shrinking. No one in his right mind said he enjoyed doing it. To the pilots, a good LSO was something between a doctor and a brother. Just to hear his calm voice on a rainy night was reassuring. Many LSOs made it a point of knowing every pilot on a carrier, calling them by their first names, regardless of rank, as they came in to land.

Charlie Tinker, an LSO the year before, said, "I had a standard phrase to tell a pilot after he called the ball. 'We've got thirty-five knots down the angle and you're doing fine.' Or whatever else might pop into my mind to relax the guy. You had to make the pilot fly it all the way. You couldn't just wave him off, because the poor bastard might not have any fuel left. On the bad nights, with the monsoon churning up the sea, the deck heaving, I'd end up going to see the flight surgeon after I brought the planes in. My stomach would be so knotted I'd get the dry heaves. He always prescribed the same thing: a small bottle of 'medicinal' brandy."

J. P. O'Neill, a stocky, redheaded Irishman, a pilot of Squadron 162, was the *Oriskany's* senior LSO in 1967, and served as Ron Coalson's teacher. "One night the ship was in and out of rain squalls," John Hellman said. "There was no horizon, just blackness. I said, 'Hey, J. P., I can't see anything.' He said, 'Keep it coming, you're looking fine. I've got your approach light.' I said, 'But I can't see anything.' He said, 'I'll tell you. Just keep it coming.' As I went over the ramp, I saw the lights on the deck. After I got out of the cockpit I went to him and said, 'Thanks J. P. Love you.' He said, 'Anytime.' "

It was not all sweetness between the LSO and the pilots. He graded them on how well they landed and the grades were posted on the bulletin board in the ready room. A commanding officer could see who was having trouble getting aboard. The pilots, as fiercely competitive about their landing grades as they were about everything else, sometimes argued with the LSO and asked that a video recording of the landing be replayed on the TV monitor, though it was usually like arguing with a baseball umpire, with no better results.

Some pilots cared little about how well they landed but simply wanted to get aboard the first time. When landing at a ground field, a pilot cut the engine as he touched down. On an aircraft carrier he went to full power, so that if he missed all four wires with his tail hook he would do what amounted to a touch-and-go and be able to fly off for another pass at the deck. Missing all the wires and flying off was called a "bolter." The target wire to catch was the three wire, numbered from the rear, since that represented the safest position between hitting the back ramp and overshooting the deck. A few pilots were known for aiming their planes at the deck and taking whatever wire they could get.

"Dick Wyman's attitude was, 'Screw the LSO. I'm going to land the airplane,' " Ron Coalson said. "He wouldn't do what you told him at all. His way was to get all the wires in front of him and then rotate the airplane slightly before it touched down, to drop the tail hook. That was okay if you had the ability, and Wyman had the ability, but it was dangerous. The LSO worried about the influence that might have on a less talented pilot who might try to emulate the heavy and wind up smashing his airplane into the ramp. I think that's why we as LSOs didn't like Dick's attitude. J. P. would call him on it. But Wyman would laugh, give a thumbs up, say 'Righto,' and go do it again."

Ironically, Ron Coalson disliked carrier landings so much that his avoidance of night flying won him the nickname of "No-Nights." Though no one questioned his innate courage, some pilots theorized that Coalson suffered a psychological block because of his work as an LSO. Just to *watch* an F-8 land at night was frightening. Coalson disagreed with the theory and said, "I don't think I was so afraid I wouldn't go up at night. It was just that I was afraid enough so that if the airplane wasn't in perfect working order, I wouldn't go. Other guys weren't like that. Dick Wyman had different criteria than I did. If a plane had a hydraulic leak or something, why shit, Wyman would take it up. He knew his limits, knew he could handle the problem. I knew I couldn't handle it, that it would psych me out at night. So they called me No-Nights, and I laughed. No way was I going to get sensitive about it. If I'd shown any resentment, I would've been crucified. That's the way the squadron worked. We were honest with each other, had to be, to fly in combat together day after day."

Rich Minnich was the squadron's scheduling officer, and he discreetly protected Coalson by dividing up the flights in such a way that Ron's name seldom appeared on the night schedule. Minnich sympathized with Coalson, for he himself had trouble getting aboard at night. One night Minnich landed so hard it blew the struts out and started a hydraulic fire that burned up his airplane. He got out of that one without a scratch, though his luck was destined to run out in a few months.

Ron Coalson. Few officers in the United States Navy looked as good as he did in a uniform. He was six-three, lean and handsome, with black hair and hazel eyes. He had a deep, resonating voice, which, heard on a tape recorder, could make a stranger say, "I like that man." There was something vulnerable and guileless about Coalson. He had been on a spiritual quest since his college years, when he majored in psychology and minored in philosophy. His father, a B-17 navigator, was shot down and killed over Belgium in the final days of the war. His older brother, a helicopter pilot in South Vietnam, was wounded in action at the time Ron decided to enter naval aviation.

"I really liked the military and believed all the stuff they told us," Coalson said. "I was the kind of guy who wouldn't smoke while wearing my uniform, wouldn't put my hands in my pockets. I was absolutely gung ho, probably to the point of a Marine Corps type of enthusiasm. Perhaps not being raised with a father made me like being part of the system, being in the midst of elite men."

Coalson was selected as a regimental subcommander in flight school. Chuck Rice, a cadet under his student command, recalled that Coalson was a stickler for haircuts. Chuck and Ron were to become the best of friends, and later Chuck would be shot down while flying Coalson's wing. "Chuck was a super guy," Ron said, "very low-key and laid-back. But he was a professional who took great pains with his uniform and looked like a naval officer."

When Coalson reported to Squadron 162, one of the first officers he saw was Dick Wyman. He squared his shoulders, locked his elbow, and gave Wyman a salute that snapped like a flag. Wyman glanced at him and said, "That's a bunch of horseshit; I don't do that." Coalson was hurt. "I had rendered him the proper military courtesy and he mocked me. He was well dressed and looked good. He was a combat-experienced lieutenant, and I thought he should have had more respect for himself. Later I understood that although he outranked me, he considered both of us junior officers and thought we were equal."

Ron Coalson knew how to fly F-8s very well, but he discovered there were a lot of other things he had to learn about being a fighter pilot. "We were in the club at Miramar and a gorgeous woman came up to me and said, 'Here's my name and number; give me a call.' I noticed a ring on her finger. I said, 'But aren't you married?' She said, 'Yes, I am. But my husband is going to sea tomorrow.' I wasn't ready for that. I didn't know it went on. I wadded the piece of paper up and threw it away after she left. I had turned twenty-three. This was life in the fast lane. I had to play catch-up. And consequently I overdid it. I drank scotch whiskey because of that—and it was awful. But fighter pilots drank scotch. Why? Because bourbon was considered a redneck drink and nobody was interested in being a redneck. They were fighter pilots and fighter pilots were the epitome, they thought, of everything a man should be—sophisticated, gallant, suave—they wore ascots and all that."

Coalson soon felt comfortable as a member of the squadron. His entry, he thought, was made smoother by Black Mac. "Black Mac was a disgrace to the navy as far as his appearance was concerned," Ron said. "He looked like a slob. His stomach hung over his belt and he drank more beer than anybody I ever knew in my life, concealing it in his room on the ship, cases and cases of Budweiser. But the man had incredible enthusiasm and was a hell of an airplane driver. He was awesome, he really was. If you had a weakness and tried to hide it and Black Mac found out, it was history. He laid it on the table and you realized it was okay to have a weakness, because the very next hour he was doing it to somebody else. We had a unity we might not have had if Black Mac hadn't been there."

In Japan Coalson first saw Black Mac's afterburner trick. "We were standing away from the bar and a Japanese waitress, five feet tall, white kimono, trim and proper, brought us a tray of drinks. Black Mac had a mouthful of lighter fluid. He lit his Zippo and blew a huge fireball right in front of her. We called it the night the slant-eye became a round-eye. Her eyes got so big it was unbelievable. The club manager asked Black Mac to leave. But of course that happened to him more than once."

Ron fell in love with the daughter of a U.S. Navy captain. She was a slender blonde, beautiful and elegant. "She was dancing with somebody at the officers' club in Japan, and it was one of those things where your eyes meet and bam! I was struck down." He spent the rest of the time the ship was in port taking her to dinner, going sailing. "It finally ended months later. She wrote me a Dear-John letter, saying her father had warned her that pilots were fast and had no substance. She ended up marrying a young ship's commander, a black shoe."

Coalson was assigned as John Hellman's wingman. Hellman was a lieutenant commander, a native of Seattle, Washington, who looked—

and acted, some in the squadron thought—more like a sedate banker than a fighter pilot. Hellman was solid and dependable, not given to excess. He took Coalson on his first flight over North Vietnam on his twenty-fourth birthday. Coalson was shot at for the first time at Thud Ridge.

"White puffs of flak were exploding everywhere. I could see the muzzle flashes of the guns. It looked like a bunch of sparklers on the ground. With the headset plugged in, you were hearing the pilot chatter, plus the electronic sounds of the anti-SAM gear, hearing quite a bit of noise. Suddenly everything fell silent, and I was shocked. What happened was that I'd accidentally unplugged my headset. Should I take my hands off the airplane and plug the cord back in? Or should I just leave and return to the ship? I pickled off my bombs—I don't know where they landed—and headed toward the coast. I was weaving in and out, jinking, hauling on the stick to make sharp turns as an evasive maneuver. I looked down and saw some A-Fours outrunning me and wondered why. Then I realized, 'Hey, you're doing it wrong. Look at those guys, they're just moving their airplanes easily into evasive turns.' So I leveled my wings, came out of afterburner, and returned to the ship. I was sweating, absolutely soaked. I was adrenalized, peaked, it's unbelievable how you felt.

"When John Hellman got back, he said, 'Come on, let's go to my room.' I was still in a kind of daze. I went to his room and he handed me a cold beer. It was the first time I'd been invited to my flight leader's room for a drink. It was a rite of passage. 'You've been shot at, so now you can drink with us. You didn't run.' In a sense, though, I did run, because I didn't effect the proper bomb delivery. He began to talk about what we'd done, how I had to improve. He said, 'You lost me,' which was true. I returned to the ship alone. He was low-key about it, and he put me on the right track for future flights."

From his first days in flight training, Coalson had wanted to be an LSO. It became an intense but inexplicable urge. "Something appealed to me about watching the airplanes and being able to help them," he said. "It was a very important duty, a place for me. I didn't fit in on other jobs." In J. P. O'Neill he found a teacher who was anxious to communicate everything he knew. Everybody agreed J. P. was an excellent LSO. He understood how the pilots felt, knew what was required to get them aboard. He gave Coalson a radio headset and a

157

waveoff switch and let him practice bringing the planes in, always at his side.

"I made a mistake one night," Coalson said. "A junior officer, a friend of mine, was coming in and was too high. I told him, 'You are high, way too high, make a big correction.' But I let him keep coming and finally he landed with a bang. I don't know why the airplane didn't break up. J. P. looked at me and said, 'I can't believe you did that.' Having him say that was the worst punishment I ever received in the navy. He had the highest standards, and I'd not measured up. I handed him the pickle and the radio and stood there for the rest of the recovery. I was devastated to have failed him."

Eventually, Ron Coalson was to become one of the finest LSOs in the United States Navy. And it was all due, he said, to a redheaded Irishman.

On July 19, 1967, Coalson stood on the LSO platform, waiting for Herb Hunter and Lee Fernandez to return from Co Trai. The planes would first fly by the right side of the ship at eight hundred feet and make a thirty-degree turn that would bring them around and put them in the groove to land. A plane touched down every thirty-five seconds. Coalson wondered if Cal Swanson was in the air tower with his stopwatch. Swanson demanded the squadron adhere precisely to the correct interval between landings. If you were five seconds off, he told you about it. There would be no need to check on Herb Hunter. Herb, a former Blue Angel, could really fly that plane.

Coalson's preoccupation was with Fernandez. In a way, he and Lee were a lot alike. Coalson had been asking questions his whole life. Big questions. What does it all mean? Why are we here? Lee questioned things too, was very introspective. But Lee's questions, unlike Coalson's, were not concerned with the cosmos. When Lee asked, "Why are we here?" he meant *here*, right now, in Vietnam.

"Lee was bothered," Ron said. "Not because he was afraid. But in a moral sense. The more he seemed to ponder the war, the worse he got at the boat. It worked on his head. I mean, he was dangerous, absolutely awful at bringing the airplane aboard the ship. And yet he continued to fly."

9

THE MORNING of the Co Trai strike did not start well. The day before, two pilots were shot down not far from Co Trai. One was picked up and the other was left on the ground overnight. Shortly before Herb Hunter and Lee Fernandez were catapulted off the *Oriskany,* an attempt to pull off another rescue like Butch's was made, only this time it failed. The rescue helicopter was shot down and the crew killed. The pilot who was the object of the attempt was left on the ground and presumably captured, and another A-4 was downed during the operation. The failed attempt cast a pall over the ship. There was little talking in the ready room, as the pilots listened to the radio transmissions of Herb's and Lee's strike group.

Though Lee had never flown against Co Trai, the target held a special significance. The previous year he had been in F-8 training at Miramar when Terry Dennison was shot down on Cal Swanson's strike. Dennison was several months ahead of him in the replacement air group. Lee did not know Dennison personally, but the death affected him, as it did the other young trainees at Miramar, because Dennison was fresh out of training and they realized they soon would be facing their own Co Trais.

Exactly what happened on July 19, 1967, Lee Fernandez later blocked out of his mind. He remembered his anxiety as they crossed North Vietnam's coastline. But he could not recall details of the strike itself— the roll in, the flak, whether his bombs hit the target. The horror started when he noticed the small hole in Herb Hunter's right wing. It looked insignificant and must have been caused by a small-caliber bullet. But Herb was losing fuel fast.

Hunter and Fernandez dropped to seven thousand feet and flew slower to conserve fuel, while another plane went ahead to warn the *Oriskany* of Hunter's damage. The hole did not seem to be particularly dangerous, but two of Herb's seven hundred and fifty-pound bombs had failed to release from the same wing and were jammed, adding excess weight to the plane. The combined problems could mean serious difficulty in landing.

When Cal Swanson learned of Hunter's battle damage, he went to the air traffic control center to talk to Herb on the radio.

"Superheat-Two, this is the skipper. I understand you got a hit in the wing."

"Roger. I'm losing fuel."

"What about the hydraulics?"

"I'm out on one system and maybe the other too."

"What's your fuel state?"

"Eight hundred pounds. I'm going to be overweight with hung ordnance. Do you think I can bring it aboard?"

Swanson made mental calculations as they talked. A hydraulic failure would keep Herb from being refueled by a tanker. The hung bombs were a problem, but Herb was a remarkably good pilot.

"Affirmative," Cal said. "You'll have one shot at the deck. If you don't catch a wire, you'll have to eject."

Swanson made his calculations with the belief that Herb Hunter was fifteen miles from the *Oriskany*. Which was wrong. Hunter was actually *fifty* miles out. Hunter and Fernandez were making their plans to land also based on a mistaken assumption. The ship they had in sight was not the *Oriskany* but another aircraft carrier, which, coincidentally, was sailing directly behind their ship.

"That's not the *Oriskany*," Herb Hunter suddenly radioed. "It's the *Bonnie Dick*. I can land there."

Cal Swanson was surprised. He did not know the *Bon Homme Richard* was sailing behind the *Oriskany*.

"I've got to shift frequencies to talk to the *Bonnie Dick*," Herb said.

"Okay," Swanson said. "Take a shot at it. But if it doesn't look good, go ahead and get out." He was not sure Hunter heard his final transmission.

"It was a terrible coincidence," Lee Fernandez said. "The *Oriskany* had been alerted and I'm sure if we had made it to the ship, Swanson or the air boss would have told Herb to eject. As it was, we didn't realize it was the *Bon Homme Richard* until we were almost upon it. The LSO had little time to assess the situation. Herb was making a straight-in approach, tough in any circumstance, and because of hydraulic problems his wheels wouldn't lock down, so he had to blow them down with emergency air. Then he discovered his wing wouldn't jack up, which was necessary for the landing with an F-Eight.

"Why he attempted to land, why the LSO allowed him to, I don't know, except that a decision to eject is difficult to make, unless there are clearly no alternatives. I think he'd given up on hopes of saving the airplane intact but thought he could throw it at the wires and pray it would stop. As he dropped to the deck, obviously not going to catch a wire, I yelled for him to eject. I wish I had yelled that earlier. He hit hard: the bombs were knocked off, the two landing gear collapsed, the little fuel left burned up in a second.

"I screamed as I saw his plane go off the deck into the water. I yelled with rage and disbelief that the war could do this to such a man. In a daze, I flew around to check the spot where he went down. I saw a partially opened parachute underwater. The impact must have triggered the ejection. The helicopter recovered his body. Somehow I made it back to the *Oriskany*. I landed on the first try. I relived the crash over and over that night."

Stunned, Cal Swanson went to his room and wrote Nell. "My remorse is heightened by the fact that I could have ordered him to bail out," he told her. In his letter and the one he wrote the next day, Swanson displayed a rare emotion, perhaps feeling through Herb's death an intimation of his own mortality. He and Nell had a close, trusting relationship, but not a very passionate one. After unburdening himself about Herb's death ("I can't let the young fellows know how it affects me"), he closed, "And, Darling, remember, I love you with all my heart and soul. No one could ask for a finer mate than you."

Cal filled out a casualty report on Herb. It would be radioed up the chain of command and flashed to Miramar. In a few hours the dreaded black government car that sent shivers through the wives of pilots as it passed through their neighborhood would pull into Herb's driveway. A crisply uniformed officer would get out and ring the doorbell. Diane would answer, the frozen shock on her face saying she already knew. Cal decided to postpone writing a letter to Diane. Tomorrow, he would do it then. What he wanted now was a drink. He opened the small wall safe in his room and took out a bottle of scotch. He remembered that the form letter he'd sent the wives would reach Diane at the time she learned of Herb's death. *We all know the risks involved, yet we accept these risks because we feel the gratification and satisfaction associated with military flying far exceed the hazards involved.* How callous it would sound. He poured another scotch.

Bob Punches was one of the pilots in the ready room, shocked by what had happened. "Lee Fernandez came in and sat down in his chair," Punches said. "He was sickly white. He refused to take off his flight gear. We had to force the story out of him. 'Come on, Lee, what happened next?' He didn't want to talk about it. Lee, I think, already had guilt feelings about what he was doing. After Herb's death, he was never the same."

The squadron was shaken by Herb's death and also puzzled. It didn't fit. No one blamed Swanson for not ordering him to bail out. Everyone wondered why Herb, an excellent pilot, took such a high-odds risk. He knew the F-8 better than that. Black Mac had his theory, which Dick Wyman and others in the squadron conceded might not be too far from the mark.

"In a meeting the day before," Black Mac said, "the air wing commander had really laid it on about how we were losing too many airplanes. 'If you possibly can,' he said, 'bring that airplane back and try to get it aboard.' Herb was a professional. He was trying."

---

10 · Dick Wyman

ONLY DUMBSHITS get shot down. How many times did I think that! "If I don't do anything stupid," I'd say, "I'll stay ahead of the game and survive." When someone got killed, I thought it was because he did something wrong—and in many cases that was true. Of course, it wasn't always so. But I never thought I was going to die. Not once did it enter my mind. They weren't smart enough to shoot me down, I thought. If you lived with the reality that your chances were probably no more than fifty-fifty, you would get numbed. So only dumbshits got shot down.

I discovered something about fear. You go over the beach and you're extremely alert. You don't blink. Your mouth goes dry. You couldn't spit if your life depended on it. Your heart starts beating like you're running a four-minute mile. But it's not a bad environment to work in, it really isn't, as long as you keep it under control. I'd tell my wingmen, "If you're scared and can't control it, you're probably going to get shot down." Because the guys who were frightened stiff would fly in a straight line, forget to make evasive maneuvers, and they'd catch some shrapnel or take a missile up their tail pipe.

Every time I exited the beach and aimed the airplane toward the ship, which was maybe fifteen or twenty minutes away, I suffered a letdown and got the shakes. I smoked a cigarette after I came off a strike. It was against the rules. If you had an oxygen leak and lit up, you could blow yourself out of the sky. I smoked Luckies then. I don't smoke any longer, thank goodness—I quit completely. But in those days I kept a little ashtray in the right knee pocket of my G-suit. I would be shaking so much I'd have to use both hands to put the cigarette in my mouth.

Subconsciously, I guess, I made exceptions for my friends who were shot down. They weren't exactly dumbshits. I could figure out another excuse for them. But the last thing I wanted was to go to the funeral or be around the widow. Lee Prost's wife, I treated her terribly. The day we went to a memorial service for him at Miramar she cried and wailed, and it was like somebody tearing a knife through my gut. I couldn't talk to her for more than a year. She kids me about that now. And Rich Minnich's wife, she used to come spend time with us, a month, two months, and I never said a word about Rich. I didn't even call Herb Hunter's wife after I got back to the States. I guess it was my way of self-protection. I felt inadequate. My wounds and their wounds. I just dodged them.

That's why I got so mad with Cal Swanson after Herb Hunter was killed. Swanson wanted someone who knew Herb well to escort the body to Cubi Point. I told him I didn't want to do it. He said, "There's no discussion. You're going." So I flew to Cubi with Herb Hunter in a green rubber body bag wedged between me and the next seat of a supply plane. I told the prop pilot to radio and have an ambulance meet us at the airfield. We got in after dark. No ambulance. I sat on the runway with Herb's body for forty-five minutes. When it finally arrived I was so mad I was ready to beat up the driver. Then I went to the officers' club and stayed till closing.

Next morning I had a big breakfast and hitched a ride on a radar plane back to Yankee Station. I was in a hurry to return to the squadron. I didn't want to miss any flights. The bastards would get ahead of me.

11

JIM NUNN did not get to bed until midnight on the evening of Herb Hunter's death. He wrote a long letter to his fiancée to tell her what had happened. The incident had a particular impact on Nunn because he and Lee Fernandez were roommates on the *Oriskany* and had been in the Seventeenth Company at Annapolis. They had crewed together for four years, the high point of their athletic careers coming in their junior year, when the Naval Academy finished number two in the nation for the three-mile race, losing to Cornell for the championship. Jim liked and respected Lee and was worried about how he might react to Herb's death. Like Fernandez, Jim Nunn was something of an enigma to the squadron—but for different reasons. Jim was obviously intelligent and had excelled at every point along the way, but sometimes he seemed to be slow on the uptake, which, coupled with his great size and Tennessee drawl, led some pilots to call him "Jim Numb" or "Tarzan." He was very athletic, yet at the same time appeared surprisingly clumsy.

"Nunn reminded me of a football player on a basketball court," Bob Punches said. "He was the type to be sitting at a restaurant table and accidentally knock over a coffee cup. Or reach behind him and unknowingly hit somebody in the mouth. Something of a klutz. But a nice guy."

Nunn had flown as Swanson's wingman the year before and become his protégé. Swanson clearly preferred Nunn to Fernandez, and Nell and Jim's future wife also had become fast friends. Jim and Cal made a public relations tour after Swanson took over the squadron, flying to Florida to give a pep talk to pilots in training. It was Jim whom Cal had called on to fly rescue cover after Butch Verich was shot down. And again, after Herb's death, Nunn was scheduled for a flight early the next morning, which meant he would get no more than three hours sleep.

"I saw Nunn in the ready room just before he was scheduled to take off," Bob Punches said. "He had on his flight gear and was sound asleep in his chair. I said, 'Jim, you want me to take the flight for you?' He looked at me bleary-eyed and said, 'No, I've got it. Thanks.' I figured I'd probably have the next flight, so I put on my gear and went to the air tower. I was sitting up there when it happened."

"I went to the aircraft," Nunn said, "and I told myself, 'Well, here it is two hours before the sun comes up. I'm tired and I've got to be careful.' In the dark, you signal the catapult officer you are ready by flicking on your external lights. It usually takes about five seconds after that until he brings his arm down and touches the deck for the launch. After about thirty seconds, he was still looking at me and I at him and nothing had happened. I got worried and said to myself, 'Maybe he can't see my exterior lights.' I took my left hand off the throttle and moved it to the right side of the cockpit to check the light switch. As I moved my hand, they fired the catapult."

Bob Punches could tell something was wrong. The plane didn't sound right. It wasn't at full power. He knew Jim Nunn was going into the sea. He watched as Nunn's plane pancaked off the front of the ship. That's it, he thought. No one survives something like that. Punches ran down six flights of steps to the flight deck and headed to the bow. The *Oriskany* was thrown into reverse, all back full, to keep from running over the spot where Nunn went under. By the time Punches reached the bow, the airplanes had all been shut down and the flight deck was quiet. Everybody stood at the edge of the ship, staring at the dark sea.

"It was like hitting a grove of saplings in a car at eighty miles an hour," Nunn said. "That kind of stuttering, jarring shock of deceleration. If I hadn't been in such great physical condition, I would've been knocked out or broken my neck. The airplane rolled on its side. I pulled the ejection curtain and was blasted downward into the water. The seat separated and the parachute streamed out behind me. I pulled the toggles to fill the flotation gear and released the shoulder fittings of my parachute. Then I went up and up. I finally broke the surface and, gasping for air, got a lung full of jet fuel vapor. I turned on my strobe light."

"We saw a *blink-blink-blink* in the darkness," Bob Punches said. "Everybody yelled, 'Look! The pilot!' A spotlight was turned on the water from the bridge. Nunn was bobbing up and down like an apple."

Nunn was in a daze when he got to the ship. His only apparent injury was a strained neck, which would prevent him from flying for several months. "Skipper, oh Jesus Christ," he said to Swanson, "I've cost you an airplane." Cal told him not to worry about it and helped escort him to sick bay. Nunn was, everybody agreed, incredibly lucky. Only two other navy pilots had survived an underwater ejection. For the moment, no one spoke about the obvious: that Nunn had committed the military equivalent of driving down the wrong lane of a freeway. As Cal wrote to Nell, "Don't spread it around, though it is common knowledge, but Jim just plain screwed up. We lost an airplane by his violating two fundamental rules: i.e., never take your eyes off the cat officer and never take your hand off the throttle. Jim did both and got fired while he was dicking around in the cockpit."

Swanson was upset. His squadron was responsible for three of the ten aircraft lost by the *Oriskany* after only a week on Yankee Station. He was dubious about Butch's shootdown, though he could not be absolutely certain it was caused by pilot error. He had come to believe, as did Black Mac and Dick Wyman, that Herb Hunter had killed himself while trying to prevent another airplane loss. But even reaching for all extenuating circumstances, Jim Nunn's loss was inexcusable. It went against the most elementary rules of pilot training.

When a pilot committed a major error, the navy authorized that an aviator's disposition board be convened to examine whether he should be allowed to continue flying. Some pilots had had their wings lifted for making errors less serious than Nunn's. Just to convene a disposition board, whether a pilot was found negligent or not, meant a blot on his career.

"I sat down and agonized," Cal said. "Should I convene a disposition board? He had been my wingman, had flown well for me. I guess the thought crossed a lot of people's minds that favoritism was involved. Subconsciously, I may have felt protective. I'd overheard some of the comments about him not being the swiftest person. There were no secrets in the ready room. But I didn't think they saw the same qualities I did—his strength of character, his motivation and intensity. All good traits, I thought, for a naval officer. And I considered his airmanship to be excellent, even though he did tend to horse the airplane because he was so big and strong. As a skipper I had to act as a sort of grand jury in deciding whether he should be given a board. And I decided against it. My reasoning was that he was a good pilot and would be an asset to any squadron."

Chuck Rice, on the USS *Ranger* off the California coast, was fresh out of F-8 training and trying to qualify for carrier landings. Shortly after Nunn went into the ocean, Rice's superior walked into his room waving a message. "Chuck," he said, "you're going to One Sixty-Two. Jim Nunn has hurt himself and he's coming home." Chuck Rice finished his qualifications, and then took a quick leave to tell his parents goodbye and to store his Porsche.

12

AFTER HERB HUNTER was killed Lee Fernandez drew closer to Bob Punches. If the squadron had an odd man out, even more so than Lee Fernandez, it was Lieutenant Punches, a twenty-nine-year-old former marine enlisted man from Michigan. Fernandez and Punches talked about the morality of the war. Bob Punches listened to what Lee had to say, though he did not share his opinion that America was wrong. And though Lee didn't agree with Bob, he listened to his arguments in support of the war, for he knew that Punches was a man of absolute integrity.

Two years earlier, as he sat in a bar on the Fourth of July, Bob Punches had decided to change his life. He had recently heard a talk by Herb Philbrick, the former FBI undercover agent whose anti-communist exploits were turned into a TV series called *I Led Three Lives*. Philbrick said, "If you want to be a Christian, make a commitment and live like one. If you don't, then don't. But there's no in-between way." Bob's father had been a bartender whose own drinking caused his mother much pain. His brother-in-law was killed in a drink-related car accident. Punches suddenly realized that countless families were wrecked, thousands of innocent people killed, all because of alcohol. He put down his glass and walked out of the bar.

Shortly after he was assigned to the squadron, Bob Punches joined the other pilots at the officers' club and, nursing a Coca-Cola, watched them play dice games. Herb Hunter stopped the game and said, "We've got a great squadron. We're all gung ho. We don't have any pansies, except for one guy here who doesn't drink." Everyone looked at Punches. He returned their stares. Someone else said, "Well, I don't think you have to drink to be a man." There was an awkward silence. Hunter turned red. The following day he apologized to Bob.

Not long afterward, the squadron had a meeting of all hands. "One of the men," Punches said, "started talking about how the girl he was out with the previous night never had oral sex before. He described the procedures he used and everything, very graphically. I got up and walked out. Somebody asked me why, and I said, 'Because we're supposed to be talking about professional matters.' " Bob Punches had a commitment to his wife. He let the others know he found their adulterous tales hypocritical and disgusting.

Thus in two quick encounters Bob Punches struck at the heart of the fighter pilot's social code. He was against wine, women, and—though he expressed no opinion on it—presumably song. A lesser individual might have been exposed to some sort retribution by his peers, especially by men as proud of their image as fighter pilots. But Punches was an extremely capable aviator, totally self-contained, and the sincerity of his Christian beliefs did not cross the line into self-righteousness. He was accepted, if a bit gingerly, and respected by the other pilots.

Before they left Miramar Cal Swanson told Punches to fly as his wingman on an exercise. When they returned to the base, Swanson said, "I've never had anybody stay on my wing like you. You were like glue." From then on Punches flew with Cal. Bob was impressed by Swanson's knowledge and his technical ability, though less so by his human touch. One day over North Vietnam Bob did a barrel roll to evade a missile and saw that it was headed for Cal's tail pipe. "Superheat-One, break hard starboard!" Punches yelled. When they got back to the ready room, Swanson said in front of everybody, "That was a close one, wasn't it? I really appreciate your saving my ass." But there was usually little communication between them.

Every night Bob read three chapters of his Bible. He began each morning with fifteen minutes of quiet time, filled by prayer and meditation. He attended church services on Sunday morning and talked to the chaplain several times a week. When the *Oriskany* was in port, he was the only squadron member to be found painting an orphanage or playing father-for-a-day to an Asian child. He chipped in for squadron parties, but told the organizers he wanted his contribution to be used only for food. He began to take a closer look at his squadron mates.

"At the East Coast squadron where I was assigned before I got to One Sixty-Two," he said, "the guys put on coats and ties to go to a party. Here everyone dressed loose and the energy was explosive. Black Mac would be sending out his fireballs and everybody screaming. Guys drank champagne and then broke their glasses against the fireplace. I said, 'Gee whiz, what kind of outfit is this? These guys are all wild men.'

"When I saw Dick Wyman and learned we were about the same age, I said, 'My goodness, he's lived some other place besides this earth.' He looked like he'd been pushing time. One thing I respected about Dick, though, I never heard him speak about his wife in a derogatory way, or talk about anything he did on a cruise. He wasn't a bragger. He respected his wife. But he was very much a fighter pilot and accepted the fighter pilot image.

"As I watched Black Mac, I realized that a lot of his fear came out of his mouth. He started talking a lot more before a mission to get himself pumped up. The week we arrived on Yankee Station he had made one mission and was scheduled to make another, and I saw him in the ready room rubbing his hands together. I said, 'Hey, Mac, why are your hands all wet?' He said, 'Oh, it's nothing,' and kept rubbing them. He was scared, actually scared. It made me wonder if I should be afraid too. For me, fear was acquired. I learned to respect what could happen to you."

Bob Punches was generally tolerant of the foibles of his squadron mates, but at times he felt it a matter of principle that he speak out. One such time occurred the night he walked into the ready room and found it filled with officers and enlisted men looking at a pornographic movie. "I went to see the chaplain and told him. I said, 'I'm confused about what I'm supposed to do. They're showing a porno movie in the ready room and, besides that, we're not supposed to fraternize with enlisted people. All of them, officers and enlisted men, are in there screaming, laughing, and smoking.'

"The chaplain said, 'Well, those things happen on the ship. The men are under a lot of pressure, and they've been at sea for a long time. I know it's wrong, and I understand your feelings, but maybe we shouldn't do anything about it.'

"I said, 'Thanks a lot,' and left. I was disturbed by his casual reaction. I talked to Cal Swanson the next day and told him what was going on. He said, 'That won't happen anymore. Thanks for telling me.' I never saw it again."

It was out of respect for Bob Punches's sensibilities that the squadron developed a tacit policy of excluding him from its more unorthodox endeavors. The porn movies continued. And twenty years later, Bob Punches still did not know that drinking parties were frequently held in the ready room on days when bad weather prevented flying. The tradition had begun under Commander Bellinger, who, when the opportunity presented itself and business came to a halt, would fill the ten-gallon water can with Hawaiian punch, medicinal alcohol, and whatever other ingredients were available, and allow his pilots to work off their tensions by getting smashed. Captain Iarrobino knew what was going on but turned a blind eye so long as it didn't get out of hand. Captain Billy D. Holder, who replaced Iarrobino after the fire, tried to establish himself as a strict disciplinarian and court-martialed a young officer from the ship's company for bringing alcohol aboard. But the only effect of his edicts on 162 was to cause the ready room door to be locked and a guard posted outside when a party was going on.

"Every eight days or so we had a standdown lasting anywhere from twenty-four to thirty-six hours," Black Mac said. "The squadrons would have a ready-room party. Sometimes we mixed up a raunchy punch; other times people brought their own bottles. Guys all over the ship were buying skin flicks in Hong Kong. We would lock the ready room door and have a moviethon. Ready Room Four was known as a place where you could show your movie and the chief master at arms couldn't touch you."

"The conventional wisdom was that lots of pure oxygen would revive you quickly," Dick Wyman said. "So when you had a hangover, you went to the airplane, put the mask on, and sucked like crazy. It didn't work, though. You always felt bad. The catapult stroke would just tear your head off. You felt like you were going to black out. But fighter pilots were supposed to be able to handle it. That was the image. A fighter pilot was a hard-drinking, hell-raising, fast-moving guy."

Meanwhile, Bob Punches worked out his tensions by jumping rope between parked airplanes. He completely wore out a jump rope he bought at the Pearl Harbor naval exchange. He and Lee Fernandez jogged almost every day on the flight deck. Afterward, they showered and had a Coke and talked.

"Maybe because Lee was quiet I gravitated toward him," Bob Punches said. "Or maybe he came toward me. We were good friends. The question he always brought up was, 'Why are we in Vietnam?' "

13 · *Marilyn Elkins*

I WAS TEACHING at a junior high school in Nashville, located near the state penitentiary. Most of my kids lived there so they could visit their fathers. *Popular Mechanics* was my reading classic. Most of them were waiting till they were old enough to leave school to get a job. I had a whole bunch of applications and we did mock job interviews. The school authorities were bothered that I wasn't teaching Shakespeare and the required courses. I had trouble with the language arts supervisor who came by one day and saw my students reading motorcycle magazines. They wouldn't fire me, though. To get fired in a public school, you had to be blatantly immoral or so incompetent you couldn't read or write. I resigned and returned to graduate school, this time to get a master's in English at Vanderbilt.

I was writing Frank. The navy sent me advisories about what I should, or should not, talk about in the letters. They kept changing the rules. Whatever the rules were, I went by them. I mailed Frank a package once every two months. I sent playing cards, vitamins, toothpaste. I sent cigars and photos of me and other people in his family. Each month, I was becoming more disenchanted. I felt not enough was being done to help the POWs.

Allard Lowenstein, who was a congressman in Washington, had been a friend of Frank's when they were at Chapel Hill. I wrote Lowenstein to tell him about Frank, and he later came to Vanderbilt to speak. I went up and put out my hand, and he said, "You must be Marilyn." He was one of the few politicians I'd ever met who depended on reason in his public speaking rather than hearts and flowers. I was really impressed with him.

Al Lowenstein and I spent a long time talking about whether I should go public to bring attention to the POW issue. Would publicity hurt their cause, as the government was saying? Al felt that predictions of negative repercussions were exaggerated. How could you expect to remedy a situation when you were keeping it more and more in the dark? Still, I didn't want to come out and say exactly what I believed. Everybody told me, "How is your husband going to feel if somebody sends him a news clipping and there's his wife saying the war is wrong?"

Three pilots were released by Hanoi. I went to hear one of them speak. He told about the American choir he'd seen in Hanoi at Christmas and the blond pilot who sang tenor. I was sure it was Frank. I talked to the POW in private, trying to get more details, but he was noncommittal and didn't try to encourage me.

I joined the League of Families, a group composed of the relatives of prisoners of war and the missing in action, and began attending their meetings. Sybl Stockdale, Jim Stockdale's wife, was one of the league's organizers. She was saying we've got to stick together, do this, do that. It was like rah-rah-rah. I tried to set up a meeting between Sybl and Al Lowenstein. He was offering to do things through his contacts in terms of getting letters to POWs. She wouldn't talk to him, though, because he was against the war. I considered that totally irrational. Nor did I like the other extreme, on the left. One was just as bad as the other to me. Daniel Berrigan, the Jesuit priest, wrote an article for the *Saturday Review* titled "The New Man: The Complete Soldier" and said that the American military man has become "an obscene biological charade," wearing his uniform like "the skin of a predator." He made all these statements describing military men as though they were all alike, none of which fit me or my husband. I wrote a letter the magazine published in reply and said they "are not insensitive robots as he suggests. By his own insensitivity to those men, Mr. Berrigan qualifies as a candidate for another form of 'new man'—man so prejudiced against the military that he cannot see its members as capable of individual lives, consciences, or suffering."

Berrigan was claiming it didn't matter what happened to the pilots as prisoners of war. I said, when you say it doesn't matter what happens to them because their beliefs are different from yours, you are doing exactly what they are doing in regard to the North Vietnamese, when they say the Vietnamese don't matter. If you deny anybody's humanity, you've made a mistake. And once you've said yours is the only answer, you are in trouble. So I talked to Sybl Stockdale and people who felt like she did. And I talked to people like Cora Weiss who were against the war. I tried to put together a realistic picture of what was happening and what I could do.

I lived quietly. I remember that Ray, whom I'd dated off and on in college, wanted me to come over to see him. I always made sure somebody else was with us and I was never alone. It was ridiculous in a way. But I didn't want, you know, well, it was strange. I just wanted to do something to help Frank.

Al Lowenstein was a friend of John Seigenthaler, editor of the Nashville *Tennessean*. I wrote Seigenthaler and told him that my husband was a friend of Al's and was missing in action and that I was bothered that the missing seemed to be forgotten. He sent a reporter named Kathy Sawyer to interview me. Kathy was pretty, single, about a year older than I. Not long afterward, she went to work for the Washington *Post*. Kathy did a story timed to come out on the anniversary of Frank's being missing. Some of the other articles I'd seen in various papers about the POWs I thought were bad. Those with the pilot's medals spread out everywhere, the flag in the background, the God-is-on-our-side type of stories. I thought what Kathy Sawyer did was much better than that. I was hoping to make the world, and particularly the American people, aware of the fact that there were all these men who'd been missing for so long and nobody knew anything about them. It was pretty well received. I got a few negative comments. And some obscene phone calls. Not about the war, just heavy breathers and such.

I tried to stay busy. I went to school during the day and worked at a dress shop in the evenings. I didn't really need the money, but I wanted something to do. I also did some TV stuff. I was on talk shows where people phoned in. I got questions about money, about my personal life, things that had nothing to do with the POWs. Somebody always wanted to know what I did for sex. Of course, they didn't put it that way. "What do you do for a social life?" The TV interviewers used euphemisms like, "Do you think your husband has passed away?" And I'd say, "You mean, do I think he's dead?" And they would look at me thinking, "Oh my God, this woman is hostile." I wasn't. I was just trying to be clear.

14

CAL SWANSON was disturbed when he learned the name of an officer whom the Navy Department had assigned as a replacement to the squadron. In Cal's opinion, Julian Arthur (not his real name) was the worst possible choice. Swanson hurried to see Burt Shepherd, the air wing commander, and told him of his reservations. Commander Shepherd agreed with Swanson. Together they rushed a confidential message to the Bureau of Personnel saying they did not consider Julian Arthur a suitable replacement and asking for an alternate.

Swanson later denied that Julian Arthur's suggestions of effeminacy, which all the squadron members recognized to one extent or another, had influenced his decision to oppose Arthur's assignment. "There's no real mold for fighter pilots," Cal said. "But I could foresee that he and I were not going to work in sync. The thought that he was perhaps different crossed my mind, but that wasn't a trait that would have influenced me to oppose him. He was an excellent pilot, but I'd always found him aloof and difficult to conduct a dialogue with."

Julian Arthur was a bachelor who talked frequently and lovingly of his mother. He wrote her every night. While other pilots had their hair cut short, he wore his fuller, with a wavy, pampered look. He spoke precisely, almost with a lisp. Nothing was said aloud, but glances were exchanged, eyebrows lifted, when he walked into the ready room.

Cal Swanson realized it had been a mistake to oppose Arthur in such a precipitous manner. Had he given it a little thought, he could have figured out the attempt was doomed to fail and would only sour his relationship with Arthur who, given the gossip quotient of naval aviation, was bound to find out about it. Julian Arthur was cool and correct when he reported to Swanson. For a few days Cal thought perhaps Arthur did not know about his opposition. But then it became evident that Arthur was snubbing the squadron's senior officers, refusing to eat with them at their reserved table, preferring instead the company of the junior officers, most of whom were flattered by his presence at their table and who found his subtle wit entertaining.

Ron Coalson was one of the junior officers who liked and respected Julian Arthur. "He was almost prissy," Coalson said. "But he could fly that airplane better than anyone else and that took all the prissiness away. He walked to the beat of a different drummer, that's all. I think there was a cleavage in the squadron between him and Swanson, with the junior officers liking him the better."

Dick Wyman wasn't among them. "Beyond the question of whether he was effeminate, I didn't like him because he was such an asshole," Wyman said. "He would say and do things to hurt people. I remember the first time we were in the club at Cubi Point together. Black Mac was laughing and telling his jokes. 'Har! Har! Har!' Well, that was Black Mac. I knew him and loved him. Suddenly Julian Arthur picked up a scotch and water and poured it over Black Mac's head. We'd just come off the boat and nobody was drinking much. Black Mac said, 'Why'd you do that?' Arthur said, 'Because I don't think I like you.' He started associating with the junior officers and promoting the idea that if he ever became skipper things would be different. He had the character of a snake. Swanson obviously knew that and tried to keep him out of the squadron."

Looking back, John Hellman decided that Julian Arthur, despite the prickly aspects of his personality, probably had a more mature attitude about being a fighter pilot than the rest of the squadron. Arthur was in a technical sense the best pilot, and he saw no need to engage in the kind of competitive jostling that was prevalent among the others. Like Bob Punches, he was secure and without the compulsion to prove himself. But Hellman too realized that Arthur's differentness came at a cost to squadron unity.

"As it turned out, my intuition was on the mark," Cal Swanson said. "We didn't get along. He was in there every night writing a letter to his mother. Never once did he come to my room with work I'd requested. If I wanted something, I had to go to his room."

Except for a brusque exchange of words on the flight deck one day, Swanson and Arthur maintained a distant but correct relationship. The squadron knew, however, that something was not quite right between the two men.

15

THE PROBLEM continued to grow between Cal and Pat Crahan. Crahan did not let an opportunity pass to remind everyone that he was a short-timer and being held in the navy against his will. Swanson, for his part, was determined to make him toe the line. Cal was the leader on Crahan's first strike on North Vietnam. In the confusion, Pat forgot to turn on his master arming switch and failed to drop his bombs. He jettisoned them over the ocean on the way back to the ship. Swanson pointedly told him that because of his failure, the mission would not count toward an air medal.

"That's fine with me," Pat laughed. "I'm not over here to win a medal."

Swanson's exasperation with Crahan finally pushed him into the error of losing his temper in front of the squadron. It happened on a night when Crahan had trouble getting aboard. Pat disliked night landings and wasn't very good at them. On his first pass he forgot to lower his tail hook and boltered. When he tried again, he missed the four wires cleanly. Going around once more he did the same thing. He was now low on fuel and would have to tank. Aerial refueling at night was not easy. The tanker unreeled a sixty-foot rubber hose from underneath its belly. At the tip of the hose was a fabric-covered opening shaped like a cone, three feet in diameter. The F-8 pilot pushed a button in his cockpit to extend a probe about four feet long on his plane's left side, and then maneuvered to stick his probe into the cone-like basket. When the pilot plugged in, clamps on the basket locked the probe into place with a solid clunk. The tanker refueled him within a minute or so at the rate of two hundred gallons a minute. The difficulty came in trying to put the probe in the basket. If there was any turbulence, or if the tanker pilot did not fly smoothly, the rubber hose with its basket flopped around in the air, making it like trying to spear a fish.

After tanking Pat Crahan returned to make two more passes at the deck but failed to get aboard. He went to tank again. "How about an extra five hundred pounds?" he asked. The tanker pilot could have squirted the extra fuel and nobody would have known the difference, but he said, no, it was against regulations. The *Oriskany*'s control center heard the conversation and told the tanker to give Crahan the extra fuel. The tanker pilot made an issue of it.

Even more nervous after the argument with the tanker pilot, Crahan failed once again to catch a wire when he tried to land. The ship was preparing to launch another strike and could no longer wait for him. He was ordered to fly to Da Nang, the nearest land base, to refuel there and then try once more to get aboard. It was Crahan's first time in South Vietnam. When he landed at Da Nang the base was under a mortar attack. The U.S. Marines were not happy to see him. They ran to his plane, inserted a fuel hose, and quickly returned to the safety of their bunkers.

Crahan was anxious to get away from the exploding shells. The encounter somehow steadied his nerves for flying and he landed on his first try when he reached the *Oriskany*. The entire ship was aware of what had happened. It was part of the competition among the various squadrons that a pilot who had trouble getting aboard became the object of good-natured razzing. Though it could happen to anybody, it was treated as a teasing humiliation for the pilot's squadron. No commanding officer liked to see the can tied to the tail of his squadron, and Cal was irritated even more than usual that Crahan was the cause.

"Swanson said something about me being a lousy carrier pilot as I walked into the ready room," Crahan said. "Maybe I've blotted out exactly what he said. But in our relationship, he had to say it publicly. He wasn't going to get me alone to say it, because I probably wouldn't have gone. I was getting my ass shot at for no apparent reason and if he said I did something wrong my attitude was, so okay, sue me. The fact that he chewed me out in front of everybody didn't bother me as much as it did some of the other pilots."

"The leadership principle is that you criticize in private and praise in public," Ron Coalson said. "We resented the way Swanson handled the situation with Pat Crahan."

"I thought," Bob Punches said, "that some day the same thing was going to happen to Cal—and then what was he going to say? I had no idea it would happen so soon, in fact, the very next night."

It was the night of August 6, 1967, and Cal Swanson had been under stress since the *Oriskany* arrived in the Tonkin Gulf. The ship had lost fourteen airplanes during that time. Four pilots had been killed; two more were listed as prisoners of war. Eight days before, the *Oriskany* had been sailing twenty miles behind the USS *Forrestal,* when Swanson spotted a huge cloud of black smoke billowing in the sky. It was an accidental fire aboard the *Forrestal,* and it brought back the horrors of that day on the *Oriskany* the previous year. The *Oriskany's* first line period was scheduled to end at six o'clock on the morning of August 7. For the past month Cal had seldom slept more than three or four hours a night. He was set to fly to Bangkok, along with several other commanding officers, for five days of rest and relaxation. His anticipation of the holiday perhaps caused him, he said later, to lose his edge and led to the trouble he had in getting aboard the ship, his worst time ever.

"I walked into the ready room," Ron Coalson recalled, "and Rich Minnich, the duty officer that night, was telephoning Pat Crahan. Rich said, 'Pat, get down here. The skipper's going round and round.' I took off my flight gear and hung around. I knew they were setting Swanson up, and I wanted to see the fireworks. Rich called the TV room and said, 'This is the duty officer of One Sixty-Two. I want a video of the F-Eight that's boltering replayed continuously till I tell you to stop.' The TV was on, the volume full blast. The LSO was saying to Swanson, 'Skipper, you're doing the same thing every time. You are getting too low in the middle. You're going over the top in close. You've got to correct that sag at the start, or you're going to bolter all night.' "

When Swanson went to tank he discovered that the light on his probe was out and there were no bottom lights on the tanker. It was difficult to see what he was doing and he missed the basket the first time. Down to four hundred pounds of fuel, or about five minutes of flying time, he drove in and missed again. He began to talk to himself. "You are going to plug this thing in, or you are going to bail out. Which is it to be?" He continued speaking to himself, quietly, deliberately, as he maneuvered his plane. It worked. Just before he was about to run out of gas, he felt the solid connection of the probe entering the basket.

16 · Dick Wyman

IT'S ABSOLUTELY NECESSARY to think you are the best pilot in the world. If a guy doesn't have supreme confidence in himself, he is probably going to get killed. I saw guys lose confidence and that was the end. Therefore the unwritten rule was that you didn't chew somebody out in public. The pilots who were good were the ones who had the intensity, the edge, and anything pointed to destroy that was madness.

So we began to gather in the ready room when we heard Swanson was having problems getting aboard. Every time he tried to land and missed the wires we loved it. There were ten ready rooms in the air wing, all of them connected by an intercom system. When anybody did something wrong, all the ready rooms would push your button and rattle bells and blow horns to razz you. It was done in fun. Everybody was razzing us, as Swanson boltered time and again. They didn't know that we ourselves were cheering. Finally, after six or seven tries, he landed.

"Here's what we are going to do," we said. "Everybody sit in their chairs. Stare straight ahead. Absolute silence."

Swanson walked into the ready room. The TV set was blaring out a replay of his bolters. He said, "Jesus, I—" He looked at us. No one said a word. No one smiled. "I, uh, I—" He realized he'd been had. His face turned beet red. He walked out, slamming the door. We cheered. He never again chewed out anyone in public.

17

ON AUGUST 9, 1967, the day after Cal Swanson arrived in Bangkok, the Stennis subcommittee opened hearings in Washington into the conduct of the air war. Cal and three other commanding officers from the *Oriskany*—Burt Shepherd, Bryan Compton, and Don Willson—were taking an unofficial holiday to buy some Thai silk, hit a few clubs, and maybe get a massage. They knew as little about the split between Defense Secretary Robert McNamara and military leaders, a split that the Senate subcommittee would shortly reveal, as did the general public in the United States.

While most aviators thought restrictions should be removed from the bombing, few had the time or the inclination to dwell for very long on questions of higher strategy. Much of what Squadron 162 knew about the air war debate came from a day-old *Stars and Stripes* newspaper or from the press digest prepared by the ship's public affairs office. In fact, they probably knew less about the overall progress of the war than an average reader of a large American newspaper. Except for dropping bombs, pilots on Yankee Station were strangely isolated from the war they were fighting.

Cal Swanson's only brush with the Washington bureaucracy had occurred a few weeks earlier, when the Pentagon sent a team of investigators to find out why the *Oriskany* was losing so many airplanes. The answer to that, said Cal, was because the North Vietnamese had expanded their air defense system. Hanoi alone was now protected by fifteen missile sites and five hundred and sixty antiaircraft guns. As a result of the investigation, the squadron modified its tactics, adopting a steeper dive angle on bombing runs—sixty degrees instead of forty or forty-five—which narrowed the pilots' exposure to antiaircraft fire, while doing little for accuracy. But those were technical details. The Washington investigators said nothing about targeting, and Squadron 162, whose morale as a unit was high despite certain personality conflicts, remained under the impression that the bombing of bridges, no matter how small, was helping to win the war and everything was generally going okay.

That was not the impression of Admiral Grant Sharp, who was in charge of running the air war. On a bureaucratic level, where wars were fought with words instead of bombs, Sharp was almost in open revolt against the policies of Robert McNamara. The admiral's suspicion that McNamara's heart was not in the fight had hardened into conviction. The previous October, after McNamara returned from a trip to South Vietnam, he had recommended the creation of an electronic barrier between the North and the South as a means of preventing infiltration, a thinly disguised admission that he believed the bombing could never accomplish the job. His defense of the bombing, when questioned by the press, took on a vaporous air that could not be faulted on grounds of loyalty to Johnson administration policies, but that made it sound as though he was less than convinced himself. The bombing, he said, was designed to reduce the flow of men and supplies to the South, to raise the cost to North Vietnam, to boost the morale of the South Vietnamese, to supplement the land campaign in the South— designed, in fact, to do practically everything but serve as a "credible threat" to force the North Vietnamese into concessions, which was the rationale he had given President Johnson two years before. Indeed, there was a suggestion that Robert McNamara, like many other Americans, was bewildered by what was happening in Southeast Asia. In June 1967, he ordered a secret study made to determine how America had become involved in Vietnam, a study leaked to the press four years later, known as the Pentagon Papers.

The Stennis hearings were to be the showdown between Robert McNamara and the military establishment and would effectively end his seven-year term as secretary of defense. The stage for the encounter was set a month earlier at a conference in Saigon, when Admiral Sharp let McNamara know he was ready to fight it out with him. After learning in mid-June 1967 that McNamara planned to go to Saigon in July, Sharp started lining up the generals and admirals who commanded the war in a unified front of opposition to McNamara, who, he cautioned them, was leaning toward imposing even more restrictions on the air war.

"I told them at the Saigon conference I would give my views on the importance of our air campaign in North Vietnam, particularly in the northeast quadrant, and that the firsthand knowledge of commanders on the scene would be most helpful," Sharp said. "The importance of our conviction that we needed to continue the air campaign in the northeast could not be overemphasized. . . . Statistics, I stressed, would be essential."

To ensure no slip-ups, Admiral Sharp made a special trip to Saigon on June 28. He particularly wanted to make sure General William Westmoreland knew what he planned to tell McNamara and would back him up. He also wanted to coach Vice Admiral John J. Hyland,

Seventh Fleet commander, and General William W. Momyer, Air Force commander in Vietnam, on what to say. Sharp then ducked back to Honolulu, and returned to Saigon a week later.

When the conference opened, Sharp reviewed the air campaign and quickly went to the attacks on North Vietnam's petroleum storage areas in June 1966. He knew that McNamara and his civilian aides viewed the attacks as a failure. The secretary had not recommended another escalation of the air war from that moment on. "The enemy," Sharp told the conference, "had been publicly forewarned of our intent and had therefore been able to disperse his POL supplies widely enough that our strikes were not as effective as they could have been with the element of surprise in our favor."

Moving to the present, Sharp said they had struck the Hanoi thermal power plant near the center of Hanoi a few weeks before, on May 19 and 20. "However, the immediate outcry from the North Vietnamese government had been so effective in Washington that on 23 May we were again told not to operate within ten miles of Hanoi. Strikes against such significant targets had thus been interrupted and real pressure on the enemy had once more been removed. . . ."

"In closing," Sharp said, "I would like to emphasize one point that General Westmoreland has already made." He told the conference that the North Vietnamese held the initiative in the ground war in the South, that "political restraints rule out any assumption of a strategic offensive on our part. We must await his moves at places and times of his own choosing." That was not true for the air war in the North, he said. "Here we hold the initiative. We are conducting a strategic offensive forcing the enemy into a defensive posture. He is forced to react at places and times of our choosing. If we eliminate the only offensive element of our strategy, I do not see how we can expect to win."

Sharp presented his recommendations to McNamara on several charts. He wanted to close the Haiphong harbor by bombing or mining; to destroy the six basic target systems with integrated attacks; and to change some of the operating rules of the air campaign, removing, for example, the ten-mile prohibited zone from around Hanoi. Essentially, Sharp recommended the same things the Joint Chiefs had recommended shortly after the air war began in March 1965. Two years later, the military mind had not changed.

Robert McNamara realized he had been sandbagged. When the

briefings were over, he said, "General Westmoreland, that was a fine presentation," and left.

"The next day," Sharp said, "I remarked to General Wheeler that I was damned annoyed at McNamara for turning to Westy at the end of the presentation where I was the senior officer present, to say he had made a fine presentation, without saying anything to me. Wheeler replied, 'The reason he didn't say anything to you was that he was furious at you because of your presentation.' "

Sharp was satisfied that he had headed off any attempt by McNamara to limit further the air war. Nevertheless, it became clear two weeks later, on July 20, 1967, when President Johnson authorized the next series of bombing targets, that the administration was still adhering to what Sharp called "a strategy of equivocation." The sixteen new targets were outside the prohibited areas around the centers of Hanoi and Haiphong. "And so, once again," said Sharp, "the increasingly divisive issue of the air war in the North had been brought to a boil only to be pushed onto the back burner and allowed to simmer, to no one's satisfaction."

It was time, Sharp thought, for political action to force the issue. On August 9, 1967, he was scheduled as the leadoff witness at the Washington hearings, closed to the public but open, as was usual in such cases, by the participants' leaks and self-serving statements to the media. The subcommittee consisted of senators John Stennis, Stuart Symington, Henry Jackson, Howard W. Cannon, Robert C. Byrd, Margaret Chase Smith, Strom Thurmond, and Jack Miller. "They were," said the Pentagon Papers, "known for their hardline views and military sympathies. They were defenders of 'air power' and had often aligned themselves with the 'professional military experts' against what they considered 'unskilled civilian amateurs.' They viewed the restraints on the bombing as irrational, the shackling of a major instrument which could help win victory."

Lyndon Johnson, faced with having his bombing policies raked over by the Senate's chief hawks, decided to try to cut the legs from under Sharp and his parade of generals and admirals by amending the list of July 20 to include sixteen additional targets, six of them within the usually inviolate ten-mile prohibited zone encircling Hanoi. He authorized for the first time an attack on the Long Bien (formerly Paul Doumer) Bridge, which, to Harrison Salisbury's surprise, had not been hit immediately when the air war began.

With Johnson's ploy, announced the morning Sharp was scheduled to testify, the bombing had come full circle. It had begun not as an attempt to break the back of North Vietnam in a traditional military sense and cause Hanoi's surrender. Rather it had been launched, in effect, as a means of influencing North Vietnamese opinion, of forcing Hanoi into concessions, McNamara's "credible threat." The strategy of trying to stop infiltration, of interdicting men and supplies headed to the South, had developed simultaneously with the failure of its original purpose. Now the bombing was being used to manipulate not North Vietnamese but American opinion, to help Robert McNamara and Lyndon Johnson out of domestic political trouble, to show that, despite what the military establishment and Senate hawks claimed, the administration was pursuing the air war in a diligent and effective manner.

"It was obvious to me that the secretary of defense hoped to spike my guns by granting these new targets right before I was to testify," Sharp said. "That hope proved futile, however, since it came out almost with the first question that we had just received the authority not only to strike certain lucrative targets heretofore denied us, but also to re-strike some targets that had been removed from the authorized list. The significance of this turn of events was not lost on the senators, and they made quite a point of it."

Robert McNamara, whose testimony came August 25, 1967, was the last ranking witness to appear before the subcommittee. He took issue with Sharp and his subordinates and defended the administration's policy of limited bombing, which he claimed to be successful in terms of its carefully tailored aims. He discounted the value of closing the Haiphong harbor, an action military witnesses had stressed they believed would help bring the war in the South to an early close.

Primed by Sharp, a senator tried to maneuver McNamara into openly confessing his lack of conviction about the effectiveness of the air war by asking if he favored stopping the bombing around Hanoi and Haiphong and limiting it to the area above South Vietnam's border. This proposal had in fact been given serious consideration by McNamara and his civilian aides as a way of de-escalating the air war, while continuing to support U.S. troops fighting in the South. McNamara, however, avoided giving the senator a straight answer. Instead, he made his case obliquely, sounding like a businessman reading the bottom line of somebody else's company report. Some $320 million worth of North Vietnamese facilities had been destroyed, he said, with $911 million worth of U.S. airplanes lost, while about 2 percent of North Vietnamese infiltration to the South had been stopped.

"Those who criticize our present bombing policy do so, in my opinion, because they believe that air attack against the North can be utilized to achieve quite different objectives," McNamara told the senators. "These critics appear to argue that our airpower can win the war in the South either by breaking the will of the North or by cutting off the war-supporting supplies needed in the South. In essence, this approach would seek to use the air attack against the North not as a supplement to, but as a substitute for the arduous ground war that we and our allies are waging in the South."

It was the new McNamara arguing against the old.

The Stennis subcommittee report, hurriedly released on August 31, 1967, urged President Johnson to widen the air war and abandon his policy of "carefully controlled" bombing, revealing publicly for the first time the split between McNamara and the military establishment. With an election year coming up, Lyndon Johnson was thus forced into the position of having to choose between the men who wore stars and his defense secretary. In an unscheduled press conference called the next day, Johnson denied there were any differences among his advisers, but at the same time began to back away from McNamara.

Nine days later, on September 10, 1967, Johnson authorized the bombing of Cam Pha, North Vietnam's third largest port. Cam Pha was a clear signal to McNamara. U.S. planes had wiped out a flak site three months before near the Cam Pha harbor, touching off a row with the Soviet Union, which charged that during the attack the Americans had hit one of its merchant ships, the *Turkestan,* and wounded two crewmen, one of whom later died. The Pentagon apologized to Moscow rather abjectly and said efforts would be made "to insure that such incidents do not occur." McNamara specifically advised against attacks on Cam Pha during his testimony before the Stennis subcommittee. Johnson's decision to overrule him could only be taken as a personal rebuke.

On November 1, 1967, Robert McNamara played out his part in the game by formally—though secretly—recommending to Johnson that the bombing be stopped and that no more U.S. troops be sent to South Vietnam. Johnson released the news two weeks later that he was nominating his defense secretary to be the new president of the World Bank.

Robert McNamara had once jumped on the hood of a car at Harvard and told student protesters that he was tougher than they were. On the day he took his leave of the Pentagon, he choked up and cried. Over the years he refused to comment about the war and the decisions he had made, though nearly twenty years later, after the conflict had receded in the public mind, he emerged as a commentator on air warfare—this time concerning nuclear weapons, which he seemed to want to reduce to the lowest possible numbers while still maintaining a credible retaliatory threat—or mutual deterrence, as it was now called.

18

ON AUGUST 25, 1967, the day Robert McNamara testified at the Stennis hearings, Cal Swanson was sitting in his plane to the rear of the flight deck, waiting to move forward to be launched, when another aircraft skidded into him, pushing his plane to within eighteen inches of tumbling over the ship's side. The Washington hearings were having a direct effect on the life of Squadron 162. In trying to undercut Sharp's testimony, President Johnson removed the restriction on hitting the Hanoi thermal power plant a second time, which Sharp had complained about at the Saigon conference. Bryan Compton led the *Oriskany's* attack, and Cal was saved twice by pilots who warned him in the nick of time about the flak and missiles closing on his tail pipe.

They dropped the new Walleye bomb on the power plant, scoring five hits out of five. The Walleye was a TV-guided glide bomb with an eight hundred and thirty-pound warhead. The first of the so-called smart bombs, soon to be followed by more advanced laser-directed weapons, the Walleye represented a great improvement in the accuracy of air-dropped ordnance, since it could be locked on the target prior to release, with the TV eye then guiding it toward the aiming point. Of course, there were ways to outsmart even a smart bomb, and the North Vietnamese quickly learned them. The next time American planes came to bomb the power plant, the Vietnamese put a smoke generator on the back of a truck and drove it around the building, changing the surrounding contrast and the target's visibility, confusing the TV eye.

Nevertheless, the Walleye was the most accurate bomb in the U.S. arsenal and its new availability had played a large role in President Johnson's decision to authorize the bombing of the thermal power plant (another target Harrison Salisbury was surprised to find not hit) for the first time on May 19, 1967. This was a further indication of the Johnson administration's concern for preventing civilian casualties, though an appreciation of the fact was lost to opponents of the war, who considered one bomb dropped, one civilian killed, too many. Whether that concern stemmed from political or moral reasons, government officials, especially those who had turned or were turning against the air war, actually tended to overestimate the number of civilian casualties in their secret communications with one another.

In August 1967, the seasoned journalist David Schoenbrun visited North Vietnam. The thrust of his reporting was that the North Vietnamese showed no signs of weakening under the bombardment, indeed seemed more determined than ever to resist, but he also noted the accuracy of the bombing. Around that time, the North Vietnamese announced that five hundred civilians had been killed and eleven hundred wounded during the first six months of 1967. Since the North Vietnamese had no apparent reason to minimize their civilian casualties and may have even found it advantageous to exaggerate, this meant, by their own figures, that an average of about three civilians were being killed and six wounded each day in the whole of the country. The effectiveness of their bomb shelter program and evacuation of all but key personnel from the cities undoubtedly helped account for the relatively low figure. But considering, too, that three times the total amount of bombs dropped on Europe and Japan combined during World War Two were ultimately to be dropped on Indochina— much of that in restrikes on the same few targets—this did not seem to suggest that the administration was waging a campaign of indiscriminate bombing but was, as the Stennis subcommittee unhappily observed, following a policy of careful control.

By the time McNamara testified at the Stennis hearings, Johnson's civilian advisers had, for all practical purposes, narrowed the debate over the bombing policy into a consideration of three options, which they described in terms of a funnel strategy having three possible courses of action. They would come up with nothing new during the remaining life of the Johnson administration. As they formulated it, the president could either (1) close the funnel at the top; (2) attack what was inside; or (3) block the funnel at the bottom.

Closing the funnel at the top meant mining Haiphong and the two other major ports, entry points for 85 percent of North Vietnam's supplies. It also meant heavily attacking the rail lines near the Chinese border, which was what the military establishment had wanted to do since the air war began. Johnson's civilian advisers had consistently opposed this option out of fear that it might escalate the conflict into a confrontation with the Soviet Union or China.

Attacking what was inside the funnel, that is, hitting the supplies after they were offloaded from Russian ships or Chinese boxcars and bombing industrial targets in the Hanoi-Haiphong area, was basically the strategy that Johnson had pursued. The cost had been high—six hundred and forty-seven planes lost to date, with hundreds of pilots killed or languishing in prisons. Yet the policy had not succeeded and still carried a seeming risk of confrontation with the Soviets, who issued vague warnings frequently enough against the bombing to keep Johnson's civilian advisers worried and unsure.

Blocking the funnel at the bottom—concentrating air attacks in the southernmost part of North Vietnam, the area above South Vietnam's border—was an option developed by a key assistant to McNamara, John McNaughton, who had grown increasingly disenchanted with the air war and who had influenced the thinking of his boss. It was a way of scaling down the political costs of the air war in terms of the antiwar movement and international opinion, of reducing the risk of confrontation with the Soviets, and of cutting the loss rate of pilots and planes (since the funnel's bottom was less heavily defended than its top), while aiding U.S. combat troops by continuing to try to interdict men and supplies flowing into the South. The option carried an implicit admission of American defeat in trying to break Hanoi's will through the bombing of its industrial base. But it nonetheless gave disenchanted advisers a fallback position that could be argued out with facts and figures in front of Johnson without making it appear that they were giving up.

Some of Johnson's civilian advisers supported various refinements to the options, but essentially the president was left with three choices that ranged, by administration standards, from hawkish to dovish. As always he sought the middle ground, which meant continuing to attack what was inside the funnel. (Later, when he announced his decision not to run for re-election, Johnson did not stop the bombing but simply chose the third—and most dovish—option his advisers had been offering him for eight months, that of blocking the bottom of the funnel.)

In a speech at San Antonio, on September 29, 1967, Johnson launched a new peace initiative, saying, "The United States is willing to stop all aerial and naval bombardment of North Vietnam when this will lead promptly to productive discussions. We, of course, assume that while discussions proceed, North Vietnam would not take advantage of this bombing cessation or limitation." After it became clear that the initiative, like others before it, had failed, he began to authorize more targets to be hit in the Hanoi-Haiphong area, including many of the fifty-seven targets that had been turned into a point of contention at the Stennis hearings, when the military charged they had been permitted to hit only three hundred and two of the three hundred and fifty-nine targets the Joint Chiefs had recommended.

It was in this way that the pilots of Squadron 162 found themselves flying more and more against targets in the Hanoi-Haiphong area during the latter part of 1967. While Johnson was not ready to mine the Haiphong harbor, he was amenable to letting the military try to isolate the port city by attacking its bridges. The effort started on August 30, 1967, when twenty-four planes from the *Oriskany* dropped the Haiphong Highway Bridge, southeast of the city. Within weeks the city's four major bridges had been bombed. The North Vietnamese quickly repaired them, as they did the Paul Doumer Bridge in Hanoi. The following month the navy hit the bridges again.

By October 1967, two hundred thousand tons of supplies were stacked up on the Haiphong docks. As the North Vietnamese correctly assumed, the Americans would not be permitted to bomb the docks, so their supplies were safe. The *Oriskany*'s pilots could only take heart from the intelligence reports that indicated the frequent day and night alerts were slowing work on the docks. Unloading times for ships had increased from thirteen to forty-two days.

For a while navy pilots thought they had won the battle of Haiphong. After the fifth day of successive attacks, they were astonished to arrive over the city without being fired on. Had the Vietnamese given up? Certainly they had run out of missiles and were low on ammunition. Two planes circled Haiphong for fifteen minutes without finding an active flak site. The phenomenon lasted two days, until bad weather forced the cancellation of all strikes for the next three days. After the skies cleared and the Americans returned to Haiphong, they were greeted by the familiar SAMs and shellbursts.

All civilians except those vital to the defense of Hanoi and Haiphong were ordered to leave. Workshops and offices near military targets were moved out of the two city areas. Despite the heavy bombing, the war in the South continued at its usual pace. The North Vietnamese began to divert more of their supplies from Haiphong to the port of Sihanoukville, in Cambodia, where they could be transported easily into adjoining South Vietnam.

Robert McNamara's stand at the Stennis hearings had been disclosed in the subcommittee report and press leaks, but it wasn't until October 10, 1967, that he himself publicly revealed his disaffection with the air war, saying, "All of the evidence so far is that we have not been able to destroy a sufficient quantity to limit the activity in the South below the present level, and I do not know we can in the future."

Rear Admiral Malcolm Cagle said, "To the pilots who were risking their lives daily under the restrictive targeting system and flight rules imposed by Secretary McNamara, who were not allowed to destroy the supplies where they could be seen, it was a disheartening judgment."

That was undoubtedly the feeling of the military brass and those who were paying close attention to the push-and-pull going on in Washington. But actually morale remained high on the *Oriskany*, which had lost twenty-four planes—nearly 40 percent of her combat aircraft—since July, and McNamara's disaffection was hardly noticed by the carrier's pilots. The constant danger of flying Alpha strikes, as the pilots called major attacks in the Hanoi-Haiphong area, brought Squadron 162 closer together. Cal Swanson even found a few good words to say about Pat Crahan, who ended his tour in September and was returning to the States to be discharged from the navy.

"I must confess," Cal told Nell, "I've gained a great deal of respect for him on this cruise. He has ended up with four air medals and has, to date, flown more hops than anyone else. He's a gutsy little bastard, and his terminal fitness report will reflect it. I'm going to miss him."

Pat remained less enthusiastic about Cal and the navy, but he too had mellowed under the comaraderie of shared danger. Not enough, though, to resist trying to get in one final dig. His crew painted the logo of United Airlines on white paper and taped it over the tail of his plane. As he moved up to be launched for his trip homeward, Crahan waved to Swanson and other high-ranking officers in the air tower, who looked down in surprise at the UA logo on the F-8 fighter.

The jest lost some of its sweetness soon after he was airborne, when the paper on his tail suddenly ripped away with the sound of a violent explosion. The navy had run a study to determine the last phrase or word most frequently spoken by pilots who were shot down. It turned out to be "Aw, shit!" and an island not far from Haiphong, where numerous Americans were downed, was given that name. Now Pat heard himself utter those fateful words. For an excruciating minute, he thought that he was doomed to crash at sea and that the navy would have the last laugh after all.

19

ONE EVENING Lee Fernandez asked Cal Swanson if he could talk to him in private.

"Sure," Cal said. "Why don't you meet me in my room."

Lee arrived a few minutes later. He looked a little tense.

"Come on in, Lee," Cal said. "What can I do for you?"

"Skipper," Lee began quietly, "I don't think I can go over the beach any more. I feel badly every time we drop bombs. I may be killing somebody, and that's not my nature now. Even if I had a MiG in my sights, I don't think I could pull the trigger."

"Well, that's surprising to hear," Cal said. "It's certainly inconsistent with our mission."

"From what I've seen, Skipper, what I've read, I don't think this war is right. Basically, we're intervening in a civil war between the Vietnamese."

"I disagree, Lee. The North is trying to take over South Vietnam, like the communists are trying to do all over the world. Here's a small country asking our help in maintaining their freedom. Do you think when the going gets tough we should just pull out and leave?"

"South Vietnam's governments—and there have really been a lot of them in the past couple of years—haven't been known for their popularity with the people. They've not had much of a reputation for being fair, honest, or democratic. Maybe that's why communism seems to thrive in the South."

"No, I don't think so, Lee. I remember when I was assigned to Saigon, we had a daily briefing about the communist atrocities being committed in the rural areas against the peasants. In fact, I visited some of the villages and hamlets right after I got there. I was just appalled. I think if you'd seen some of those atrocities you might have a different attitude."

"In my opinion," Lee said, "the most important question to be asked by individuals and by a country about a foreign war is: 'Is this war, is this cause worthy, not only of the spending of so great an amount of money and resources, but more important, is this cause worthy of the act of sending a large number of our young men to a foreign country where many will die?' And I don't believe by defending the government of South Vietnam from a communist takeover we are in any way defending the United States."

"Are you sure you're not trying to rationalize because—"

"Because I'm scared? Yes, Skipper, that's part of it. I'm afraid. I don't want to die for a cause I believe unworthy. And Herb Hunter's death had a great effect on my decision. The death of someone like him, one of the finest men I've ever known, cannot be justified by this war. It was just a tragic waste. I knew after he was killed I didn't want to go over the beach again, but I put off telling you."

"Maybe there are other reasons you aren't going into. How about your carrier performance? You've had a high bolter rate recently. Something is wrong. Is it your eyesight?"

"Well, I—"

"You sure this is final?"

"I've thought about it a long time, Skipper. It's not a quick decision."

"Okay, then the easiest way out would be for you to turn in your wings."

"I'd like to continue flying if I can. In some noncombat capacity. I like flying. I just can't out of conscience do this kind of flying any longer."

"Look, there's no way I'm going to transfer you to a utility squadron. You are assigned here for a tour of duty. If you can't fly in this squadron, you can't fly anywhere. Consider yourself grounded as of now."

"I don't quite see the logic of that, Skipper. There are lots of pilots in utility squadrons who would love to be transferred to a fighter squadron, to get a chance at combat. Why can't we make an exchange?"

"Because you're here. This is your duty. If you can't fulfill that duty, we'll have to take other measures. As I say, the easiest way would be for you to turn in your wings. If you don't want to do that, we'll convene an aviator's disposition board to decide what must be done. That could get messy, I warn you. It could lead to a court-martial. Why don't you think about it overnight? Hey, look, I've got to run. I'm already late for a CO's meeting. Think about it, Lee."

LATER THAT EVENING Swanson told Burt Shepherd and the *Oriskany's* captain about his conversation with Lee Fernandez. Captain Billy D. Holder, John Iarrobino's replacement, was a capable officer but without the degree of equanimity of his predecessor. Cal was taken aback when the captain angrily said he was in favor of lifting Fernandez's wings and court-martialing him for cowardice. Cal perceived the danger of moving too quickly and strongly against Lee. The year before the executive officer of the other F-8 squadron—the one who was to become an admiral—was allowed to turn in his wings without prejudice on a combat tour. Could they afford after that to try to court-martial Lee for doing the same thing?

Something else, too. Newspapers had been running stories for months about the army doctor—what was his name? Levy?—who was court-martialed for refusing to teach Special Forces soldiers his medical specialty, dermatology. The media had puffed him into a celebrated antiwar protester. Lee Fernandez had more impressive credentials as a protester than the skin doctor. Lee was a young, articulate Naval Academy graduate, a fighter pilot with two commendations for bravery, whose record was excellent in every way. If his case became a public issue, it would surely give the navy a black eye, not to mention how it would make Fernandez's squadron commander look to his own superiors, who would hardly be delighted by this turn of events. After he returned to his room, Cal gave his conversation with Lee further thought.

Lee Fernandez was also thinking about their conversation. When he went to talk to Swanson, the only reason he had in mind for wanting to quit flying was his feeling that the war was wrong. But Cal had added a worm of doubt by bringing up his problem with carrier landings. He *was* having trouble. He had flunked the depth perception test during his annual physical a few months earlier. He was otherwise in such good physical condition that the navy granted him a waiver and had recently given him a pair of glasses to correct the deficiency. Was his eyesight causing his problems getting aboard ship? Did that influence his attitude about flying combat? Lee decided, to be honest, that he should list his eye problem as a secondary reason for his decision to quit. He decided, too, to give up flying entirely if necessary.

Cal Swanson was visibly relieved when Fernandez told him he intended to turn in his wings voluntarily and would not fight it. It was Cal's understanding that Lee would cite his eye problem as the reason for his wish to quit flying. That would wrap the matter up very neatly. Deteriorating vision was a routine cause for a pilot's request for termination of his flight status. A pilot even showed he had the best interests of the navy at heart when he withdrew for such a reason. Besides that, Swanson truly believed it would be a serious error for Lee to proclaim himself against the war; he believed such a move would mark him as unpatriotic and follow him for the rest of his life.

Cal was surprised, then, to receive the next day the following letter.

From: LTJG *Leabert R. Fernandez, Jr., USN, 678079 / 1310*
To: *Chief of Naval Personnel*
Via: *(1) Commanding Officer, Fighter Squadron ONE SIX TWO*
          (2) Commander Carrier Air Wing SIXTEEN
          (3) Commanding Officer, USS ORISKANY (CVA-34)

Subj: *Termination of Flight Status; request for*

1. It is requested that my flight duty status be terminated. The following are my reasons, and they are listed in order of importance.

a. It is contrary to my personal convictions and to the dictates of my conscience that I continue to engage in the direct destruction of human life in connection with this conflict.

b. It is not my desire to continue to expose myself to the long-term and calculated risk of death which is inherent in the duties of my present billet.

c. My motivation toward flying has suffered somewhat during the past eight months due to the above-mentioned feelings and convictions, and also due to some difficulties in connection with carrier operations.

2. The difficulties associated with carrier operations are reflected in an increase in my bolter rate during this year's carrier qualification exercise and cruise deployment as compared with that of last year's. I feel that this problem is at least in part the result of the deficiencies in the sight of my left eye. I was granted a waiver for these deficiencies in February 1967.

3. This request in no way reflects on my motivation to continue duty in the field of aviation for the remainder of my obligated service. Indeed, since this is what I know and like best in the navy, it is my desire to remain in this field as a 1350 designator.

Leabert R. Fernandez, Jr.

Cal Swanson talked to Fernandez again after he received the letter. This time he was on the verge of losing his temper. "About your desire to keep flying," Swanson said, "forget it. You are going to lose your wings. No question. So face the fact. You are allowed, of course, to say whatever you wish in your termination letter. But I think the whole slant of it is a big mistake. You don't want to put a black mark on your career by saying you are opposed to the war."

"I don't plan to make the navy a career," Lee said.

"It doesn't make any difference," Cal said. "These things tend to follow a guy around the rest of his life. In fact, you may be laying yourself open for a court-martial."

Lee Fernandez refused to back down. Swanson left and returned with the air wing commander. Burt Shepherd, a tall man with an imposing physical presence, spoke to Fernandez in a conciliatory manner. He asked Lee to take out the part of his letter referring to his opposition to the war. It was for his own good, Shepherd said. Leave it in and it would hurt him in the future. Fernandez listened to the arguments of the two officers, then said he was satisfied with his letter as it stood. Shepherd insisted that he take it back and rethink his position overnight. Fernandez agreed. The next morning he resubmitted the letter, unchanged.

Cal Swanson and Burt Shepherd agreed privately that it was best to handle the problem with Fernandez as quietly as possible. To make an issue of it, as the *Oriskany*'s captain wanted to do, might let a snake out of the box that could bite them all. In his letter of endorsement, attached as regulations required to Fernandez's request for termination of flight status, Swanson ignored the question of Lee's opposition to the war and emphasized his declining carrier performance, his eye problem, and suggested that his recent marriage to Dorothy had negatively affected his flying ability.

"It should be noted that throughout both deployments, during which he has flown a total of eighty-six missions, LTJG Fernandez has never shirked his duty to fly against the enemy, nor has he ever inexplicably rejected an airplane in which he was scheduled," Swanson said in his endorsement. But the eye problem and Lee's marriage, he concluded, "have had a more profound influence on LTJG Fernandez's airmanship than he will admit. Thus, it is considered in the best interests of the service to terminate LTJG Fernandez's flight status at this time, without further action."

Burt Shepherd forwarded the letters to Washington without comment.

"In my endorsement I tried to blow enough smoke about the effect of his marriage and his eye problem to distract higher authority," Cal told Nell. "But it may not work. I think he's laying himself wide open for a court-martial. God, I tried to tell him it wasn't worth it, that he didn't need to say those things to terminate his flight status. His response was that he felt that way and would be dishonest to himself if he didn't put down all the real reasons. I asked him if he thought he alone could change the national policy, or if he wanted to be a martyr. No, he just had to say what he felt. He'll be lucky to get off unscathed."

As Swanson hoped, his endorsement did blow enough smoke to distract "higher authority." Either that or someone in the navy's personnel bureau recognized the makings of a public relations flap if Fernandez was not allowed to go quietly. In any case, Lee was agreeably surprised to be reassigned to shore duty, first in the Philippines, then, after the *Oriskany* returned to the States, at a naval air station in California, where he completed his obligated service without controversy and resigned. After leaving the navy he became an accountant. He wrote letters to congressmen and others expressing his views against the war and stood firm as an individual in protest, but it was not in his nature to use his position as an Annapolis graduate and a former fighter pilot to seek publicity.

Cal Swanson called a squadron meeting—which, as agreed to beforehand, Lee did not attend—and announced that Fernandez was terminating his flight status. Swanson did not disclose Lee's reasons and no one asked. It was the prerogative of a naval aviator to turn in his wings, and his fellow pilots traditionally accepted the decision without questioning him. Most of the other pilots knew only that Lee had quit flying.

"I suppose that eventually the word got around, but I'm not even sure about that," Lee said. "Black Mac and I had a talk about it when I was with the Beach Detachment in Cubi Point. He was very open-minded and told me that he respected me for going through what I did, even though he didn't agree with my views. The only other person whom I told about my reasons was Bob Punches. He made no comment (he was a good and loyal officer), but since he was quite religious I think he may have understood what I did."

After the squadron completed its combat tour, Cal Swanson sat down to write Lee Fernandez's last fitness report. His worries, it had turned out, were exaggerated. The Fernandez affair had passed almost unnoticed by anyone outside the squadron. Cal's anger with Lee had cooled. He wanted to be as fair as he could in the fitness report. He began by noting that Lee was "an excellent naval officer with professional competence and mature judgment. He is intelligent, industrious and a resourceful officer who is confident in his ability to complete any assigned administrative task. This officer approaches these duties with aggressiveness and enthusiasm; the results are invariably meritorious, punctual, and complete in every detail." Lee, he said, had flown many combat missions over North Vietnam, "doing a creditable job in the face of enemy opposition." He had never shirked or hedged his duty.

Then he came to Lee's refusal to fly further combat missions.

"Since flying ability was not a prime factor, it is assumed his reasons, as stated in the request for termination of flight status, are a true reflection of his feelings. Under the circumstances, I consider that his loyalty to the navy and the nation is barely satisfactory. In conjunction with this evaluation, it is difficult to judge LT Fernandez's moral courage. Strong in his convictions, he had the courage to state in writing,

197

and in private discussions, that he was unable to continue his role as an active participant in the Vietnamese war. He could have discontinued flying for reasons other than those stated. Yet, his rationalization, no matter how strongly debated, is not in harmony with traditions of courage and dedication handed down through generations of American military men. As a result, I feel obligated to rate his moral courage as barely acceptable."

20 · Dick Wyman

I KNEW Lee Fernandez was having problems with himself. He had physical courage; he went over the beach; he wasn't a slouch or a dud. I talked to him a couple of times about the war, though he didn't confide in me. I was polite and friendly to him but that was about it. His wife was a good friend of my wife. I don't want to say Lee was different. But of course he was. I think being the type of person he was, he was really disturbed by the war. Still, in 1967, a lot of guys were beginning to turn in their wings, and you never heard them say, "I'm turning in my wings because I'm scared to death and don't want to die." It was always, "I'm turning in my wings because I don't agree with the war." Vietnam was the only war in history with no cowards. We're all afraid and cowards exist in the natural scheme of things. But Vietnam didn't have any. Not even any old-fashioned draft dodgers like other wars always had. Just draft resisters. Every single one of them believed the war was wrong.

Well, each guy builds his own excuse. The executive officer who quit and later became an admiral didn't say he was quitting because he was scared. He had a pretty intricate rationale to offer. So when somebody quit, he was suspected by the other pilots of being frightened to death and just not able to admit it. There were so many things going on, you were so busy, you didn't have time to sit down and analyze the guy. Even with Lee, I probably felt a little secret contempt, felt he couldn't hack it. At the same time, I kind of admired him for standing up and saying "I don't agree."

By 1967 the war had become a sensitive issue. It was like talking about religion—you avoided it as much as possible. I passed around some of my books, and we discussed them. But I think there was almost a feeling that if we got very deep into it, if we really examined the war, we would find it was bullshit. So we never really looked at it that closely. I think we were afraid we would cut the legs off some guy, destroy the last prop he had going, and he might say, that's it, I'm turning in my wings. And you said, "If that happens, who's going to be flying with me next?"

After reading books on Vietnam, I had questions about the war, especially about the way it was being fought, but you could drive yourself crazy with questions. Blind military discipline. That was a necessary part of it, to do what you were told to do. I was a professional naval officer, hired by the taxpayers of the United States, and I intended to do the job I was assigned in the best possible manner. So you put the questions out of your mind and said, "If they want me to bomb that bridge today, tomorrow, and the next day, by God, I'll do it." The way to survive was to keep your enthusiasm up.

IV

October 26, 1967

The Captive

1

ON THE MORNING of October 26, 1967, Dick Wyman, Ron Coalson, J. P. O'Neill, and Chuck Rice walked to the *Oriskany's* wardroom and ate an early lunch. The meal was nothing special—pork chops and rice—(not like Wednesday night's steak and baked Alaska), but as was generally the case on the *Oriskany* the food was well prepared and tastefully served. The four men joked that since they were scheduled to fly at noon, they would get back in time to eat another lunch before the pork chops ran out. A mission over the beach and back usually took no more than an hour or an hour and a half. Today they were assigned a strike on Hanoi, which the pilots called "Downtown." The name was taken from Petula Clark's 1965 hit, with its lyrics, *Everything's waiting for you . . . Downtown.* A big memorial service to remember the victims of the fire one year ago had been planned but canceled because of the heavy flight operations.

In spite of the danger they faced, the four officers were in high spirits and at ease. Though Chuck Rice had arrived on Yankee Station only two months before, he immediately had found his place in the squadron, and no officer since Herb Hunter had been better received. Like Hunter, Chuck Rice was easygoing, with a cheerful, friendly personality, and the ability to poke fun at himself. The son of a TWA pilot, of medium build, handsome, with hazel eyes and brown hair, Rice was born in Augusta, Georgia, and reared on Long Island, New York. Two squadron members—Ron Coalson and Bob Walters—knew Chuck Rice when they were in training together, and they gave him such good reviews that this squadron waited skeptically to see if he measured up. Coalson and Walters met Chuck on the flight deck when he arrived and grabbed his gear. "We might have got you in a little trouble," they told him on the way to the ready room. "You're going to take some static but don't worry about it."

Rice entered the ready room, and Dick Wyman walked up and

silently looked him over from head to foot. Then Wyman shook his head and said, "He doesn't look like he walks on water to me."

Everybody laughed. Chuck was left standing in the middle of the floor, looking confused and embarrassed. In the following days he showed he could take the hazing that went with being a "new guy." Cal Swanson considered himself lucky to have such a fine junior officer assigned to his squadron.

The evening Cal told Chuck he would be flying as Dick Wyman's wingman, Wyman invited him to his room for a talk. Dick took out two beers from his small refrigerator and handed one to Rice. He said, "Okay, Chuck, you're going to be my wingman. I want you to understand, we're going to be the best team in the squadron. From now on I don't ever want to hear you say anything derogatory about me in public. If you don't like something I do, we come back to this room and you can chew me up one side and down the other. But don't ever walk into the ready room and laugh and joke that Dick screwed up this or that. Dick Wyman never screws up in public but in private. And it works both ways. I'll never do it to you either."

Before taking off on their first mission, Chuck said, "Dick, I don't know what I'm doing."

"I know," Wyman said. "Forget about everybody else. Stay on my wing. Don't lose me."

"Fine. But what about dropping the bombs?"

"Stick with me as I roll in. When you see my bombs come off, punch your button."

"After we made our run and headed back to sea," Rice said, "Dick put a cigarette in his mouth and lit up. 'Check me over.' I moved out and looked for oil leaks or damage, then came back and gave him a thumbs up. He did the same for me. There was a shared sense of relief. We'd made it. Ten miles from the ship, he stubbed out his cigarette, put his mask on, and we were back to business.

"One day we returned from a mission and everybody said, 'Jesus, you got five missiles shot at you today, Chuck.' They were patting me on the back. Ron Coalson said, 'Five of 'em, what did you think of that?' I gave him a dumb look and said, 'Ron, all I saw was Dick Wyman's helmet.' I had no idea what had happened to us. Outside the ready room, Dick Wyman put his arm around me and said, 'Don't sweat it, you did good today.'

"That's the way my first five missions went. It took me that long before I even realized where Haiphong was. We went to the target and I'd start hearing chatter over the radio, SAMs here, SAMs there. I never saw anything. I just stayed on Wyman's wing. And he never lost me. To do a barrel roll and not throw your wingman out, you've got to be awful gentle, awful patient.

"Then Wyman began to urge me to look around. He didn't say, 'Okay, get out there.' But he kept pressing. I never lost him but I got sucked behind several times. He said 'Dammit, you're no good to me back there and I can't help you either. Lag behind me and you're going to get your shit blown away.' There was no doubt: Dick Wyman wanted to take care of me and make me into a super F-Eight driver. He was meticulous. He taught me a lot of things. Flying isn't just driving an airplane. A guy can be a helluva pilot, but if he doesn't use his head he's not going to be where he ought to be, and Dick had some of the best headwork in the squadron.

"He was very adamant about not taking unnecessary chances. 'Don't try to be a hero,' he told me. 'But, by God, get your bombs on the target like we're supposed to do. You've got to know your limitations and pay attention to them, because there are a lot of dead guys who didn't.' He taught me how to beat the game while staying within the rules. He said, 'On a bad night when you've got a pitching deck with green water coming over the bow and the ship's captain decides everybody is going flying and you're feeling scared as hell, don't try to argue with him that the weather is too bad. Say 'Yes, sir.' And then go out and get in your airplane. Preflight it real well and you're going to find something wrong with it.' You could find something wrong with an F-Eight in a second and have a legitimate reason for not flying."

There was only one thing that Wyman seemed to be inflexible about, a little excessive. He was anxious to shoot down a MiG. He warned Chuck not to get in his way if they saw enemy planes. "I'm in the lead and I get the first shot," Wyman said. "If I mess up, you can have at him. But don't go trying to take the lead away from me."

Wyman's attitude was shared by the more aggressive members of the squadron. A fighter pilot who had not shot down an enemy plane was like a professional football player who had spent his career practicing but never played in a real game. MiG activity had increased in the last few months, and as their second and final tour on Yankee Station approached its end, some of the pilots became obsessed with downing an enemy plane.

Just the day before, on October 25, 1967, that obsession had almost led to tragedy. After two years of waiting, the pilots had been authorized to hit the Phuc Yen MiG base for the first time. As Cal Swanson and Bob Punches headed to the target, Cal saw an airplane. "He was coming from the direction of Phuc Yen and he looked exactly like a MiG," Swanson said. What happened next was never clear. Swanson said that he realized at the last moment the plane was not a MiG but an American A-4 and that he pulled away. Others claimed that Cal fired a Sidewinder missile at the American.

"The pilot Swanson shot at came back and complained to his squadron commander," Black Mac said. "He was usually a mild-mannered guy, but that day he was livid, mad as hell. Swanson missed because his missile wasn't in range. Just dumb luck he didn't shoot the guy down."

John Hellman was not ready to condemn. "When a strike group is coming from the target area it's chaos and difficult to define an airplane. I say this in defense of Cal's shooting the missile. I asked myself if I had been in the same situation what I would have done. Would I have fired at the plane? I think not, but you have to be careful in making a judgment about what happened. Of course both Swanson and Wyman were hellbent on getting a MiG at whatever cost."

In any event, the prospect of running into MiGs partly accounted for the high spirits of the four officers on October 26, 1967. The target was the Hanoi power plant. They were told to stick around and fly MiG cover after it was hit. Chuck Rice thought he might even have a chance to down an enemy plane himself.

2 · Chuck Rice

WE WERE GOING to tank and get a whole bag of fuel before we crossed the beach, so if we ran into any MiGs we would have plenty of gas. Up there tanking, Dick Wyman's generator failed. He said, "I've got to go back to the ship." I said, "Roger." That left me and Ron Coalson and J. P. O'Neill, who was the flight leader. Dick Wyman had once told me, "Don't you ever, ever go across the beach as a solo." I'm sitting there flying by myself and I'm saying, "What are you going to do, Rice? How long do you go before telling J. P. you're not crossing the beach as a single?" I was ready to call the ship and say, "Where do you want me to dump my bombs? I'm coming back."

Well, J. P. O'Neill, one of the nicest, dearest guys in the world, knows the situation, and about halfway to the beach he says, "I'll be the lead, Ron you be the section leader, and Chuck you fly on Ron's wing." He was telling us he would fly as the single, while Ron and I flew together. That seemed to solve the problem.

The strike group leader called, "Superheats accelerate!" He wanted us to go ahead and take out the flak sites around the target. The strike group had twenty-five planes, and Ron and I and J. P. were on the outside. I was looking around, expecting to see a MiG at any moment. I glanced at Ron and J. P. and saw they were already making a turn. In an F-8 carrying bombs, once you get slow it takes a heck of a lot of afterburner to catch up. Why'd I get slow? Because I made a mistake. When I started to turn I ended up sliding outside Ron's radius of turn. Once you slide outside you are sucked behind.

Ron knows where I am—I'm behind him, I can help him, but he can't really help me. I was busy looking at Ron and J. P. Ron said, "Chuck, you got one at ten o'clock." When a missile was fired, you sat and looked at it through the canopy. If it started to move, it wasn't you. Well, this one didn't move. And right behind it came another. So I'm looking at two of them. They had started firing two at us in trail, because we were outmaneuvering them one at a time. You might get away from the first one, but the second had time to make the correction.

I said, "Holy Shit!" I lit the burner and started down. My thought was, "Should I roll over the top or go underneath?" You could do it either way. You could do a barrel roll or go underneath it and force it to come down on top of you. "If I go underneath I know I'm going to have tons of airspeed," I said, "I can really be smoking. But if I go under I'll be looking at six thousand feet when I'm trying to pull up. And at five hundred knots air speed, with bombs, I'm not going to pull out, I'll crash into the ground." I would have to ditch my bombs to go under. So I said, "Okay, I'll take it over the top." That was my second mistake. I decided later that I would have had a better chance if I had ditched and gone underneath.

I waited and waited, watching the missile come at me, until I couldn't take the anxiety any longer. Then I started the maneuver of rolling around the missile. I did what I was supposed to do, flew an arc around it. The missile looked like a telephone pole going by, that's how close it was. I heard a boom! I thought, "I made it." I started to roll out. I didn't even get my wings level, when the airplane just blew to hell.

I daresay what I'm about to tell happened in no more than three to six seconds, but it seemed much longer. It hit, a tremendous jolt, and scared the shit out of me. Fire came into the cockpit. I got burned on my eyelids and neck and hands. I had vowed I would not jump out of an airplane as long as I had altitude and could make it go. A pilot's greatest fear was to be captured. We'd heard about Ev Alvarez and Stratton, and everyone said, "God, I can't go through that." The second biggest fear was of being maimed. Getting killed was the least worry, because if it happened you wouldn't know anything about it. I said, "I've got to get this airplane out of here."

Well, it won't fly. "You're going to die." I said that out loud. I tried to reach for the ejection handle. The airplane was shaking so violently that I couldn't get a hold of it. I put my left hand on the radar scope, threw my shoulders back against the seat so it wouldn't rock, and with my left hand braced, my head down, I grabbed the ejection handle, thinking, you're going to break your back but you are getting out of here.

I pulled. The next sensation I felt was a violent tumbling. I didn't feel the seat separate, the chute come out—just tumbling. Suddenly I'm in a totally different war than I was familiar with. The war I'd fought till this point involved the sound of my own jet engine and the radio voices of men either high-pitched in panic or calm and cool, with puffs of exploding flak outside my canopy, and the white contrails of jets streaming around.

Soon as I punched out, it's windy and I'm hearing all this noise. Flak and missiles exploding, the roar of bombs going off, the sound of the whole strike group, instead of just the sound of my engine. And the smell! Even that high up I could already smell North Vietnam. Night soil used as fertilizer. The country smelled like shit.

There I was. If you've ever seen a five-year-old kid who just lost his mother in a shopping mall, that's what you've got in that parachute floating down. Mrs. Rice's little boy, Chuckie, age twenty-four. It was the worst despair I'd ever felt in my life. And I started to cry. I said, "This can't be happening to me." Floating down. Tears pouring out of my eyes.

I'm still in the air and the realization hits—I've got to get out of North Vietnam. I said, "I'll run to the coast, maybe get picked up by a helicopter there." I knew there was no chance for a rescue where I was coming down—four miles from Hanoi. I'm not a jogger, never was a jogger, and I've got lots of gear on me, yet I felt I could run it to the coast.

I tried to move my chute. I pulled on the risers hard as I could, but it's not going anywhere, I'm not going to drift to the coast. I heard a big *boom!* and looked behind me. My airplane exploding. As I got closer to the ground, I could see a lot of people in a big circle in a rice paddy. They were looking up at me. As I moved to the left or right in the air, the circle moved to the left or right on the ground. It's obvious: I'm about to land in the middle of those peasants. I'll hit the ground, draw my pistol, break out of the circle, and head for the hills.

I landed and scrambled to my hands and knees. I got my pistol out. I could hear the high-pitched sing-song of their voices and smell the stench of my new world. As soon as I started to move, all hell broke loose. People in the circle started shooting at me in the middle. They're crazy! They're shooting at each other while trying to hit me.

I stuck my gun above the rice paddy, in surrender, and kept my head down. They closed in on me. I had some pretty good flight gear and boots, and that's a poverty-stricken country—you'd think they would save that stuff. But they cut my gear off with a machete. I tried to help them, to explain, but they kept batting me down, and finally I just lay there, in shock, numb. When they finished I was left with my old aviation-cadet T-shirt, blue on one side and yellow on the other, and a tank suit I always wore. I never wore underwear, because I figured if I jumped out I would be in the water. I had on white wool socks.

I believe I'm alive today because the people in charge were the militia. If you got shot down in the backwater rural areas, you hoped the farmers caught you, because they were curious about Americans and you weren't bombing them all that much. But in the areas near the cities, which were getting hit pretty hard, you hoped the militia caught you, because the villagers there wanted to slit your throat.

They tied my hands behind my back with rope and marched me to

209

a nearby village and stuck me in a shed. My eyes felt burned; my neck hurt; my hands looked bad. They turned out to be superficial flash burns. A Vietnamese came in, took the ropes off, and tied my hands in front. Then he offered me a cigarette. I remembered my survival training and thought, "It's starting already. Take the cigarette and you've sinned for life, gone against the Code of Conduct." I didn't smoke cigarettes anyway, just cigars. I said, "No, I don't want it."

Two militia men retied my hands behind my back, blindfolded me, and marched me out of the shed. I could see out of the blindfold a couple of feet in front of me. They took me to a ditch and told me to get down on my knees. I felt a gun barrel pressed against the back of my head. "I've seen this in World War Two movies," I thought. "You're about to die. At least you'll never hear the gun go off."

Villagers around me were screaming and yelling, chanting slogans against America. My mind was blank. I'd given up. I was numb, just waiting for the bullet. They made me stand up and marched me to another place and forced me to kneel down. "Oh, they didn't want to shoot me over there. They're going to do it here." Again, I could hear people screaming and chanting. After a while, they made me get up and marched me to another location. The same thing happened. I said, wait a minute, this is a hate rally. They're using me to psych up the local populace for the war against the United States.

They took the blindfold off and pushed me toward a jeep. Farmers lined the path. They were in a frenzy against me. The militia prodded them back with their rifles. A little old man, looked like Ho Chi Minh with a white beard, ran out of the crowd and leaped off the ground— that's how short he was—and hit me with all his force in the throat. Maybe because I was in a state of shock it didn't feel like much. But when he hit me a rifle butt came from the other direction and I could hear his skull crack. He went flying back into the crowd. "You bastards," I said. "You get them all riled up and then beat the shit out of them."

They put me in the jeep and pulled the flap down over me. They drove me through other villages and sometimes opened the flap, letting people point and jab at me, but I wasn't taken out of the jeep. At three that afternoon I arrived at the Hoa Lo prison—the Americans called it the Hanoi Hilton. I was put in a cell and then taken for interrogation.

The interrogator we later called "Oney" for ONI—Office of Naval Intelligence—because he was not army but navy and wore blue instead of green. He seemed to interrogate most of the navy guys. He asked my name, rank, service number, and date of birth. As the Code of Conduct allowed, I answered in full. Then he started asking other questions.

After about fifteen minutes of hearing me say, "I can't answer that," he smiled and said, "As a matter of fact you will answer all of my questions."

Oney was a son of a bitch but a polite son of a bitch. He was slender, mousy dark hair, small bones. He spoke fairly good English and had a better grasp of American sarcasm than most Vietnamese, so you couldn't slip something past him. "You are not the first American we've had here," he said. "I can assure you, you will answer my questions. I'll let you think about it for thirty minutes. Then we'll try again."

When he returned, he asked, "What ship are you from? What squadron?"

I repeated my name, rank, and service number.

He smiled pleasantly and said, "Well, I guess it's time to begin."

Two men entered the room. Their basic method of torture was to tie you up where you were eyeball to eyeball with your ass. They had a twenty foot nylon strap about a half inch wide. They tied the strap around my elbows and pulled it until they were tight together. They brought the strap down and tied my wrists. Then they put shackles around my ankles and ran a bar through the shackles to spread my legs out. They brought the strap over my back, put it under the bar, and pulled the bar up until I was forced into a ball, straining every muscle in my body.

A piece of iron covered by a cloth was stuffed into my mouth. It made me nauseous. A couple of POWs threw up with the gag in their mouths and the Vietnamese couldn't get them untied in time and they died. One American vomited and knew he had to get it all out through his nose if he didn't want to die—and he did. I was in agony for fifteen minutes and then everything started to go numb. They rolled me around on the floor, kicked me in the kidneys, and stomped on me. After about twenty minutes, they loosened the strap so my circulation would come back, and then tightened it again.

Night came. I lost track of time. The torture continued. I think it was probably some time during the second day when I broke. They got me to the point that I didn't care any more. I just wanted it to stop. "You've blown it, Rice," I said. "You're useless, a nobody, a traitor, not worth a damn." I was heartbroken. I had tears in my eyes. I knew I had capitulated.

Oney said, "Get up and sit on the stool."

I tried but couldn't get up. I crawled on my hands and knees to the stool. The guards lifted me up. The first question was about military information. The escalation of the bombing around Hanoi had started, I believe, on October 24, and the interrogator was anxious to know what the Americans were going to bomb next. I never went to strike ops to see in advance what we'd be hitting. I only knew the same morning what the target would be.

The Vietnamese showed me a map. I said, "That bridge. We're going to bomb that bridge."

"You're lying," he said. "That bridge has been down for three weeks."

Our biggest fear was that the North Vietnamese would ask us for information they were convinced we knew but which in fact we didn't have. In that case, you were liable to die under torture, because it was almost impossible to persuade them you really didn't know.

I was desperate. With tears in my eyes, I yelled, "Dammit, I don't know!"

If it had been, say, Cal Swanson, a senior officer, they wouldn't have eased up. But I still had my ensign ID card (I was really a lieutenant junior grade), which indicated I'd just turned twenty-four and had been on Yankee Station only a short while. I think he realized that I was ready to tell anything I knew.

But then Oney asked for the name of the *Oriskany*'s skipper.

"The captain of the *Oriskany*? It's Captain . . . Captain—shit, I can't remember."

I really couldn't. Oney found that hard to believe.

3

CHUCK RICE'S SHOOTDOWN uncovered a dispute that had been simmering for some time in the squadron, which took the form of a question. In the event one plane malfunctioned before or after takeoff, should the other three continue the mission and thus break the integrity of the two-plane support system? Cal Swanson and J. P. O'Neill said yes. Other squadrons, they argued, used the three-plane element. In a meeting called to discuss the matter, Dick Wyman was asked what he thought. "It's not smart," Wyman said. "I don't think you can look out for more than one guy and do it right."

Black Mac and other officers agreed with him. When Chuck Rice was downed, they took it as proof that the three-plane element was foolhardy. Swanson came in for criticism and a rumor started that J. P. O'Neill was a jinx. "I never heard the word *jinx* actually used in connection with J.P.," Ron Coalson said, "but something was going on. I think he knew what people were thinking. So I went to his room after Chuck got shot down and said, 'Look, Paddles, I just want to say that I would go to hell and back with you.' " Ron had seen a parachute, and though John McCain, an admiral's son and later an Arizona congressman, went down about the same time as Rice, Coalson was sure it was his roommate whom he had watched floating down.

Rich Minnich had earlier moved in with them, and that night, as they were lying in their bunks, Minnich said, "Chuck, I know you'll forgive me for saying it. But better you than me."

Ron Coalson grinned and looked at Minnich with understanding. Rich was not being heartless. Like Ron, he was sad about Chuck getting it. But you could not let the loss of a friend start eating at you. And several months later, when Rich Minnich got shot down, Ron Coalson lay in his bunk and repeated the incantation: "Rich, I know you'll forgive me. But better you than me."

Ron Coalson noted that Herb Hunter, Chuck Rice, and Rich Minnich were all shot down while flying a plane with the number 206. He began trying to avoid being assigned that number. He also noted that an unusual number of pilots were shot down after losing money in a card game the night before. Such was the case with Rice and Minnich. One night, when a pilot from Frank Elkins's old squadron lost nearly three hundred dollars in a game, Ron watched to see what would happen. "After losing the money he told us, 'I'll write you guys a check tomorrow.' He stood to leave and then said, 'No, I'd better pay you tonight.' The next day he got hit and jumped out and the North Vietnamese shot his face off in the chute. That was the last time we played poker."

Dick Wyman normally put a downed pilot quickly out of mind. But with Chuck Rice it was different. Wyman felt badly about Rice. Chuck was his wingman and he hadn't been there to protect him. At least, thought Wyman, Chuck had been trying to carry out his assignment. It made Wyman all the more angry with E. D. Goodpaster (not his real name). To Wyman, Goodpaster was the worst kind of officer, a navy bureaucrat who hedged on his missions, who was afraid to take the necessary chances. After Chuck Rice was downed, Wyman's relations with Goodpaster grew increasingly strained, which threatened Wyman's career, since he was assigned administrative duties as Goodpaster's assistant in the maintenance department.

Goodpaster was a senior lieutenant commander, pleasant-looking, six-two and balding, which made him seem older than his age. He had worked in the Bureau of Personnel, BuPers, at U.S. Navy headquarters in Washington. "He was in a position where he could pull strings to get the squadron he wanted and for some reason he picked One Sixty-Two," Cal Swanson said. When Goodpaster checked in, Swanson told him, "You'll be the maintenance officer. If things work out you can have one of the other jobs for the second cruise." Goodpaster replied that he would not be making a second cruise, which surprised Cal, because everybody usually made two.

"He told me, 'I've got arrangements to be recalled to Washington when this tour is over.' " Swanson said. "He had his career all lined up, to the exact time he was going to make admiral. It appeared he'd joined the squadron simply as a ticket-punching thing. He needed a combat tour on his record."

Swanson was not satisfied with Goodpaster's performance as maintenance officer. Cal was always concerned—excessively, some pilots thought—with the availability of airplanes. He wanted his squadron out there with every launch of strike aircraft. Swanson believed that Goodpaster did not make sure the enlisted crew repaired malfunctions quickly enough. There were also instances of airplanes being fixed but not placed in the lineup soon enough to make the next launch. Swanson decided to take the matter into his own hands. He called a meeting of the maintenance department and chewed everybody out. Goodpaster was angry. "You undercut me," he told Cal after the meeting.

"I wouldn't have," Swanson replied, "if you had done the job yourself."

Swanson learned of another problem when he overheard a conversation between two junior officers. Goodpaster and one of the junior officers were on standby alert that night, with Goodpaster scheduled to be launched first, if the necessity arose.

"Well, you better plan on being launched," one j.o. told the other. "Goodpaster will never make it." The implication was that Goodpaster was finding phantom malfunctions to keep from flying missions.

When Goodpaster did make it over the beach, his actions usually angered Dick Wyman. "Two times he left his wingman and wouldn't answer when I called," Wyman said. "I found his wingman and brought him out, which meant my wingman and I had to stay in there longer and get shot at. You'd find him out over the water and say, 'Where did you go?' And he'd say, 'Didn't you see that SAM site? I went to knock it out.' A cock-and-bull story."

Goodpaster was affable and generally well liked. Some pilots were reluctant to believe he intentionally shirked his duty. Besides, they pointed out, Goodpaster was older and had a growing family. Maybe he felt he had more to lose. Wyman wasn't buying that. Look at Dick Leach, he said, a guy with four kids. Leach was losing weight, practically worrying himself to death. Before a hard mission he would go to the chapel and pray and then sit in his ready room chair all night, unable to sleep. "I don't mind telling you," Leach would say. "I don't like it. But I'll go and do the best I can." Wyman admired Leach for his honesty. He always felt good flying with him over the beach. Goodpaster was another matter.

The squadron was assigned one day to hit some flak sites at the edge of Haiphong. When they were ordered to accelerate ahead of the strike group, Wyman decided to keep his eye on Goodpaster. He followed him and watched as Goodpaster dumped his bombs in a rice paddy and then turned toward the ocean.

"His wingman stayed with us," Wyman said. "After we came off the target, Goodpaster started calling. He wanted to rejoin our flight. 'He's not rejoining us,' I said. I wouldn't tell him where we were. He found us just before we got to the ship.

" 'I'm taking the lead,' he said.

" 'No,' I said. 'I've got the lead.'

" 'I said I'm taking the lead.'

"I didn't want to argue it out over the air. He was a lieutenant commander and I was a lieutenant. He took the lead and landed first. I came in right behind him.

"I was so mad I couldn't stand it. I was out of my airplane in a heartbeat. He was unstrapping and just starting to throw a leg over. 'You rotten son of a bitch,' I said. 'Get out of there and I'm going to kick your ass all over this deck.'

"He stepped back into his airplane and said, 'What's the matter with you?'

" 'You dumped your bombs and left us up there.' I said. 'I watched you.'

" 'I did not,' he said."

When they reached the ready room Wyman was trembling, almost unable to control himself. He was convinced that what he considered Goodpaster's cowardice was endangering lives. If Goodpaster couldn't take it, Wyman believed, he should quit and get out before he got somebody killed. Other pilots in the ready room were muttering that they would refuse to fly as Goodpaster's wingman on any of the big strikes. Goodpaster acted as though nothing had happened. "Did you see that Sam site I got?" he said to the others.

"Bullshit!" Wyman snapped. "There wasn't any Sam site." He went to the map and jabbed at it so hard that his finger nearly went through the board. "Your bombs hit right in this rice paddy."

"Okay, Dick, pipe down and relax," Cal Swanson said.

"He's wrong, Skipper," Goodpaster said. "There was a missile site."

Swanson changed the subject and the argument ended without resolution. Cal had begun keeping records, however, to see if there was a pattern to Goodpaster's combat performance. He started the night he overheard the two junior officers talking. Sure enough, that night Goodpaster had downed his plane, claiming a malfunction.

Swanson approached Bob Punches in private to ask if he had noticed anything. Punches liked Goodpaster personally. He considered him a good naval officer in an administrative sense. Goodpaster, he thought, had a talent for writing—he also had a beautiful handwriting—and unlike Swanson, Punches thought that Goodpaster ran a good maintenance department. But, yes, Punches had to admit he had seen instances where Goodpaster obviously was not being truthful. The night, for example, they'd had a little Saint Elmo's fire in their cockpits, harmless lightninglike electrical charges caused by ionization. Goodpaster had sworn he was being shot at and almost killed.

Another time Goodpaster was leading a flak suppression mission. "He got to the target and said, 'I've got a pressurization problem,' " Punches remembered. " 'My cockpit is filled with smoke and I can't see anything.' I was flying close to him and I could see there wasn't any smoke. So Bobby Walters, his wingman, said, 'I got the target,' and we rolled in. When we returned to the ready room, he had this bull story to tell."

"I personally liked him," Ron Coalson said. "I think he did an outstanding job as maintenance officer. But he had this tremendous conflict within himself about not being able to face that he was afraid. He was scared to the point, I thought, that he drummed up mythical stuff."

Swanson wrote his wife about the problem. "Nell, I've always been a fatalist, but this cruise I've become even more resigned to the fact that you can't worry about it. It's only on one or two of the great big ones that I get a dry mouth anymore. With this attitude, you really get a lot more accomplished. We have a couple of lieutenant commanders in the squadron who are really worried about home. As a result, their effectiveness is impaired."

He told her about Dick Leach. "He wants to go home! I can't blame him, but Dick is to the point where he is counting who has how many big strikes and whether he is being given too many. He's not but the fact that he is concerned about it indicates his reluctance to be exposed. Still, he never misses a hop and does a damned good job."

Goodpaster was his big worry. "I think he's just plain scared and is fighting himself every time he thinks there is an element of danger involved. Even over low threat areas he stays so high he can't see anything. He may overcome it, but I doubt it. The other day, out of a flight of twenty some airplanes, he was the only one to claim that a missile was shot at them. I'm quite certain he imagined it. We've seen before that when one little thing goes wrong with an airplane, he immediately compounds it into many major malfunctions.

"Lastly, he exaggerates sometimes to the point of embarrassment of other members of the flight. Now, I'm the only one who knows all these things, and they haven't been discussed openly, but I also know that the junior officers don't like to fly with him. It's most unfortunate, and today, when he was scheduled to lead a flight into Hanoi, I told him beforehand, 'Be aggressive!' Well, he didn't make the flight and we don't know yet what's wrong with the airplane."

Dick Leach was hit by antiaircraft fire a week later. He made it back to the ship, though his airplane was badly damaged. Leach flew another mission the next week and was struck by a missile. He again survived and continued to fly his assigned strikes. Leach's show of courage, despite his nervousness and worry, which were evident to everyone, only heightened the contrast between him and Goodpaster.

Swanson decided the time had come to do something. He examined the records of Goodpaster's last twelve scheduled night flights to see how many times he had failed to be launched by claiming a malfunction. Then he checked the maintenance department's records to determine what action had been taken to correct the malfunctions. In nearly three-fourths of the cases, he discovered, the maintenance department had been unable to find anything wrong with Goodpaster's plane. Careful not to let anyone else know what he was doing, Swanson called Goodpaster to his room one night and invited him to sit down for a chat.

"This is very awkward for me and I hate to do it," Cal began, "but I think we better get something out in the open. I've been hearing innuendos in the ready room, and I've gone back and analyzed the situation myself, and there's evidence that you are downing the airplanes unnecessarily in order not to fly."

Goodpaster reddened. "That's not true. Every airplane I've downed has been a downed airplane."

Swanson was waiting for his denial. He pulled out the records he had collated and showed them to Goodpaster. He considered the documentation of the malfunctions his trump card, a way of approaching the idea that Goodpaster was shirking his duty without actually bringing up the word *cowardice*. Swanson wanted to avoid a confrontation over whether or not Goodpaster was a coward. Such a charge would, at best, turn into a sticky unpleasantness. At worst, it could blow up in Cal's face. Swanson would have to convene an aviator's disposition board to consider lifting Goodpaster's wings if he were to make a charge of cowardice stick. A board would require extensive documentation and hard proof, not just the angry opinion of a couple of junior officers that a lieutenant commander who was well connected in Washington had run away from battle. Besides, how would it make Squadron 162 look to have one of its members publicly accused of cowardice? And the squadron commander?

Goodpaster was a master of the bureaucratic game. He instinctively realized the weakness of Swanson's hand. There was a loophole in the records that Swanson had collated. It was not that unusual for a pilot to down an airplane and have the maintenance department unable to find the cause. The wet tropical climate, for example, could cause a short-circuit in the plane's complicated electrical system that might right itself after a few minutes in the sun. Other transient glitches were known to hit airplanes, especially the F-8. Goodpaster argued that such was his case. It was simply a coincidence, he said, that his malfunctions had come in a string at night. He spoke with indignation that Swanson would even dare to suggest otherwise. The discussion went on for twenty minutes.

"Well, I think you are getting a reputation for not flying at night," Swanson ended weakly. "And I think the only way you can disprove this is by not letting it happen anymore."

"As I anticipated," Cal told Nell, "he got mad as hell, even though I tried to present it in a positive manner. He has an excuse for everything and refused to admit he could be wrong." He warned Nell that she might encounter "icy treatment" from Goodpaster's wife, who lived nearby in San Diego.

Although he did not like to look at it that way, Swanson realized that Goodpaster had won in the encounter. Cal prided himself on knowing how the navy really worked, the difference between how it should be and the way it was. One of the frequent criticisms of Swanson by the squadron was that he was too politically aware. In Goodpaster, however, he had met his match. Goodpaster too understood the bureaucracy and its limits. Swanson's only recourse would be to give him a bad fitness report at the end of the cruise. But even that might not inconvenience a man with good connections in the Pentagon.

It was with the weapon of the fitness report that Goodpaster began to threaten Dick Wyman. As Goodpaster's assistant, Wyman would be graded by him in a report that would be entered in his permanent record and influence his future in the navy. The fitness report would have to pass through Cal Swanson for his endorsement. But Wyman knew nothing of Swanson's attitude about Goodpaster and assumed that anything Goodpaster said about him Swanson would accept. Senior officers stuck together.

Black Mac often declared with his usual bravado, "You can't hurt me with a fitness report, unless you wad it up and stick it in my eye." In public, Wyman affected the same attitude. It did not matter. He was a fighter pilot. That was the important thing. Goodpaster was a coward who was endangering the lives of his wingman and others, a disgrace to the navy. If he gave Wyman a bad fitness report, so be it. Yet underneath that was not entirely true. Dick Wyman was interested in his navy career, and he knew he was headed for trouble.

---

4 · *Marilyn Elkins*

THE VETERANS OF FOREIGN WARS invited me to a luncheon to talk about the POWs. They told me the meeting would not be political. But the VFW head got up and said, "If Bill Fulbright over in Arkansas doesn't shut up, we're going to go over there and whip his ass."

I was furious. I have a high temper. When I get mad I'm transparent. I knew I was supposed to get up and cry and look pretty and vulnerable and sad. But I was determined not to do that. "I'm only here today because I'm concerned about my husband," I said. "I'm not here to promote the continuance of the war. I'm just trying to see that my husband gets home, and I think we are getting away from the key issue."

I did not want to insult or alienate the audience. But I didn't want anybody to think I approved of what the head of the VFW said. It was at that meeting that I began to see what I was being linked to and began to reject it. I did not dislike people who were patriotic. It was the blind patriotism I didn't like. H. Ross Perot's organization phoned and asked me to help on a project and I did so gladly. I liked Ross Perot, the Texas businessman who was trying to help the POWs. He wasn't just talking, he was trying to do something.

I got in touch with the singer Johnny Cash and asked him to make a plea for the POWs on his TV show. Johnny Cash had the kind of hill integrity I was used to, coming from Tennessee. I felt he really cared and that he was patriotic. Yet it wasn't the empty patriotism of someone who always had it easy and assumed everything to be true.

The wives of POWs and MIAs were invited to Washington for a big rally. We stayed at the Marriott Hotel. There was a huge stage and we had bands, we had—why, we were dancing around the flagpole. The politicians arrived to give us a pep talk. "We haven't forgotten you. We're going to bring your wonderful sons and husbands and fathers home—tomorrow, if we possibly can." I was cynical by this time. I thought we had just become part of the government's political program, something else to be manipulated.

I sat next to a woman who could have been a linebacker for the Green Bay Packers. She had her arms wrapped around a big plastic pocketbook. Spiro Agnew arrived and started to speak. Everybody stood and gave him an ovation. I wasn't about to stand up for the man. Already, it was pretty clear to me that he was corrupt. The woman next to me said, "Stand up! You *will* stand up!" She started tapping me with her pocketbook really hard.

"I don't have to stand up," I said.

"You stand up," she said. "He's our vice president."

"He's your vice president. Leave me alone."

I wanted to do something to help Frank, not to act in a way that suggested I supported the war. After I finished Vanderbilt I flew to Paris and visited the North Vietnamese embassy but was turned away. I returned to Tennessee. After thinking about it a while, though, I decided to go back to Paris and visit North Vietnam's embassy every day until I learned something. "If the other wives think the way to get their husbands home is to continue the war effort, fine," I said. "Let them go about it the way they feel best and I'll go about it my way."

221

5 · Chuck Rice

THE INTERROGATOR insisted that I give him the name of the *Oriskany's* captain. "I simply cannot remember," I said. "How about the admiral? Or his chief of staff. I can remember their names." I definitely did not want to be tortured anymore.

When the North Vietnamese saw that I was ready to cooperate, they said, "Now you must repent of your crimes and tell the world that you are sorry." During the torture sessions they had damaged my hands so badly that I couldn't hold a pencil. They brought a tape recorder and told me to make a statement. I said something like, "I'm very regretful for the war and the damage it has done the Vietnamese." It was not that short but I tried to be that vague.

After my give-in they brought me food. That was a rude awakening. It looked like turnip green soup and the taste almost made me throw up. I fought to keep it down. "You've got to have energy if you are going to escape," I told myself. Reality hadn't set in at this point; I was still thinking about escaping. The North Vietnamese told me they were not satisfied with my statement repenting for my crimes, but I think I got away with it because of the escalation of the air war. They were shooting down guys left and right, most of them with more rank and information than I had. I think they would have pressed me more if it had been a slack time. Instead, they threw me into a four-by-eight-foot cell. It had a thick teak bed pushed up against the wall. It was the first time I had been alone since my capture. They can leave me here for the rest of my life, I thought. Just don't ever bother me again. In my mind I was a failure. I was terrified to be in Hanoi, but I felt I didn't deserve to go home. I had betrayed my country. I was not John Wayne.

I was so stiff I could scarcely move. They had pulled every muscle in my body. When I returned home X-rays showed a dislocation of all major joints. During air strikes the guard made me get under the bed. By the time I was able to bend my body into position, the attacks were almost over. After two weeks I was called out to make another tape-recorded statement, this time about President Johnson. "I'm sorry about what is happening," I said. "I'm sure President Johnson is sorry too. We want this war to end."

I really didn't know much about the war. Dick Wyman had read a great deal and he had pointed out some things to me before I got shot down. "Do your job," Wyman said. (He had no use for you if you didn't do your job, because that meant you were sending your buddy to do it for you.) "But don't be crazy. 'Cause I'll tell you something, Chuck. This thing will go on for another five years." Sitting in my cell, I remembered what Wyman said. It depressed the hell out of me.

After spending time in solitary, I was moved to a cell with an American occupant called the Duke. He was the backseat guy, a radar intercept officer, in an F-4 Phantom, and had got shot down the day after I did. I was elated to see him. I almost wanted to cry. "Remember, you are a fighter pilot," I told myself. "You've got to be cool." We stared at each other in sheer delight, not saying anything. Then we began to talk, and I thought, "How in the world am I going to tell him that I'm a traitor? I've got to let him know I gave in, or he might find out some other way."

"How did you do?" Duke asked. "Did they torture you?"

"Did they torture me?" I said. "They beat the shit out of me."

Thankfully, he said it that way. "How did you do?" He had an understanding look on his face. I decided to get it over.

"I hate to tell you, Duke," I said. "But I didn't do worth a damn."

"I didn't either," he said.

"I mean, I really did bad."

"Yeah, I know. So did I."

"Duke, I caved in."

"Yeah, thank God. So did I."

That's how our relationship began. We were both in the same boat. We felt we were traitors and could never go home again. But we had each other, we were friends. We started telling each other that we had to toughen up, to resist the North Vietnamese. Well, we did to an extent. But four years later I would've said that was a beginner's attitude. If the North Vietnamese wanted something, they were going to get it. Or else you were not going to be among those returning home.

An air force major I'll call the Baron (not his real name) was moved in with us a week later. Baron remained aloof for three days and hardly

223

talked. From what we could gather, the same thing had happened to him. He too had given in. We didn't press him. We were junior officers. We called him sir. Things began to change, though, the day the Baron muffed lighting a cigarette. The guards gave us three cigarettes a day. I didn't smoke cigarettes and Baron seldom smoked either, but Duke was a tobacco fiend. So we pretended to light up when the guard handed us a cigarette, just to get them for Duke. The guard gave you a light and *bam!* he was gone and not coming back till lunch. Baron failed one morning to get his cigarette lit properly.

Duke started yelling, "Suck, dammit, suck!"

I moved between them.

"Goddammit, Major," Duke said, "why the hell—"

"Hey, Duke, you gotta ease up," I said. "That's a major you're talking to."

"Major, my ass. He wrecked my cigarette."

Rank began to take on a different perspective.

After I returned home I saw the movie *Papillon*, and it brought back the old panic. It showed a French prison. The architecture, the cells, the mats, the irons—all were like we had. Someone walked down the hall and keys rattled. A chill ran down your spine. Then the bolt flew back—boom! The door opened—boom! And your heart stopped. If it was a Vietnamese with your bread and soup, you felt an incredible relief. A stranger, someone you'd never seen, put fear in your gut. Two guys who tortured Duke and me we called Twisted and Bent. If they were standing there when the door opened, you practically did something in your pants.

That was Hanoi for us. The sound of rattling keys and a door opening.

6

NELL BAKED Cal some cookies. She wrapped them in aluminum foil and sent the package through the armed forces postal system. It arrived a week later, with a note saying that she was doing a rain dance.

Nell knew that the monsoon season began in October and by November or December strikes on North Vietnam would be curtailed by the rainy weather and Cal would not be exposed to as much danger.

Actually, Nell was half-joking. She realized that inaction drove Cal up the wall and that he preferred flying missions to sitting around. The cookies and note were her way of playing the dutiful wife. When it came to military matters, Nell and Cal shared an understanding that surpassed most navy marriages. Dick Wyman and his wife Ardyce had an agreement not to discuss domestic or professional problems. Their letters contained the kind of playful sexual exchanges that a young couple often used to express affection. But Cal gave Nell a detailed rundown on what was happening on Yankee Station. His letters were straightforward, neither boastful nor complaining. He did not minimize or exaggerate the danger they faced and never glossed over the injuries and deaths occurring daily.

Cal wrote Nell at night during the time he was on Condition One alert, sitting in the cockpit of his plane ready to be launched in case a ship on Yankee Station came under attack. It was boring duty. Except for the muddled Tonkin Gulf incidents in 1964, the North Vietnamese had made no serious attempt to attack the U.S. ships that were often in view of their coastline. Why, no one knew. They had not hesitated to use suicidal human wave attacks against U.S. bases in South Vietnam. Why didn't they load up a MiG and send it on a kamikaze run at a carrier like the *Oriskany*? Did they have such a high regard for the Seventh Fleet's defenses? Or did they fear an attack might cause Washington to remove the restraints on the bombing?

Whatever the answer, the U.S. Navy operated in what it called a permissive environment. Whether American warships could withstand an attack in light of the technological advances made in weapons systems since World War Two would not be decided by the Vietnam War. Only a Russian spy ship, the *Gidrofon*, a converted tuna boat the Americans code named "Skunk Yankee," was there to harass them. The pilots disliked the useless but necessary duty of standing Condition One alert. Many of them, like Cal, used the time to write letters home by the red night-vision light in their cockpits.

Nell was the perfect navy wife. After all, who could understand a husband's career better than a former naval officer? Nell's love affair with the navy had begun when she was a student at Mary Washington

College in Virginia. The school was not far from the U.S. Naval Academy in Maryland, and it was almost inevitable that she should date a midshipman and fall in love. The end of the story was not all that unpredictable either: she wound up with a broken heart. That failed relationship did not, however, diminish her love for the navy, and may be suspected of enhancing it.

After taking a business degree, she went to work for Woodward & Lothrop in Washington and lived in the YWCA. She heard that the navy was offering women, in a new program, commissions as regular officers, not as clerical help or nurses, but as ensigns, equal to any man, in theory. Her mother was appalled when she told her she was thinking of joining the service, and Nell agreed to postpone her decision. Six months later she showed up one morning at the navy recruiting office. The naval recruiter looked at her. Before him stood a short but pretty young lady, well mannered, very feminine, obviously intelligent, who neither smoked nor drank. He put on his glasses and looked again. Before entering the officer training program, Nell worked in the Pentagon for an aide to General Omar Bradley. She discovered that her baby voice and giggles were an asset. A woman who wanted to get ahead learned to conceal herself around military men. She underwent basic training at Newport, Rhode Island, marching with a back pack, not minding being called the shortest man in the squad. Then she was assigned to Patuxent River, Maryland.

Her commanding officer had a beer belly and greeted her from under bushy brows, saying, "Sit down, Ensign," making no attempt to disguise his distaste. A female officer. What was the goddamn navy coming to? But Nell won him over with her cheerful efficiency, and when she got married, he gave her away at the altar.

The heart broken by the Annapolis midshipman mended but left Nell with a permanent distrust for a relationship that began with bells ringing and rockets going off. She made sure that she and the young blond officer going through test pilot school had a durable friendship before she considered his proposal for marriage. Cal was not particularly handsome or glamorous. He was, though, she realized, someone to whom you could entrust your life. One thing made her hesitant about accepting his proposal. That was his love of partying. It was odd. Cal had a cool reserve. He wasn't a backslapper or loud talker like so many officers. But he seemed to have a deep-seated need to be at the officers' club every night. It was not just the lure of drinking, for he knew when to stop; he had no problems with alcohol. She couldn't figure it out.

After their marriage, she resigned from the navy, and the social thing grew larger than she had anticipated. He was seldom there. When she had the youngest of her three children, a son who suffered damage at birth and almost died, Cal had to be called home. His relationship with the children was that of a disciplinarian who issued orders and disappeared. The photographs in her scrapbook did not show Nell and Cal sightseeing in Paris or Rome, but Nell and Cal at one social function or another, standing in the midst of naval officers who looked slightly out of focus through no fault of the camera. Nell drank little, a glass of white wine, maybe a pink lady, and she hated the late hours. But it seemed a matter of principle that Cal be the last to leave a party. If she complained, he gave her the Swedish deep-freeze, and Nell couldn't stand to have him angry and not speaking to her.

Yet on another level their relationship deepened. After Cal suffered a career setback, fired from his job as the catapult officer on the *Midway* and passed over for commander, Nell stood by him and even wrote her old contacts at the Pentagon, trying to help out. Nothing came of it, but Cal realized that he had someone with a loyalty hard to find in a time of instant divorces, a real partner. Of course Cal became a tightly wound perfectionist after his career setback, and the intensity he gave to his job seeped over to the home, where he found it difficult to resist telling Nell exactly what to do, sometimes treating her like one of his junior officers. But he trusted her as he did no one else.

Nell had done an excellent job as the leader of the squadron wives while their husbands were at war. Since the executive officer was a bachelor, the whole burden of supplying support and morale fell on her. There was lots of telephoning back and forth between the wives and frequent potluck suppers. Nell's older son, twelve and a half, took on babysitting for the squadron children. Nell developed an easy relationship with the wives. Black Mac's wife, Phyllis, sometimes said, "Mac wrote me that your husband sure is on a short chain this week." Nell knew Cal's flaws, knew he wasn't always a diplomat in stressful situations, and she replied, "Well, if they mess up, he'll tell them about it. But as long as they do their job, he'll say they are great." Nell tried not to let Cal's opinions influence her. She made up her own mind about people. About the officer called Goodpaster she was to say, "He wasn't so eager to go on flights, and that's all I knew. But he was such a nice man. I liked him very much. He was a family-oriented person, not a gung-ho fighter pilot."

Some of the wives occasionally found the bubbly personality of a middle-aged woman hard to take with morning coffee. Nell had grown up in an era when women had to flirt and giggle, do anything to hide that they were tough and intelligent, and she tended to fall back on the reflexes of a lifetime. She could also be unbending about how she thought a navy wife should conduct herself. "It had been ingrained in me over years of marriage," she said. "A navy wife doesn't make an ass of herself. She doesn't yap and she doesn't call. She waits. A lot of the younger wives found that hard to do. They would call me and I'd say, 'Just hold on. Bad news will get here before the good. Hang on. Hang on.' And we hung on."

One young wife by the improbable name of Stella Dallas seemed to look on Nell as a combination of mother and maid who should be ready to respond to any request. "Another wife," Nell said, "was on her fourth marriage and her husband on his third. He wouldn't send money and the kids had no food. We'd get together to try to figure out what to do. It was usually the younger women who had no resiliency. The older ones knew what they were getting into with naval officers. They were the finest bunch of women you'll ever meet."

The only serious problem concerned one of the wives who could not handle the pressure. She had four young children and the fear of her husband getting shot down compelled her to cry for help, which took the form of various dramatic complaints. "She had a robbery; she spilled hot grease on her foot; she had to have a D and C," Nell said. "I can't tell you how many times she was in the hospital. We stopped believing her." The problem in fact eventually led to the wife's being hospitalized for a nervous breakdown. After she recovered, she refused to speak to Nell, believing her insensitive during the hard times.

All in all, though, most of the wives agreed that Nell had done a terrific job in a position that carried no pay and no title. She was the perfect navy wife, a great asset to her husband's career, and it seemed an appropriate reward when a navy captain assigned to the Pentagon telephoned Nell to let her be the first to know.

"Don't tell anyone," he said. "It hasn't been announced yet. But your husband has been selected to command an air wing."

7

IN MID-1965, when the *Oriskany* arrived on Yankee Station for her first cruise, North Vietnam had seventy combat aircraft, the old version of the MiG. The fighters had arrived from China shortly after the Tonkin Gulf incidents, at a time when the entire North Vietnamese air force consisted of fifty trainers, fifty transports, and four helicopters. The country had only two airfields capable of handling jets. Six other fields eventually were built. For most of the war, Phuc Yen and Kep served as the main military air bases. At the end of 1965, the North Vietnamese began receiving the new MiG-21, which was as fast as most U.S. aircraft and armed with heat-seeking Atoll missiles, a formidable threat.

Under the Johnson administration's rules, pilots could engage the MiGs in the air but could not hit their bases. The Americans often flew low over the airfields around Hanoi, looked at the MiGs lined up on the runway, and passed by without firing a shot. The prohibition lasted for two years. When Robert McNamara was asked by the press why the MiG fields were not being attacked, he said that if enemy planes were destroyed on their bases, the North Vietnamese would move them farther north, perhaps into China. To the military, his explanation appeared to be based on a misapprehension, or a strategy too subtle for ordinary minds to grasp. So what if the North Vietnamese moved their bases farther north? It would simply lengthen their reaction time to American strikes.

Actually the decision not to hit the MiG bases was another indication that McNamara, McGeorge Bundy, and other holdovers from the Kennedy administration had been more shaken by the Cuban missile crisis than they liked to admit. Though not officially acknowledged by Washington, Russian and North Korean advisers supervised North Vietnam's fighter defense system in the early stages of the war, and until mid-1966 or even later sometimes flew MiGs against the Americans. It was Washington's secret worry that an attack on the MiG bases and their Soviet advisers might cause a strong reaction from Moscow.

Hitting the MiG bases made good sense tactically and might have helped spare American pilots a private embarrassment. For all their expensive aircraft and years of training, the fact was that they were not doing terribly well in air-to-air combat with North Vietnamese pilots, many of whom had driven nothing more complicated than a bicycle only several years before.

The air force and navy finished the war with a winning margin in dogfights. Two and a half MiGs were shot down for every American plane lost to an enemy fighter. But that was a far cry from the Korean War, when the ratio had been twelve to one in the American favor. Even the two and a half to one ratio may have been a bit of an exaggeration. The air force and navy occasionally tried to cook the books when they could get away with it. When Commander Bellinger went down at sea, for example, running out of gas as a direct result of having been hit by a MiG, his aircraft loss was credited not to an enemy plane but to "battle damage."

Why were they fighting less well than in previous wars? There seemed to be several reasons. The first involved what Lieutenant Colonel Charles Brown called the rocket-on-a-stick problem. Brown was the Da Nang special sector adviser and, along with Colonel Howard St. Clair and his staff, one of the Americans who held the fort until U.S. Marines waded ashore in 1965. Brown realized that the Viet Cong were equipped with the perfect weapon for the Vietnam War, the B-40 rocket. Cheap to make, easily carried by one man, with loads of firepower, it was nothing but a rocket on a stick, point it and fire. He advised the army to get cracking on developing its own. But military research couldn't come up with anything nearly as good. The B-40 rocket was too simple. American technology had become like a tailor who announced he could no longer make a coat to keep warm unless it was waterproof, fire resistant, fully reversible, with hidden pockets and a zip-out lining.

The rocket-on-a-stick problem was noticeable in American fighters. The idea behind a dogfight was to get an enemy plane lined up in one's sights and shoot. Speed and maneuverability were essential. Following World War Two, however, the U.S. began adding on other functions. Not only was a fighter supposed to gain air superiority, but it was also to serve as a bomber, do reconnaissance work, and carry a variety of accessories the technological equivalent of hidden pockets and a zip-out lining. (Commander Bellinger was waging a campaign against the navy's trend toward complicated fighters at the time that he was committed to a psychiatric ward.) The result was a loss of maneuverability. Hanoi's MiGs were lighter and smaller and harder to see than American planes. They had a smaller radius of turn and were more maneuverable than, say, the F-4 Phantom, even though the U.S. plane had greater speed.

Another problem obviously existed on the human level. It was axiomatic that Americans were never whipped or fought to a standoff by North Vietnamese pilots. According to them, anybody who showed a talent for dogfighting had to be a Russian, or a North Korean, or maybe an East German. American pilots were not ready to admit that a Vietnamese with water buffalo dung still clinging to his feet might be flying circles around them.

Yet something was wrong somewhere, as seen by the fact that nine MiG pilots were credited with downing five or more American aircraft, while only two Americans—one air force and one navy—became aces in Vietnam. In Korea, forty U.S. pilots were aces. Of the North Vietnamese planes the Americans shot down, more than half were the older MiG-17, which could not hold a candle to the new MiG-21. Commander Bellinger was the first navy pilot to knock down a -21.

After the war ended and the statistics were in, the navy considered the relatively poor showing of American pilots serious enough to institute a new training program. A special unit was set up at Miramar to act as enemy fighters in practice dogfights. The "enemy" squadron flew camouflaged F-5s, which were light and small like MiGs. There would be no more horsing around in air combat maneuvers between buddies who knew each other's weaknesses. Israeli pilots were brought over to demonstrate their tactics, dazzling the Americans with their flying ability.

The media, usually alert to any failures in Vietnam, missed the story about the problems of air combat. This could be attributed partly to the fact that many pilots had a rocket-on-a-stick problem when it came to public speaking. A MiG kill was a big thing, bringing an automatic Silver Star, the third highest decoration, and publicity. Some pilots declined to be interviewed, fearing antiwar radicals might harass their families. Others preferred to remain anonymous in case they were later shot down and captured. But most of them described their victory to newsmen. And therein lay the problem. They spoke in a convoluted, technical manner that made shooting down a MiG sound as exciting as repairing a washing machine. After the novelty of the first few shootdowns, the media lost interest in this part of the war. American victories were still noted in news reports. But the eyes of journalists began to glaze when yet another pilot, his face gleaming with pride and earnestness, fell into his specialized jargon. So no one took the trouble to add up the number of MiGs shot down and compare it to the number of American planes downed by the North Vietnamese.

Taking the problem that Americans were having with air combat and combining that with the fact that MiGs were rarely seen, shooting down an enemy plane took on a greater importance than it had in past wars. A MiG kill gave a pilot a respected status that neither rank nor medals could match. Only nineteen F-8 pilots shot down MiGs during the war. Squadron 162 was tied for third place among F-8 units, with two kills. The second shootdown occurred on December 14, 1967. It was the longest dogfight of the war, a fifteen-minute chase over the rice paddies of the Red River Valley. The main participants were the commanding officers of the *Oriskany*'s two F-8 squadrons and Dick Wyman.

The encounter began shortly after 4:00 P.M. As the *Oriskany* strike group neared the coast, the radar ship coordinating the attack radioed the warning: "Two red bandits airborne at Bull's-eye." Two MiGs had taken off from the Hanoi airport. Dick Schaffert, a pilot from the *Oriskany*'s other F-8 squadron, saw the MiGs first and tried to slip up on them to get into position for a shootdown. They saw him coming and dropped their extra fuel tanks, then turned for a fight. Schaffert glanced over his shoulder to look for his wingman and saw two more MiGs that had appeared out of the sun and were tracking him for a gunnery pass. Schaffert tried to radio Bob Rasmussen, his squadron commander, but when he made a sharp turn to avoid being shot down, the pull of gravity forced his oxygen mask down over his chin and he was unable to use his radio. For the next ten minutes, he used every trick he'd ever learned to keep from getting shot down. Finally, when he was running out of gas, he managed to break off and radio Cal

Swanson the position of the remaining MiG, which had not turned toward its home base.

Bob Rasmussen, Herb Hunter's brother-in-law and a former Blue Angel, arrived about the same time as Cal and Dick Wyman. They saw the one remaining MiG and began the chase. The MiG could outturn the F-8, but the Americans had practiced working as a team to overcome the enemy advantage. Their tactics called for one American to fly behind the other and when the first was unable to follow the MiG's turn, the second would come in a sharper vertical angle to narrow the distance. They were trained to alternate in such a manner until one of them could get on the MiG's tail.

---

8 · *Dick Wyman*

I WASN'T SUPPOSED TO GO. I was the spare. Out of five airplanes from our squadron, three went down on the flight deck with malfunctions. Cal Swanson and I wound up being launched. We got over the beach and Swanson's radar failed. The flight leader operated off the radar and the wingman was visual. It was standard practice to turn the lead over to the other airplane when someone's radar went down. So I had the lead. Or was supposed to have it. Swanson didn't resign himself to flying as my wingman—he wanted it both ways. He started giving me instructions about where to find the MiGs.

"Let's go to Wichita," he said. That was the code name for an area of North Vietnam. "Let's go."

We got there and saw nothing. He had another suggestion. I ignored him. I spotted an A-4. I radioed the pilot to ask if he had seen anything. "Yes," he said, "I've got a MiG here." About that time I saw him. He was in front of me. We passed head on. He rolled and I rolled and started down after him.

"I'll get him," Swanson said.

He tried to get on the MiG's tail. The pilot went into a sharp turn and pulled his nose around. He started firing at Swanson.

"Get him off my tail!" Swanson yelled. "He's shooting at me!"

I pointed my nose up and pulled the trigger.

"Is he still behind me?" Swanson asked.

"No," I said, "we're going the other way."

I was running him hard. Each time I came down and tried to put a Sidewinder missile on him he reefed into me. When he did that, I had too much of an angle and couldn't get off a shot. I made four passes. He was running out of gas. His buddies had left him. I think he was just trying to get home. As I came off a pass, Bob Rasmussen zoomed down and fired a Sidewinder. The missile almost homed in on me. The MiG broke. The Sidewinder exploded harmlessly. The MiG was hard to see because of the camouflage. "I'm not taking my eyes off you," I said. Good eyesight was crucial to a fighter pilot. One of the problems, I think, was that Swanson and Rasmussen lost sight of the fight.

We had started at sixteen thousand feet. Now we were at treetop level. The MiG had done everything right. He was outmaneuvering me. Then I came down on him and was almost at the point of over-shooting him when he started a reverse. He must have realized it was too soon. He went back into his turn and tried to reverse again. That let me get on his tail. I fired a Sidewinder. The missile took off two-thirds of his left wing. We were fifty feet off the ground. He hit the rice paddy and exploded in a fireball that shot higher than my canopy.

I was about to run out of gas. I radioed for a tanker. He was pretty far offshore and he refused to fly closer. "I've got orders not to go over the beach," he said.

"I don't want you to go over the beach," I said. "I just want you to come closer, so I don't run out of gas before I plug in." An admiral was listening to our transmissions. He ordered the tanker to get in there and give me some gas.

The *Oriskany* asked if I wanted to do a victory roll over the ship, to celebrate the shootdown. "I don't know," I said. "Stand by one."

Swanson was flying beside me. He nodded his head, "Yes, do it."

"Roger, I'll do it," I radioed the ship.

"You are cleared for a port side victory roll," the *Oriskany* said.

After a mission one normally came around the starboard side at six to eight hundred feet and broke around to make a landing pass. This time I was going to come by the port side just above the flight deck, pop the nose up, roll the airplane all the way around, then break out

of that and land. I started my maneuver. Swanson had not said anything on the radio, but he later told me he tried to signal me with his
hands that he was going to roll around me as I did mine. If so, I didn't
see it. I went into my roll and suddenly I saw an airplane inches away,
ready to land in my face. I thought my wing was going to break off on
his belly, it was that close. I nearly died of fright. When I landed,
everybody on the flight deck said, "Jeez-sus, you really came close to
getting killed on that one." Dick Schaffert, who missed the MiG at the
beginning of the dogfight, joked that his only consolation was that Cal
and I almost ran into each other on the victory roll.

"I don't think I can get you a Silver Star for that," Swanson said
after we landed.

"Skipper, I could care less," I said. "I got a MiG. That's enough for
me."

Reporters came out to the ship for interviews. Swanson did all the
talking. It sounded as though he had fought the fight and pushed the
MiG in front of me where I finally shot him down. He said we fell
into the alternating passes as we'd been trained. But there was no alternating, except once when he got in front. As he knew, he made a gross
error by giving the MiG a shot at his tail. I didn't care, though. I knew
how it had happened.

On my first MiG encounter with Bellinger, I thought the pilots
were Vietnamese. This second time, I'd bet my shirt and overcoat they
were North Koreans. It was such a drastic change in the way they flew,
the tactics they used. Bob Rasmussen and I talked about it and agreed
that we would have liked to see the pilot get out safely. He fought well.
But he had too many guys against him. We were like a pack of dogs
on a deer. So I wasn't wild about seeing him get killed. But it was a
big high to shoot down the plane.

I received a Silver Star. After the ceremony, Bryan Compton said,
"Goddamn, Dick, I'd like to have you in my squadron." That meant
more to me than the medal. He was the best. If you had a tough
mission, you prayed he was leading it. Funny thing was, Compton
later made admiral and during peacetime everybody hated him. What
a mean, ornery bastard of an admiral he turned out to be! But on
Yankee Station he was loved, because nobody was a better strike leader.

After I got the MiG, two congressmen, one from Georgia, the other
from Maine, came aboard the *Oriskany* for a briefing on the air war.

Since I'd become a little famous and was from his home state, I was assigned as the escort officer for the Maine congressman. I had no idea about the importance of public relations in those days, and I was irritated to be taken off the flight schedule. You got points for flying missions. I hawked the ready room and took anybody's flight who was sick or couldn't make it for some reason. This way I got ahead of the others. When it was noticed that I was ahead, I would be assigned to take an airplane for maintenance to the Philippines, which was like extra leave, and I could spend the time partying.

The admiral was set to see the two congressmen at eleven o'clock that night. I expected a big gala briefing to be laid on to impress them. We walked into the war room and there was the admiral, his chief of staff, his aide, and that was all.

The admiral said to me and the other escort officer, "You can stay or leave. Whatever you choose."

"Thank you, sir," I said. "I'll sit in."

"Gentlemen," the admiral began, "this is not going to be a briefing with color slides and flip charts. We don't have the time."

That impressed me. He wasn't going to cozy up to the politicians. He was direct and matter of fact. He began describing the air war and what we were trying to do.

The Maine congressman stopped him. "Admiral, how much longer is it going to take to win this war?"

The admiral looked at him for a moment. "We know if the guy starts out from North Vietnam with ten pounds of rice," he said, "we're going to stop all but one pound from reaching the South. If he starts with ten bullets, he'll only get one down there. Beyond that, there's nothing we can do. Air power cannot stop that last pound of rice or that last bullet from reaching South Vietnam. So we'll have to stay here long enough to make him decide it's not worth starting with ten pounds to get one pound to the South. Or we'll have to decide whether it's worth our time to stay here that long."

The two congressmen looked like they'd been hit with a blackjack. They sat there stunned, not wanting to believe but knowing he had no reason to lie. Neither of them asked another question. The ballgame was over. Probably nothing had a greater impact on my thinking either. Until now I had believed somebody would come up with the magic answer and we would win. But here was an admiral saying it wasn't going to happen.

After the briefing I took the congressman back to his room. He was due to leave the next morning.

"Good night, sir," I said. "I'll see you bright and early."

"Hey, Dick," he said, "have you, uh, have you got anything to drink around here? I'd really like something to nip on."

"Sir, you know that alcohol is illegal aboard ship."

"Yes, I know. But have you got any? I'm not too fussy."

I had never met a congressman before and didn't realize that a lot of them drank like fish. I thought he was trying to set me up. I could see him going back to Washington and calling a news conference to expose illegal drinking on Yankee Station. "Lieutenant Richard Wyman, a Silver Star winner, was caught redhanded by Congressman . . ." I played dumb.

"No, sir. I don't have anything. Maybe the admiral does. I could ask his aide."

"Come on Dick. Where is it?" He was getting desperate.

"No, sir. Not me."

How the poor guy got to sleep on that noisy aircraft carrier I don't know. He left the next morning probably thinking I was the straightest arrow he had ever met, a fighter pilot who didn't drink.

9

NELL PASSED the good news to Cal about his being selected to command an air wing. But not even that could fully compensate for his failure to shoot down the MiG. "It was my biggest disappointment in two years," Swanson said. "When the MiG pulled up and got the burst off at me, I think I did the wrong maneuver. I should have rolled over the top and kept him in sight the whole time. It was my golden opportunity and I blew it."

Cal told Nell about the encounter. "Dick and I worked as a team in the classical offensive formation, and with Rasmussen there too, the MiG pilot was really in tough straits, but God was he good; so was his airplane. Rasmussen got off three missiles and some cannon fire, but missed. I got in two passes, but none good enough to shoot. Dick

Wyman got in three passes which were outmaneuvered by the MiG; then on the fourth pass, he got in the saddle and nailed the MiG-17 about fifty feet off the deck. The MiG pilot didn't have a chance. He was really good, though, and aggressive. He got one brief shot at me, but didn't hit me. Working together, we always had someone coming at him so he really had to fight defensively. This was probably the longest dogfight that has taken place over here. It lasted a good fifteen minutes, I think, and Dick nailed the guy only about fifteen miles south of Hanoi."

Cal told Nell he was putting Wyman in for a Silver Star. He liked Bob Rasmussen but was happy that 162 would be credited with the MiG kill and not Rasmussen's F-8 squadron. Cal had missed the MiG, but he was determined to do better next time.

"One thing I've got to say for Swanson," Black Mac said, "he never shirked his duty or looked for ways to keep from going over the beach. And there were a couple of skippers who did. After Wyman got the MiG, though, Swanson began taking a lot of chances. He hung around after strikes trying to suck a MiG in. It was guts balls. But a guy who did that was just asking for it. A lot of pilots weren't anxious to fly with him from then on."

Swanson's obsession with getting a MiG was diverted by his being picked to organize the *Oriskany*'s Christmas party in Hong Kong. The ship was scheduled to finish the combat tour in mid-January and return to San Diego. This would be the last chance for the air wing to join together socially. Cal's selection was in recognition of 162's status as a party squadron. Some of their shenanigans had become legendary. They were mostly things that had happened under Bellinger's command. Cal was considerably more sedate, but the reputation stuck. Money for the party came from the tailhook fund. Before a pilot landed he had to push a handle to lower his tail hook. A spotter stood beside the LSO watching through binoculars. If the pilot forgot to lower his tail hook, the spotter told the LSO, who reminded him. When that happened the pilot had to contribute five dollars to the recreation fund. Failing to lower his landing gear cost fifteen dollars, five dollars per wheel. Preoccupied and nervous after a mission, pilots forgot to lower their tail hooks or landing gear, and the fund grew. With that and other money contributed by the pilots, the Hong Kong party was certain to be the biggest in the *Oriskany*'s history.

The ship's supply plane made frequent runs to Da Nang, to pick up mail and visitors. The pilots often met the chartered Pam Am flight that left Da Nang taking U.S. Marines on R and R to Hong Kong. Cal arranged with the Pam Am stewardesses to establish "The Blue Ball Express," an informal but speedy mail service. The name was taken from Pam Am's blue globe logo and a play on words. A letter written in the morning could reach its recipient the same night. This way pilots were able to keep in touch with the British colony's attractive young ladies. Invitations to the party went out to a hundred of them. Cal arranged to buy the girls flowers and charm bracelets with the air wing insignia. He flew to Hong Kong four days before the *Oriskany* arrived. The Hong Kong Hilton's party manager was expecting him. Cal told him how much the *Oriskany* was prepared to spend, and they negotiated the details. The Hilton would provide the food and drinks. The ship would bring her own band. An officer helping Cal organize the party suggested that they rent the Hong Kong yacht and sail out to greet the *Oriskany* as the carrier entered the harbor. "Good idea," someone said. "Let's paint some signs and hang them on the yacht." They had a party that lasted till 3:00 A.M. the night before the *Oriskany* arrived and did the signs. Armed with Bloody Marys, they headed in the dark for the yacht, singing Christmas carols.

The *Oriskany* dropped hook between Kowloon and Hong Kong. The British admiralty barge arrived to pay a courtesy call. Cal and his yacht crew circled around. The signs said: WE HAVE, HAVE YOU? WELCOME TO THE LOVE-IN. STAND BY TO RECEIVE SHOT GLASS. A destroyer escort broke out her band. A sailor with a dummy made up to look like a girl danced to the music. The seamen on the *Oriskany* cheered. When Swanson got back to the Hilton, he found a message telling him to report to the ship as soon as possible. The thought hit him that his joke had not been well received by the admiral and the captain. They had made a spectacle of themselves in front of all Hong Kong. He went to the ship with dread, fearing that he had just ended his career. It turned out that he was called back to handle a squadron matter needing his decision, and Burt Shepherd assured him that the admiral and the captain had found the whole thing amusing. The party was going to be a big success.

Dick Wyman left the ship at Cubi Point and flew to Hong Kong a day early. The opportunity came at the last moment and he went without telling Goodpaster, his superior in the maintenance department. J. P. O'Neill said that he would inform Goodpaster that the air wing commander was sending him to help with the preparations. When Goodpaster arrived at the Hilton, however, he spotted Wyman and loudly called him to attention. "Goddamn you, Wyman," he said. "I'm going to fix you for not staying in Cubi Point as I ordered."

J. P. O'Neill saw the incident developing and went to Wyman's defense. "I told you why he didn't let you know he was leaving," O'Neill said.

"May I interrupt?" Goodpaster said. "I'm a senior officer and he's a goddamn junior officer and—"

"Goddamn yourself!" Wyman exploded. "You're not giving me a lecture in the Hong Kong Hilton."

The two men stood nose to nose shouting at each other. Wyman was running out of breath.

"Why are you shaking?" Goodpaster sneered.

"Because I'm trying to keep from smacking you in the mouth," Wyman said.

Other pilots moved in to separate them. Cal Swanson felt he had no choice but to side with the senior officer. The rank structure had to be maintained. He ordered Wyman to the *Oriskany*, where he was given a duty watch.

From then on, Wyman and Goodpaster were gloves-off enemies. Wyman conceded that Goodpaster got the best of the contest with a bit of bureaucratic slyness. It started when a group of them were at the officers' club and Goodpaster announced that he had given Wyman a bad fitness report. John Hellman, the admin officer, said, "Wait a minute. When I saw it, it wasn't bad. To the contrary."

Goodpaster insisted. "No, he's got a terrible black mark in his records now. He'll be lucky to get promoted."

"You know where you can stick your fitness report," Wyman said.

He refused to let Goodpaster see that he was bothered. But he was worried and puzzled as to why Cal Swanson would put through a negative report on him. Was he jealous about the MiG shootdown? Wyman was cool toward Swanson during his final weeks in the squadron. The next time he was in Washington he did something he had never done before. He went to the Pentagon and asked to see his records. Swanson had a policy of not showing his officers their grading sheets. Wyman thumbed through the files and found it. He read it and was shocked. It was not a bad fitness report. It was excellent. Good-paster had psyched him out. Three years later, when he ran into Cal, Wyman apologized and told him why he had acted so cool in those last days. Swanson was surprised. He considered Wyman one of the squadron's best officers—he liked his openness, his sense of humor, and the way he did his job—and there was never any question but that Cal would give him a good fitness report. He had barely looked at Goodpaster's draft before tossing it in the trash can and writing his own version.

Most surprising of all were the results of Cal's fitness report on Goodpaster. Bob Punches, the assistant admin officer, saw the report and could hardly believe it was so damning. "Essentially Swanson charged that he was a liar and a coward," Punches said. "There were things you didn't normally write about in a fitness report."

Goodpaster was nevertheless given command of a naval air squadron, though not a fighter unit, and then promoted to the rank of captain, which was equal to full colonel in the army or air force. Obviously it did not hurt a fellow, Swanson reflected, to be wired in at the Pentagon.

---

10 · Chuck Rice

OUR CELL was near a bathhouse used by all the prisoners in the complex. By lifting ourselves up and peeking out the window at the top we could see the other POWs coming and going. This was forbidden. If the Vietnamese caught us looking out it would mean punishment and torture. Duke got up his courage and said, "We've got to find out what's going on. I'll risk it." He stuck his head up, looked out, and said, "There's my skipper! By God, they shot him down." The next day he stuck his head up again. "Hey, there's my operations officer." That happened every time he looked out. He saw somebody he knew. Practically his whole squadron had been shot down during the October escalation. He was so depressed that he stopped looking out.

In January 1968 we were packed up and moved to another camp

called the Zoo—Duke, Baron, and me. We still had not made contact with any other Americans. The interrogator at the Zoo was a European-looking guy. He wrote and spoke fluent English.

"Who is this guy?" we asked each other. "He's not Vietnamese. He is just some asshole."

"You better wise up," the interrogator said. "I can be very tough on you."

"Nah," we told each other. "A European can't have any authority around here. He's just trying to scare us."

One day we were passing a building called the Pool Hall and I looked up at a window and saw a face. I nudged Duke and Baron and said, "Look at that. An American."

"Don't look," Baron said. "It's a Vietnamese trick. They're trying to get you to communicate, and it means trouble for all of us."

"Hey, come on," I said. "Take a look at that face. The guy's got a grin from ear to ear and round eyes. That's another POW."

Baron got nervous and returned to our cell. That was the first sign we had that he was turning paranoid. Baron believed that his interrogation had proved he was a big failure. He was becoming obsessed with resisting the Vietnamese. As we found out later, Baron as a child had been close to his mother but not to his dad, who was a construction worker. Apparently he felt he never measured up to his father's expectations. Baron was always striving and you got the idea that he was the sort everybody played tricks on back in his college fraternity. He worked hard and studied hard and was probably a good air force officer. He hadn't gone through survival school before being sent to the war, but he had seen the movie *The Manchurian Candidate*, and to him that represented an accurate portrayal of what we were up against. The commies were going to try to brainwash us and launch us against our own country.

Baron was against our communicating with the other POWs. Duke and I realized we would have to make contact without him, even though he was a major and outranked us. Everybody in the camp was trying to communicate with us, but we didn't know the code. I saw an American in a window making weird hand motions and I said to Duke, "What's the matter with that guy? You think he's gone stir crazy?" Prisoners in the next cell were tapping on our wall and it wasn't shave-and-a-haircut.

Finally, after a week, we realized what we were hearing and seeing was the alphabet in code. It was called the Smitty Harris tap code, named for the prisoner who brought it to Hanoi. It became the standard way of communicating for all POWs. The code was divided into a square, in appearance like a crossword puzzle box, with five lines across and five down. The first line across was A-B-C-D-E. To spell out a word containing one of these letters you made a tap on the wall to indicate it was in the first line across, then paused and quickly tapped out one for A, two for B, three for C, and so on. The second line was F-G-H-I-J. You began with two taps to indicate that the letter was in the second line across, then paused and quickly tapped out one for F, two for G, and so on. The rest of the alphabet was divided the same way, with K left out and C substituted when necessary, making it twenty-five letters instead of twenty-six.

Dog was spelled like this: *Tap . . . tap-tap-tap-tap. Tap-tap-tap . . . tap-tap-tap-tap. Tap-tap . . . tap-tap.*

In a few days we got the alphabet down cold. There was just one problem. Duke and I were the worst spellers in the world. Someone would tap out a message and we'd say, "No! Too fast. Do it over." And then patiently the sender would tap, T-H-E. "Oh, yeah! Got it!" We found a piece of brick dust and tried to write down the messages, to make sense of them. We would wind up with a bunch of letters and have to call time out to see if we could separate them into words. I-N-T-H-E-B-E-G-I-N-N-I-N-G it was a disaster.

After a lot of hard work we got so we could communicate. "Here are our names," we said. "We have a third guy in our room but he doesn't want us to talk." Our messages were passed around the prison. No one was concerned that Baron didn't want to communicate. That had happened before with POWs.

"When is the war going to end?" everybody asked. "What's happening out there?"

And of course the North Vietnamese had shot down two of the dumbest guys on Yankee Station. Duke and I hadn't read the newspapers. "Oh, we don't know," we said. "Maybe it will end in a couple or three years."

Next thing we knew everybody in the prison hated us. "Why didn't you jerks bring us some news?" That is now taught in survival school. If you are flying in a war and might get shot down, you are supposed to stay up on what's happening, so you can carry the information to the POW camp.

Then we sent a message: "We've got to tell you guys something. We gave in. We broke. We made tapes."

A message came back: "You poor bastards. Everybody here has been broken in one way or another. Quit feeling sorry for yourselves and learn to use the com system."

The next month the European-looking interrogator called us in and said, "Boys, I'm going to do you a favor." He didn't elaborate, but he split us up, putting Duke in another two-man room and Baron in solitary confinement. I was sent to a ten-man room. That's when my prison education really began. I was there for the next year and a half. My new cellmates had been around for some time, and they were wired into the communication system. They could com as fast as I could talk. One guy tapped on the wall; others walked back and forth memorizing the information coming in. "Okay, I got that one. You take the next." They weren't about to let me tap, so all I had to do was try to memorize things. I told them I had caved in. They laughed and said, "You are looking at ten of them." They asked what kind of interrogation I had been undergoing.

"I've got this dumbass European out there," I said. "He's been interrogating us."

"Has he been threatening you?" they asked.

"Aw, he says he's going to beat the shit out of us. But we're not afraid, because we know he's an outsider and doesn't have any authority."

"Sit down," someone said. "We've got to talk to you."

The interrogator I thought was a European was actually a Cuban who was in Hanoi on a special project to break American POWs. The ten-man room was his pride and joy. In the last six months he had beaten the holy hell out of every one of them until they broke and did what he said. He was working on a group of eighteen Americans but never dealt with anybody else. I suppose we were sort of a test project.

"You mean you've been giving backtalk to Fidel?" my roommates said. That was what they called him. "He'll rip your throat out."

I started shaking. I was a basket case. I understood then what the Cuban meant when he told me he was going to do me a favor. He would let the others tell me about him, before he worked me over. I don't think it was much of a favor. I would have rather stayed ignorant.

My roommates had developed their own code of conduct based on the realities of prison life. "Give it your best shot under interrogation," they told me. "You're going to break. But we expect you to take some hits. Don't just go in and collapse." I spent the next few days memorizing the three hundred and fifty-six names of American POWs. That was all we knew. The idea was if you got sent to another camp, you passed on all the names you knew and added any new ones to your list, so if somebody got out he could carry the names back to the States. We memorized them in alphabetical order.

There was friendship and compassion in Hanoi. But it often came about in different ways than in normal life. At times you lived a cold, harsh existence. One of the first things someone told me when I moved into the ten-man room was, "For your own well-being, if you have any knowledge that is sacred, don't tell us. Keep it to yourself. Because we'll shove it up your ass." Since life was harsh, you became hard yourself, and some of the things that happened in Hanoi wouldn't make good telling.

When I was called in to see the Cuban, I was a different person from the one he had seen before. He knew that I knew, because he smiled at me. He was a big man, about six-two, large hands with blunt nails, receding black hair, age thirty-five to forty, a blue collar worker, definitely not an intellectual. I think he had been an auto mechanic in Cuba, because he knew everything about Chevys and Fords through the 1958 models but nothing about them after that. The Cuban presented himself as Mr. Know-It-All, Mr. Big Guy, Mr. Powerful. Three or four other Cubans were also in the camp. One, a girl, read propaganda on the Voice of Vietnam. Another, whom we called Pancho, showed up from time to time. But Fidel obviously was in charge. Why was he just dealing with eighteen of us? I've no idea why we were the ones picked for the experiment. I think he was there to show the Vietnamese how to bust somebody and keep them busted.

The guards looked up to Fidel. We got the feeling, though, that the higher Vietnamese authorities were not so sure about him. They were watching closely to see how his program worked. According to the Cuban, everything came down to what he called the matchbook and the ashtray. The matchbook stood for a progressive and the ashtray for a reactionary. "You've got to decide which one you are," he said. He

245

pushed the matchbook and the ashtray in front of me. "Pick one."

I made my choice. He looked at me with the kind of interest you gave a bug about to be squashed.

---

11 · *Marilyn Elkins*

I TOLD MY MOTHER about my decision to move to Paris and go to North Vietnam's embassy every day until I learned something about Frank. "I can sit here crying and feeling sorry for myself," I said. "Or I can go and try to find out something."

"Fine," Mom said. "You should do it then."

I was getting 80 percent of Frank's salary and money would be no problem. The State Department got nervous when they learned of my plans. An official asked me to meet him at the navy recruiter's office in Nashville. He warned me to be careful about any statements I might make in Paris. "Your comments could be picked up by the foreign press and misinterpreted," he said. I should also watch out for suspicious people. A travel agency made the reservations and I checked into a hotel. On my previous trip I'd met a South African named Desmond who was living in Paris, and I gave him a call after I arrived. "First thing we've got to do is get you out of that expensive hotel," Desmond said. He found me a smaller place that was pleasant and cheap, and then took me to lunch.

The next morning I called the U.S. embassy. A number of POW wives had visited Paris and there was a contact at the embassy who took care of them. I believe I was the only wife actually to move to Paris, and so I was assigned a casualty assistance officer like everybody had in the States, a U.S. Marine lieutenant colonel. Most of the military attachés are spies, and for all I know he might have been one too. But he was the best casualty assistance officer I had the whole time. He wore one of the sharpest crewcuts around and was all marine, but he had really kind eyes. He did his job well. In fact, the Americans at the Paris embassy were wonderful. They helped me get my first apartment.

246

I lived on the rue de Rennes near Montparnasse and later moved to 99 rue Monge, almost at the foot of Mouffetard, where they have that marvelous open air market. Paris felt freer than anyplace I'd ever been. I could walk for hours, or I could go into a café and sit down without anybody thinking I was there to be picked up. I didn't particularly like the people, though. They laughed at my French and wouldn't try to communicate. Of course my accent was horrible. I had spent a week in a Berlitz course before I left, which didn't help much. I was too emotional to respond. And I tried the Alliance Française for a while after I arrived.

I went to the North Vietnamese embassy each morning, sometimes with an interpreter, sometimes alone. I usually wore bluejeans and funny-looking walking shoes. In those days, I was always either in jeans or something silk and fancy, and didn't like much in between. I rang the doorbell. A Frenchwoman about forty-five, dressed in a black skirt and white blouse, came to the door. "*Qui est là?*" she asked. "*Qu'est ce que vous voulez?*"

"*Je veux vous demander des renseignements sur mon mari,*" I said.

She peeked out at me. "We can't give you any information," she said. "Go away." She closed the door.

I rang the doorbell again. She ignored me. A policeman who was guarding the building said, "I'm sorry, madame, but you'll have to move along." I started explaining about my husband. "*Oui, oui, madame. Je suis désolé.* But you must leave."

I left and returned the next morning. I got to know when foreign visitors were likely to be there, when it would be embarrassing to the North Vietnamese to have me standing outside demanding information about my husband, and I would time my visits to take place then. Occasionally I was allowed to enter the embassy and talk to a Vietnamese who was never identified by name. They changed routinely and they all said the same thing: "Oh, Madame, we are sorry. We have no information about your husband. Even if we did we couldn't give it to you, because then all the wives with husbands missing would come over here. We are a very poor country and we don't have an embassy big enough to take care of them. Go home and tell your president to stop the bombing. When he stops the war you will learn the answer."

"I have no control of the president," I said. "I just want to find out about my husband."

247

Sometimes the Vietnamese yelled at me. I just stood there. Then they changed their tone and said, "Madame, we're so sorry." Quite often it was the Frenchwoman who did that but who, next time, would be nice. "Would you please leave us alone, Madame Elkins?" they kept asking. "We told you we don't know where your husband is. We too have kinfolk who are dying. We know you are in pain. But you would better serve your husband to go home."

In a sense, I felt sorry for the Vietnamese. You couldn't really blame them for shooting down your husband's plane when he was dropping bombs on them. Nor could you blame them for not returning the prisoners of war until the war was over. Sometimes I ran into them outside at shops or cafés. I would go over and smile and say hello. They would lower their eyes. They must have thought I was crazy.

Other POW wives visited Paris and I took them to see the Vietnamese. Nobody was told anything. After nearly two months, though, the Vietnamese realized that I was there to stay. I was not going to give up easily. Kathy Sawyer of the Washington *Post* came over to write a series of articles on what I was trying to do. Kathy and I had become friends. I hoped that she and Desmond, the South African I'd met the year before, would like each other. We arranged to have dinner one Thursday night at Desmond's apartment on the rue du Cherche Midi. After we arrived, a guy I'd never met named Jean-Jacques showed up. He had a French father and an American mother. I realized that while I was trying to fix Desmond up with Kathy, he was trying to do the same for me with Jean-Jacques.

Jean-Jacques was handsome, but I found him pretentious and vain. He had just gotten back from Morocco and was raving about the joys of different kinds of hashish. I stayed and talked because Desmond and Kathy seemed to be getting along fine, and I wanted them to hit it off. Somehow Desmond ended up taking Kathy and me back to my place. I went to bed and left them up. Next morning I found Kathy in the other bed and Desmond sleeping on the couch. They hadn't hit it off in a romantic way. I was really hung over. I wasn't used to drinking and the night before they had poured me a lot of wine.

I dressed and went to the North Vietnamese embassy. I had no translator and was a little scared, not knowing whether my language would work with the hangover. They took me right in and sat me down. For the first time, they brought me a cup of tea. Then they told me.

"Madame, your husband is dead."

"Would you—would you put that in writing?"

"No. If we do that all the other wives will come over here."

"Can you give me any proof?"

"Believe us, Madame. He is dead. We are sorry. And now please leave us alone."

"Thank you for telling me."

I returned home and said to Kathy, "Let's go to Spain."

"Okay, let's," she said.

We left the same afternoon. We flew to Barcelona and went to Sitges and sat on the beach.

"He's really not there," I said. "I think they are telling me the truth."

12

THE *Oriskany* returned to Yankee Station from Hong Kong after New Year's Day, 1968. The ship was due to leave for San Diego in two weeks. Since bad weather was limiting attacks on North Vietnam, most of the danger seemed to be over. It came as a greater shock than usual, then, when Rich Minnich was shot down. It happened on January 4. He and J. P. O'Neill were flying MiG cover near Haiphong. J. P. saw two missiles and called for Rich to do a barrel roll. J. P. executed the evasive maneuver and then saw that Minnich's plane was burning. He radioed for him to head toward the ocean. Minnich replied that he didn't think he could but would try to make the mountains. His plane suddenly spun out of control and crashed. J. P. saw no parachute, heard no beeper.

Cal Swanson could not be sure, but he believed from what J. P. said that Rich Minnich was dead. He wrote Nell that night: "I don't want any false hopes raised that he survived. Play that part down. Survival is doubtful."

It was hard for a commanding officer to know how to treat a shoot-down in his casualty report. Jim Stockdale, when he was the *Oriskany's* air wing commander, saw one of his men go down and listed him as killed in action. Stockdale knew the pilot had been married only a few months and he believed it best that the pilot's young wife be given the bad news immediately so she could restart her life. Then Stockdale himself was shot down. One of the first POWs he met in Hanoi was the man he had reported as dead. Stockdale felt guilty, believing he might have ended the pilot's marriage.

Not all squadron commanders had wives as savvy as Nell, who could, with Cal's guidance, set the right tone in describing to a wife her downed husband's chances of survival; and most officers tended to err on the side of caution in writing casualty reports. Nobody wanted to confront a distraught wife to tell her they were 90 percent certain her husband was dead. There was always that 10 percent chance they were wrong. With no body, no eyewitness to his death, they thought it best to list the pilot as missing in action. The Pentagon then hedged its missing-in-action reports to the families, straddling the fence between advising futility and holding out hope. A wife or relative who knew little about what flying combat entailed naturally reached for the hope. After suffering so long in a state of agonized uncertainty, some of them, after the war was over, found it impossible to believe the truth that they should have been told by their relative's squadron mates many years before. Further complicating the problem was evidence that suggested Hanoi did not return all the POWs and probably held on to a few.

Cal and Nell believed in facing the matter squarely. Painful as it might be, Cal wanted Rich Minnich's wife, Gail, to have an accurate idea of what happened to her husband and to understand how narrow the possibility that he had survived. Such knowledge would not make her give up hope, but it would make her more receptive to facing reality. And, in fact, she eventually remarried.

THE APPROACHING END of combat revealed a difference between the air war and the ground war. In the South, a soldier who had survived was given ritualistic respect and protected as much as possible. A short-timer: the name was almost a medal in itself. Even officers stepped out of the way of combat in their final days whenever they could. They believed there was no reason to tempt fate. But the approaching end of combat only quickened the pulses of the pilots in Squadron 162. They wanted to get as many missions over the beach as they could. And they grew angry with Cal Swanson when they discovered that he was using his position to fly more than what they considered his fair share. Not many aviators could say they had flown two hundred missions, and Cal was determined to reach that magic number.

To get two hundred might compensate a little for missing the MiG. Try as he might, Swanson could not find another enemy plane to do battle with, to redeem himself. He made a minor mark another way, becoming the first pilot to knock out a train with an air-to-air missile. A train was a more difficult target than it looked. If four airplanes carrying six bombs apiece found, say, a thirty-car train, they would have to score direct hits with every bomb, a feat made even harder by the Vietnamese trick of disconnecting the cars and letting them spread apart when planes were spotted. Swanson aimed his missile at the locomotive's engine, and that was that. John Hellman did the same thing.

On January 12, 1968, the day the *Oriskany* left Yankee Station, an awards ceremony was held on the flight deck. The air wing, the ship's company, four admirals, and a CBS-TV news crew stood amid flags snapping in the breeze and listened to the *Oriskany*'s list of accomplishments. The ship's pilots had flown an unprecedented one hundred and eighty-one strikes in the high-threat area of North Vietnam that included Hanoi and Haiphong. They had participated in the first raids against key targets such as Haiphong's shipyard, the Cam Pha port, and the Phuc Yen MiG base. They were the first to drop a major bridge in the center of Haiphong. Butch Verich had been rescued for the second time, and Dick Wyman had downed a MiG. Not mentioned was that the *Oriskany* had sustained the highest losses of any carrier. Thirty-eight out of seventy planes were lost. Fifty-two were damaged. Nearly one out of every four combat pilots was killed or captured.

Cal Swanson had achieved his goal the day before. During the ceremonies he was inducted into the 200 Mission Club, which meant he received a certificate and had his picture taken. The playing of the national anthem gave him goose bumps. He was proud to be a naval aviator, to command Squadron 162, to have served in Vietnam. He could think of only a few things the squadron should have done better. The unnecessary aircraft losses bothered him. Jim Nunn's, of course. Even worse was the one by Jim Shaw, who came off a strike with a couple of hung bombs. Swanson ordered him to divert to Da Nang.

Somehow, in perfectly clear weather, he missed the city and had to ditch at sea. Swanson was furious. Cal also regretted the day at Phu Ly they cornered some trucks but had only two F-8s available and didn't get many hits. They should have had a field day, he thought. There was another time, at Cam Pha, when they missed the piers and dropped their bombs in the water. Still, everything considered, he believed that the squadron had done an outstanding job.

Dick Wyman too was proud to have finished two combat tours. But he was less satisfied than Swanson with their accomplishments and less convinced of the necessity for the war. He remembered one bridge, not Co Trai, they had been assigned as a target. Moated it, that's what they had done, Wyman recalled, dropped so many bombs that the craters formed a water-filled trench around the bridge. But they had not hit it.

Wyman did not even like to think about the most famous bridge of the war, the Dragon's Jaw at Thanh Hoa, which stood after three years of bombing, mocking both navy and air force pilots. The air force had tried everything, even sent a C-130 transport loaded with a five thousand–pound weapon resembling a pancake to try to take it out. No wreckage could be found of the C-130 after the attack. Then the navy took its turn. More than a thousand tons of bombs were dropped and eight airplanes were lost during nearly seven hundred sorties. The story grew that the earth was divided into two spheres; one side was hinged beneath the Atlantic, the other was clamped shut by the Thanh Hoa bridge. Better they hadn't been able to drop it, joked the pilots. The world might have snapped open, flinging man and dog into the sky. What made it worthwhile for Dick Wyman were the times after a strike when an attack pilot walked up to him and said, "That was a good job you did on the flak sites. You really zapped them." Wyman felt he could stand tall at the bar. He had done his part.

Their last night on Yankee Station the squadron learned that the ship's captain had informally given his permission for them to have parties in the ready rooms. Everyone knew what that meant. Things got a little lively, Cal told Nell. "Not a drunk like it would have been last year, but still mellow." He had to pull standby duty at midnight, so unlike several members of the squadron, he felt fine the next morning.

Casualties had been so heavy (Cal was the only one in the air wing to serve a full tour as both executive and commanding officer) that the navy was suffering a shortage of aircraft. The *Oriskany* was ordered to stop off at Cubi Point and transfer planes and equipment to the carrier arriving as her replacement on Yankee Station. The ship would then proceed to Tokyo, where the squadron would take a commercial flight home. A few hours before the *Oriskany* arrived in San Diego, Cal and the others would go back aboard and do a flyby as the ship docked, as part of the homecoming ceremonies.

As they sat in the Tokyo airport awaiting the Northwest Orient flight that would take them home, Swanson was paged and called to the telephone. A navy duty officer asked if he'd heard the news. "You might not be going home," he said. "The USS *Pueblo* has just been taken captive off North Korea. This may turn into a warlike situation. Everyone will be needed."

They began to sweat out the hour until their flight was announced. Moments before they were to board Cal was paged once more. They looked at each other, crestfallen. Swanson picked up the phone, expecting the worst. "Hi, Cal," said the voice of a friend. "Just calling to tell all of you goodbye, and to wish you the best of luck in the States."

They boarded with other passengers, most of them tourists returning home after visiting Japan. When the wheels lifted up there was an exhalation and then a cheer. Soon the tourists were nudging each other and pointing to the dozen men in uniform. "Look at that guy they call Black Mac," one said. "That's what the war is doing to our men. He has been driven crazy by his experiences."

They arrived in Seattle at six o'clock the next morning. John Hellman's parents, who lived nearby, were waiting with bottles of chilled champagne. They walked to a parking lot. Standing in the vast emptiness, they held their plastic cups to a brightening sky and toasted one another.

13

ON JANUARY 31, 1968, the *Oriskany* sailed into San Diego and was greeted by bands playing and flags waving. At the same moment, Vietnamese communists were blasting their way into the U.S. embassy compound in Saigon. It was the start of the Tet offensive. Nearly every major city in South Vietnam came under attack. Militarily, it was a defeat for the communists. They managed to hold only the city of Hue temporarily and suffered heavy losses. Psychologically, it was a victory for them. Tet had a demoralizing effect on the U.S. public. After months of hearing that the war finally was being won, Americans were stunned to see Viet Cong guerrillas inside their embassy grounds.

The Tet offensive appeared to confirm a secret report on the bombing prepared by forty-seven scholars and scientists and circulated among top government officials four weeks earlier. The Pentagon Papers called the report "probably the most categorical rejection of bombing as a tool of our policy in Southeast Asia to be made before or since by an official or semi-official group." Known as the "Jason study," it was written by a group of scientists first brought together in the summer of 1966, mainly at the instigation of Karl Kaysen and George Kistiakowsky of Harvard and Jerome Wiesner and Jerrold Zacharias of MIT. The first sentence of the Jason study declared that the bombing "has had no measurable effect on Hanoi's ability to mount and support military operations in the South."

This secret group of scientists and scholars, which proved to be a kind of Manhattan Project in reverse, had a signal influence on the thinking of Robert McNamara and his civilian aides. The Jason group's first report, completed several months after attacks on North Vietnam's gasoline and oil supplies in June 1966, bluntly stated that the bombing was ineffective and nurtured the secretary of defense's growing disillusionment. The Jason group recommended the creation of an electronic barrier between North and South Vietnam as an alternative to the bombing and a means of preventing infiltration, an idea that worked splendidly twenty years later when used by Morocco against guerrillas in the Sahara desert but became known as McNamara's folly in the heavily vegetated environment of Vietnam.

The Tet offensive, combined with the new Jason study and similar analyses reached independently by the Central Intelligence Agency, ended any lingering doubts among most of President Johnson's civilian advisers that the air war should be modified. The key players were thinking of limiting the bombing to the southern panhandle of North Vietnam below the twentieth parallel. The proposal had been floating around for more than six months. In the arcane workings of the bureaucracy, the clearest sign that a unanimity of opinion was being reached could be seen by the lack of further discussion of the option in official memoranda. The partial bombing halt proposal was not included in the report submitted by the group of officials headed by Clark Clifford, the newly appointed secretary of defense, who was charged with reassessing Vietnam policy in the wake of Tet. The Clifford group merely noted the split between the civilians and the military. The bombing limitation option had gained such support that it was obviously considered too important to be included in a formal memo as just another possible course of action but was something to be emphasized in person and in private to President Johnson, which reportedly was the way Clark Clifford handled the matter.

After the Stennis hearings in August 1967 failed to open up the air war as Admiral Grant Sharp had hoped, military leaders scaled back their expectations and focused on trying to loosen political control of the bombing in the Hanoi-Haiphong area. The Joint Chiefs still made pro forma requests to mine the Haiphong harbor. But in one of the last major arguments for a wider war before Tet they listed the elimination of the Haiphong and Hanoi prohibited areas as their first priority. The prohibited zones had been established in December 1966, after the first bombing of Hanoi, which was followed by the reporting of the New York *Times'* Harrison Salisbury describing the damage to civilian areas.

The Joint Chiefs reacted to Tet by recommending that the prohibited zones be reduced to three miles around Hanoi and to one and a half miles around Haiphong—in effect, to the cities proper. "A reduction in the control areas," the Joint Chiefs said, "would expose approximately 140 additional miles of primary road, rail and waterway lines of communication to armed reconnaissance, as well as hundreds of miles of secondary lines of communication, dependent upon NVN reactions and usage."

For anyone worried about civilian casualties, they added: "There have been repeated and reliable intelligence reports that indicate civilians not engaged in essential war supporting activities have been evacuated from the cities of Hanoi and Haiphong. Photographic intelligence, particularly of Haiphong, clearly shows that materials of war are stockpiled in all open storage areas and along the streets throughout almost one-half of the city. Rather than an area of urban living, the city has become an armed camp and a large logistics storage base."

It was too late. The minds of civilian officials in the Pentagon were already made up. All that was left was for them to construct a bureaucratic rationale for stepping down the air war. That was set forth in a memorandum prepared by the office of Assistant Secretary of Defense Paul Warnke. The memo was concerned with countering the Joint Chiefs' request to reduce the prohibited zones around Hanoi and Haiphong. But it did more.

The bombing had begun as a political ploy to threaten the North Vietnamese and was transformed ipso facto into a tactical weapon to stop infiltration. Now Warnke's memorandum returned the air war to its roots. Suggesting that the interdiction effort had failed, Warnke called the bombing in the Hanoi-Haiphong area "primarily a political tool." If the bombing was back to being a political matter, at least in the upper part of North Vietnam, it would be much easier for civilian officials to argue to stop it than if it were adjudged to be a military tool of crucial importance to American soldiers fighting in the South. Moreover, the weather was bad and strikes were limited around Hanoi and Haiphong. Even Secretary of State Dean Rusk, normally a hardliner, was won over to the point of view that the U.S. wouldn't be giving up much to call a partial bombing halt.

Like millions of Americans, Cal Swanson turned on his TV at 9:00 P.M., on Thursday, March 31, 1968, to watch President Johnson's address to the nation. Swanson was assigned to Pax River as assistant director for surface tests while awaiting his turn to command an air wing. He was in a test pilot role. He remembered how that had once seemed so exciting. After flying strikes off the pitching deck of an aircraft carrier, he found his job boring. He had to force himself to keep up his enthusiasm. Swanson settled down in front of the TV with a double martini, to which he added a long slice of kosher pickle.

Tonight, I renew the offer I made last August—to stop the bombardment of North Vietnam. We ask that talks begin promptly, that they be serious talks on the substance of peace. We assume that during those talks Hanoi will not take advantage of our restraint.

We are prepared to move immediately toward peace through negotiations.

So, tonight, in the hope that this action will lead to early talks, I am taking the first step to de-escalate the conflict. We are reducing—substantially reducing—the present level of hostilities.

And we are doing so unilaterally, and at once.

Tonight, I have ordered our aircraft and our naval vessels to make no attacks on North Vietnam, except in the area north of the Demilitarized Zone where the continuing enemy build-up directly threatens allied forward positions and where the movements of their troops and supplies are clearly related to that threat.

The area in which we are stopping our attacks includes almost 90 percent of North Vietnam's population, and most of its territory. Thus there will be no attacks around the principal populated areas, or in the food-producing areas of North Vietnam.

Even this very limited bombing of the North could come to an early end—if our restraint is matched by restraint in Hanoi. But I cannot in good conscience stop all bombing so long as to do so would immediately and directly endanger the lives of our men and our allies. Whether a complete bombing halt becomes possible in the future will be determined by events.

Cal Swanson was surprised by President Johnson's closing announcement. (*Accordingly, I shall not seek, and I will not accept, the nomination of my party for another term as your president.*) But he was not moved either way by the decision to call a partial bombing halt. At this time, Cal knew, there was only an average of four good days of bombing weather per month around Hanoi and Haiphong. He too believed the U.S. was not giving up much.

No one expected Hanoi to react favorably to the bombing halt. But three days later the North Vietnamese indicated they were ready to open direct contacts with the U.S., which could lead to a peace settlement. Then began a long public struggle over how and where the talks would be held.

No sensitive targets were located in the southern portion of North Vietnam, and U.S. military commanders were allowed, for the first time, to run the air war as they saw fit. For seven months, until the bombing was completely stopped on November 1, 1968, the full weight of the air war fell on the small panhandle region of North Vietnam. When American journalists were invited in 1985 to Vietnam for the tenth anniversary of Saigon's fall, they reported that they saw remarkably little bomb damage in the upper part of North Vietnam. Hanoi itself appeared little touched. But the sparsely populated panhandle area, they said, looked like moonscape.

As the 1968 presidential race between Richard Nixon and Hubert Humphrey went down to the wire, the question of a total bombing cessation became enmeshed in political intrigue. It was thought that a bombing halt might help elect Hubert Humphrey and the Democrats. Hanoi seemed ready to concede a point in the prenegotiation stage (agreeing to sit at the same table with Saigon government representatives), and a halt was called at the last moment before the election—which did help Humphrey, but not quite enough.

Richard Nixon was given aid on the bombing halt question by a short Harvard professor with blue eyes and pudgy hands. Henry Kissinger had occasionally advised the Johnson administration on Vietnam and had involved himself in secret attempts to get negotiations started. During the presidential campaign he played a double game, passing on to Nixon information about the bombing halt that he received in confidence from Johnson administration officials. Considering the manner in which Nixon and Kissinger were to run their own bombing policy in Indochina, it was not a totally inappropriate beginning for a partnership.

By the time of the bombing halt, Cal Swanson had all but lost interest in the war. He volunteered to return to Yankee Station as an air wing commander but was turned down because he already had put in two full tours. He was given the air wing on the *Forrestal*, which was heading to the Mediterranean, and his thoughts turned to the problems of Europe and the Middle East. He believed that the pilots of Squadron 162 had seen the last of Vietnam. For them, the war was over.

V

July 19, 1972

Attack on Co Trai

_1_

ON THE MORNING of July 19, 1972, the USS _Oriskany_ prepared for the first strike of the day on North Vietnam. John Hellman had not slept well and his hands shook as he drank a cup of coffee. Hellman was, he admitted to himself, a nervous wreck. He had never been in worse shape. It had started when he learned they were going to hit Co Trai.

Terry Dennison, shot down at Co Trai on July 19, 1966, was John Hellman's roommate. Dennison was an athlete, a golfer, and had a nice personality. Hellman remembered that Terry had been elated to be going on the strike and that he himself had been disappointed not to be picked instead. After Dennison was shot down, Hellman gathered his personal effects and sent them to Terry's wife, who was their next-door neighbor in San Diego.

Then Herb Hunter, July 19, 1967. Hellman and Hunter were close. Their families often dined together. Hunter's death, coming after Dennison's, hit Hellman's wife hard. Two of their best friends had been killed and she was fearful that her husband would be next. Barbara became extremely nervous. Nell and the other wives thought her actions were increasingly erratic. Hellman saw the problem developing but shut it out of his mind. He told his wife not to worry, nothing could happen to him.

That was the shield of a fighter pilot. Nothing could happen. He was invulnerable. Sure, Hellman was always scared on a mission. The hardest part for him came from takeoff till he reached North Vietnam's coast. He would be sweating, his stomach churning, everything drawing up to the center of his chest. But once he got over the beach everything eased off. He had a job to do and he did it.

Now that protective armor was gone. For the first time, he believed that something could happen to him. No. Something _was_ going to

261

happen at Co Trai. He could feel it. It wasn't just the coincidence of dates, everything taking place on July 19, two friends getting killed. He had always hated Co Trai, the very thought of it. Out of luck or answered prayers he had never flown against the bridge.

The idea that John Hellman should refuse to fly the mission was impossible for him to consider. He was a conscientious officer. He disliked anyone who shirked his duty and put a further burden on his comrades. Besides, he was now a squadron commander. What would the other men think of their leader refusing to fly because he had a premonition he might be killed? How Belly Bellinger would have laughed at that. Cal Swanson too never missed a strike. Hellman had not especially cared for Bellinger, and Swanson reminded him of a guy in a hurry to get somewhere. When Hellman took command of his own squadron, however, he discovered there were things a CO had to do for the benefit of the squadron that he might not personally like to do. He had come better to understand Bellinger and Swanson. And he knew he could not refuse to fly the mission against Co Trai.

A few minutes were left before the briefing began. Hellman was a Catholic and religious. He decided to go to church. He would spend the remaining time praying. That had helped before in bad times.

2

FOUR YEARS after the bombing halt, the *Oriskany* was back on Yankee Station to hit once again the small bridge that had been bombed so many times that the cycle had become like the planting and harvesting of rice in the nearby fields. The Americans bombed; the North Vietnamese repaired.

The air war had never really stopped. American squadrons did not pack up and go home after 1968. They continued to fly frequent reconnaissance missions over North Vietnam and shifted the weight of their interdiction effort to another target—the Ho Chi Minh Trail in Laos. North Vietnam's supply system was fed by Soviet ships through Haiphong and by China through railroad lines. The supplies were then moved to the southern panhandle city of Vinh and from there to the Laos border, where they entered the Ho Chi Minh Trail. Though only two hundred and ten miles in length, the Ho Chi Minh Trail was a spidery network in mountainous jungle, hard to see and hard to hit, estimated to contain more than three thousand road miles. The trail had been bombed since 1965, but after the 1968 bombing halt, U.S. flights tripled over Laos, from one hundred and fifty to four hundred and fifty sorties a day.

With Laos being hit hard, Richard Nixon decided to expand the bombing to the third country of Indochina, Cambodia. He blamed the move on the Viet Cong offensive in South Vietnam, which was launched scarcely a month after he was inaugurated. The Americans, under General Creighton Abrams, who replaced General William Westmoreland, were also on the offensive. Whether the communists were reacting to American activity on the battlefield or conducting their operations as part of a talk-and-fight strategy was not known, although it was likely a combination of the two.

At any rate, Nixon took the Viet Cong offensive as an attempt to humiliate him. He believed the communists were not giving him a chance to demonstrate how he intended to pursue the Paris peace talks. The offensive began, moreover, the day he was to leave for his first presidential trip to Europe, adding a further sting. Nixon's means of retaliating for the Viet Cong offensive were limited. He and his advisers considered it impossible to resume the bombing of North Vietnam. The bombing halt had raised hopes for peace, and Nixon had campaigned for president on the pledge to find a solution to the conflict. With this in mind, he decided to respond to the offensive by bombing North Vietnamese sanctuaries inside Cambodia, which had been off-limits to American planes since Cambodia was considered a neutral country. Nixon was supported by his national security adviser, Henry Kissinger, who would later say in his memoirs that a failure to react to Hanoi's offensive "could doom our hopes for negotiations; it could only be read by Hanoi as a sign of Nixon's helplessness in the face of domestic pressure. . . ."

The attacks on Cambodia were carried out not by dive-bombing tactical aircraft but by the huge strategic B-52s, which dropped large strings of bombs over a wide area. One B-52 could carry twenty-four tons of bombs, more than all the planes of Squadron 162 combined. To keep journalists from learning about the bombing, a plan of deception was devised. Twelve of the sixty B-52s sent on the first mission dropped their bombs on targets inside South Vietnam, while the others hit Cambodia.

Such was the beginning of the covert missions. B-52 crews were routinely briefed for attacks inside South Vietnam and after the briefing some crews were taken aside and told that while in the air they would receive special instructions from a ground radar station. The ground stations in effect took over flying the B-52s and with computers guided them to their targets in Cambodia. The secret missions were publicly announced as having taken place inside South Vietnam. The deception was not revealed until the Watergate investigations in 1973.

The bombing of Cambodia, which began March 18, 1969, was an example of how the air war was to be conducted for the next three years—with secrecy, duplicity, and official lying. This phase ended when Hanoi launched a conventional ground attack involving tanks and large-size infantry units at Eastertime 1972. Nixon dropped his covert policy and resumed the overt bombing of North Vietnam; and the *Oriskany* was brought back to attack the Co Trai bridge.

The bombing policies of the Johnson and Nixon administrations were different. While air war strategy was hammered out by a variety of officials during Johnson's time, in the Nixon administration it was determined almost entirely by two men, the president and his national security adviser. The role of one was easier to describe than the other.

Besides his proven brilliance, Henry Kissinger had a sense of humor, ostensibly but not really self-deprecating, which meshed perfectly with the humor of the Washington press corps, many of whose members, from small towns in the South and Midwest, tended to mock in the same way as the Jewish immigrant their feelings of displacement and success. Partly as a consequence, Kissinger enjoyed better press relations than probably any government official since John F. Kennedy. His supporters in the media considered him a masterful practitioner of realpolitik, and his detractors seemed unable to come up with a stronger condemnation than to charge him with deviousness, which was, it had to be admitted, mother's milk for many of history's most successful diplomats. Even a highly critical biography later written by Seymour Hersh, the reporter who gained fame for exposing the My Lai massacre, seemed to bounce off Kissinger like bombs off the Thanh Hoa bridge.

What could be said about Kissinger's role in formulating bombing policy was that he continued to play the double game that he had played during the presidential campaign—this time with the media, portraying himself as a moderating influence on Nixon, while in private giving the president advice that would have singed a hawk's feathers. He was caught out during the 1972 Christmas bombing, when the press started speculating that Kissinger had opposed Nixon's controversial decision to use B-52s against Hanoi. He would deny in his memoirs that he had told journalists he opposed the bombing, but would add: "I did little to dampen the speculation, partly in reaction to harassment of the previous week, partly out of a not very heroic desire to deflect the assault from my person. . . ."

Nixon's attitude about the bombing was more clear-cut and differed from that of Lyndon Johnson. Whereas Johnson had found military leaders too aggressive, Nixon found them overly cautious. In 1972, at a tape-recorded meeting at the White House, Nixon said, "The bastards have never been bombed like they're going to be bombed this time, but you've got to have weather."

"Is the weather still bad?" John Mitchell asked.

"Huh!" said Nixon. "It isn't bad. The air force isn't worth a—I mean, they won't fly." The contrast to Lyndon Johnson, who had vigorously opposed military attempts to hit targets like Fuck-Yen, as he called it, was considerable.

The limiting factor on Nixon, of course, was that Lyndon Johnson (unwisely, Nixon thought) had closed down the bombing of North Vietnam, and until 1972 he felt politically constrained from overtly restarting it. By early 1971, though, his policy had become one of more aggressive action. Pilots flying recon missions over North Vietnam were first told to flee if they were threatened by ground fire or missiles. Now they were given permission to hit flak sites when their electronic gear warned them that radar had locked on their planes. These and other strikes, the Pentagon said, were a matter of "protective reaction." Sixteen bombers, a small strike group, were often sent to escort one reconnaissance plane. They usually found something to react to.

A Pentagon official was quoted by the New York *Times* as explaining, "Look, these so-called reinforced protective reaction strikes amount to a limited, selective resumption of the bombing. But they are limited in time and in geographic area. But, as the president and Mr. Laird have said repeatedly, we don't intend to allow Hanoi to take advantage of our troop drawdown to threaten a rout against those who remain. Every once in a while we feel we have to remind Hanoi of this."

Nixon's policy of protective reaction, though prompted by the continuing North Vietnamese buildup, was, at best, less than straightforward, and soon led to outright duplicity by the air force. General John D. Lavelle, the Air Force commander in Saigon, secretly authorized at least twenty-eight bombing missions on restricted targets in North Vietnam in late 1971 and early '72. After some of the missions, he ordered pilots to report falsely that the raids were in response to enemy attacks. Lavelle was exposed by a sergeant who wrote his senator about the lying. Lavelle believed the Pentagon and White House were aware of and approved of what he was doing. Nonetheless, he was fired from his job, demoted one rank to lieutenant general, and forced to retire.

The protective reaction charade was dropped when the North Vietnamese launched their massive ground offensive on March 30, 1972. Hanoi's leaders later claimed that they were trying to grab as much countryside as they could in preparation for a negotiated settlement. Nixon and Kissinger had seen the offensive coming and had warned the Soviet Union and China that the U.S. would react strongly. Hanoi apparently believed that Nixon's hands were tied by the antiwar movement. North Vietnamese troops scored an early success, forcing the South Vietnamese to abandon fourteen bases below the Demilitarized Zone. A month later the provincial capital of Quang Tri fell. Near Saigon communist troops laid seige to An Loc. It looked as though the Saigon government was doomed.

Nixon's response, whatever his critics may have thought, had the distinction of being direct and unambivalent, something rare in decision-making for the Vietnam War. He ordered more B-52s to Southeast Asia, more aircraft carriers to Yankee Station, and sent other planes to Thailand and South Vietnam. General John Vogt, the new Air Force commander in Saigon, met with the president shortly after the offensive began. Nixon, said Vogt, "wanted somebody to use some imagination—like Patton," telling Vogt at one point, "I expect you to turn back the invasion and we will emerge with a victory. We will not abandon Vietnam."

"When I received the first proposals for bombing North Vietnam from the Pentagon during the first week of May," Nixon recorded later, "I hit the ceiling. Their proposals were a timid replay of the Johnson bombing campaign from 1965 through 1968. In a long memorandum to Kissinger, I wrote, 'I cannot emphasize too strongly that I have determined that we should go for broke.' I went on to say that we were in danger of doing too little too late and that it was better to err on the side of doing too much while we had maximum public support. 'I think we have had too much of a tendency to talk big and act little,' I wrote. 'This was certainly the weakness of the Johnson administration. To an extent it may have been our weakness where we have warned the enemy time and time again and then have acted in a rather mild way when the enemy has tested us. He has now gone over the brink *and so have we*. We have the power to destroy his war-making capacity. The only question is whether we have the *will* to use that power.' I made it clear that I had the will to take strong actions and was prepared to risk the consequences."

Besides ordering the bombing of North Vietnam, he also gave the long-sought permission to mine the Haiphong harbor.

"It was," Henry Kissinger said, "one of the finest hours of Nixon's Presidency."

By July 19, 1972, as the *Oriskany* prepared once again to hit the Co Trai bridge, Hanoi's offensive was coming to a halt. Air power had indisputably played a decisive role in stopping it. But it was air power used against communist troops in South Vietnam. What effect the bombing was having on North Vietnam was not yet clear.

3 · Chuck Rice

THE CUBAN INTERROGATOR wasn't ready to resort to physical torture. I was a challenge to his theories on how to break a prisoner. After I made the wrong symbolic choice between a progressive and a reactionary, he offered me a cigarette. I refused it.

"But you smoke in your room," he said.

"Yeah, just casually. Normally I smoke only cigars."

That was a mistake to say to a Cuban. He got up and walked out and returned with a Havana.

"Smoke that," he said.

"Thanks, but I don't really care to smoke it."

"I don't give a damn if you don't care to smoke it. Put it in your mouth and light it. Right now."

I did as he said. Lord, it was hard to appear as though I wasn't enjoying it. I sat there puffing away and feeling a little foolish. The cigar was about three-quarters gone when the Cuban said, "We're finished. We'll talk tomorrow. Tell the guard to take you to your room."

I wasn't about to walk out smoking a cigar. Everybody in the prison watched the door to the interrogation room. The word would be out that Chuck Rice was taking special favors from the Cuban. As I left, I slowly took the cigar out of my mouth and hid it in my sleeve.

"Charles . . ."

I turned around.

"Take the cigar out of your sleeve and put it in your mouth."

I put the cigar in my mouth and went to my room. I told everybody what had happened. They said, "Oh, he's done that before. Enjoy your cigar." I didn't light it again, but I chewed on it for a week.

Next time I was called in, I made the wrong choice again between a progressive and a reactionary.

"I'm really trying to reason with you," the Cuban said. He snapped his fingers and a guard brought in the ropes and irons. "I'll give you a couple of more minutes to think about it."

He left and returned with a small tape recorder. "This is your last chance. Do you want to talk?"

"I can't," I said.

He turned on the recorder. It was a tape of classical music. We listened for a while and then he said, "I'm going to give you one more day. Think about it."

This went on for a period of weeks. It was an effective technique. I got to the point where I wanted him to torture me, to get it over with. The anxiety of not knowing when it was going to happen was terrible. One of the other POWs advised me to agree to write a propaganda statement when the Cuban asked. "The reason I say this," he said, "is that Fidel has broken other guys and when he got them to the point they were ready to write, he told them they didn't have to, he just wanted to make sure they would do it."

I decided to try it. One day he brought me pencil and paper. "Fine," I said, "I'll write. What do you want me to say?"

"First write your name," he said.

I wrote *Charles D. Rice.*

"That's all I want you to do. Next time I tell you to write I don't want any shit out of you. Understand?"

That was the last I had to do for the Cuban. Ironically, he was losing his prestige with the North Vietnamese on account of his treatment of my former roommate, the Baron, who had begun to resist in almost a suicidal manner. Baron had been saying before the Cuban split us up that he had to do something to redeem himself. Duke and I said, "Right, we've got to get tough. But, hey, we're not traitors. Because if we are so is everybody else in this camp."

Baron, though, decided to quit bowing to the Vietnamese. You learned to bow when you were first captured. It was something they demanded. The Cuban took on the Baron as a special project. He intended to break him bad. His prestige as Comrade Big Brother was on the line. He tortured Baron and took him to a room we called the coal bin, on the other side of the camp. He tied him up the same way they did me my first day, and left him like that overnight. Another POW held in the next cell saw what happened.

Baron screamed all night, the POW said, until three in the morning. Then he stopped, didn't make a further sound. Next morning, when the Cuban and the Vietnamese came, they were visibly stunned by what they found. Baron looked seventy years old. His hair had turned white overnight. He had snapped his wire and become a doddering old man. "Now what the hell are we going to do with him?" was the Vietnamese attitude. "The Americans know he is alive and in our hands." The Cuban tried to persuade them Baron was faking. They kept him out of the public eye for a while, then transferred him to our room. The Cuban not long afterward left Hanoi and we never saw him again.

Before he snapped, Baron believed *The Manchurian Candidate* movie represented the way it really was. Now he became convinced that everybody in our room was a Russian dressed as an American, including me. "I don't know what you've done with Chuck Rice," he said to me. "But you are not him." We treated him very carefully and with a great deal of frustration for the next year and a half. He knew that holding the index and little fingers out like horns meant bullshit in POW code, so he walked around the camp like that, challenging the

269

Vietnamese. He stopped talking, except for the occasions when he spewed out grit and hatred. "You guys are Russians. But I'm not giving in."

Once a little pudgy, he dropped to below a hundred pounds. We organized two five-man teams, a morning and afternoon shift, to force him to eat. You had to suffocate him until he needed air and opened his mouth. You never stuck your hand in his mouth because you'd lose a finger. We had a teak stick and worked that in. One man fed him, another kept his mouth open with the stick, two held his arms, and someone sat on his legs. He was a ninety-pound weakling who got terribly strong at times. Feeding him took an hour and a half. He drooled. In the mornings he was wet, and we rotated our clothes to keep him dry. A guard walked in one time. We all bowed. Baron stood there. The guard took a piece of fan belt and slashed him across the face. A giant purple welt instantly appeared. Baron did not blink an eye. The guard was so shocked he backed out of the room and closed the door.

We begged the Vietnamese to send him home. We told them that everybody would understand that he had problems—the Americans would love them for showing humane treatment. Instead, they took him to the hospital and gave him shock treatments. He returned and you could see the marks of the electrodes on the side of his head. He would come back, his eyes blank, and lie in a fetal position. Finally they took him out of our room and put him in solitary. We kept up with him for a while but eventually lost track. He died sometime around Christmas 1970.

The Vietnamese were erratic in their medical treatment. Sometimes they gave no help to POWs; other times they were fairly competent. Some Americans, for example, who suffered broken legs at the time of their capture had pins put in and were taken care of, while others with the same problem were not. I turned out to be one of the lucky ones when I came down with appendicitis. I'd had severe cramps a couple of times. Then I got pains really bad one morning. The Vietnamese came in, blindfolded me, and took me to a place for X-rays. "We need to operate," they said. "But we won't do it without your permission."

The pain had subsided, but I thought if I turned them down and it really was appendicitis, they might not do anything the next time. "Okay, operate," I said.

Within fifteen minutes I was in an open air operating room, with water on the floor and a nurse running around barefoot. The surgeon was either Russian or French, a roundeye, and wouldn't talk to me. By early afternoon I was back in my room.

We settled down to prison life. Time passed slowly. We tried to do what we could to oppose the Vietnamese. There were a few POWs who were legendary and who gave us a benchmark to work for in our resistance—men like Jim Stockdale, Robbie Risner, Jeremiah Denton. It was hard not to be impressed by them and want to live up to their standards. Their attitude was, do the best you can. They were never holier than thou, never suggested that someone who failed after trying to resist did not measure up. We could always tell Jim Stockdale when we saw him across the camp, with his white hair, his stiff-legged walk like Captain Ahab. The guards hated him.

After two prisoners tried to escape in 1969, the Vietnamese cracked down. They were not real good sports about escape attempts and were determined to put a stop to our communication system. Nobody in our room was nailed, but they got guys on the other side of us. The senior ranking officer in one building was tortured so badly that he gave up his command for three months. Then he said, "I think I've got my moxie back. I'll take charge."

My room was broken up; there was a lot of reshuffling; and I ended up moving into a cell with two other prisoners, one of whom was Ev Alvarez, the first POW in Hanoi, who was shot down at the time of the 1964 Tonkin Gulf incident. One morning I jumped up and screamed, "Dammit, Nixon! Why don't you stop this war? I'm supposed to be out of the navy and getting on with my future, and here I sit in this godforsaken hole."

Ev Alvarez looked at me calmly. "Chuck, don't sweat it," he said. "After the first five years it's a piece of cake."

"Five years! I'll never be here that long. I can't take it for five years."

How wrong one can be.

Our attitude about the war began to change. You began to ask questions, to look at it from the Vietnamese standpoint as well as your own. When you realized how the peasants were suffering, you felt compassion for them. Still, you wanted America to win. A few prisoners began collaborating actively, but everybody else let the North Vietnamese know that we remained strongly against them. We sometimes told our interrogators, "We are going to win."

"No, it will be us," they said.

"We don't think so. Time will tell,"

"Yes. You may stay here many, many years."

"Maybe. But if you don't kill me, I'm going home some day to America, and you'll have to stay here for the rest of your life. So you'll lose anyway." They hated us when we said that.

For me, prison turned out to be an education, not only in learning about Vietnam but also in boosting my general knowledge. The POWs' average age was thirty-four. More than 80 percent had college diplomas, and many had advanced degrees. I was a young guy. I learned a lot.

By 1970 the pressure had eased a bit. The publicity campaign spearheaded by the POW families, along with the attention the Nixon administration gave the problem, achieved results in terms of the kind of treatment we were given. Then in November 1970 we heard gunfire and bombing and learned that the U.S. had made an abortive attempt to free POWs who were no longer held at the Son Tay camp. The next morning the Vietnamese were in a panic. Usually they never moved us in groups of more than ten to fifteen. But two days after Son Tay, trucks started pulling into our camp and they loaded us up like there was no tomorrow. Everybody from our camp and other outlying camps was moved to the Hanoi Hilton, where the Vietnamese figured they could turn back any rescue attempt.

For the first time we were all together. A formal military structure was secretly established. The ranking officer, an air force colonel, was our camp commander. Rules and regulations were laid down. The communication system began working so well that it became bureaucratic and you almost resented it. In the first years we loved to have contact with other Americans. Now we were together and the military mentality began to reassert itself. The leadership made rules that were discussed, changed, modified, remodified. We spent much of our day memorizing how we were supposed to handle this or that problem with the Vietnamese.

The next big upheaval came after Nixon restarted the bombing in 1972. The Vietnamese seemed to sense they were going to get hit by the B-52s. That was why they took two hundred prisoners and moved us, in May 1972, to a camp near the Chinese border, an area off-limits to American planes. I remained there until the ceasefire was signed. The Vietnamese were worried about keeping us alive. If the B-52s accidentally wiped out the other POWs at the Hanoi Hilton, they would still have us to use as bargaining chips in the negotiations.

---

4 · *Marilyn Elkins*

AFTER THE North Vietnamese told me Frank was dead, I started going out with other men. I deliberately chose people I would not consider a replacement for him. I did not consciously sit down and say I can go out with this one or another because I could never fall in love with him in quite the same way I fell in love with my husband. But I seemed driven to choose someone exactly the opposite of Frank in character. The first was an American nearly twenty years older than I who lived in Paris and owned bars and restaurants. He was a con artist but the most entertaining guy I've ever known, a good personality but not a good person. I suppose one could say I was compensating for all those years of not going out. I began to sleep till after noon, then rise to have a croissant and coffee, leave late for dinner, and dance at Régine's. I would wind up at a bar in Montparnasse called the Rosebud and return home about six in the morning.

He had a couple of children by a Frenchwoman he lived with off and on. She was his age, and I'm sure it was not pleasant for her. She followed him to my apartment building one day. When she saw me, she said, *"C'est dégueulasse!"* He told her to shut up, not to make a scene. We talked about marriage now and then, but I didn't want to have a permanent relationship with someone whose word of honor was meaningless.

I had been accepted at Emory law school the year before but didn't go. After staying out one night with him, I decided I couldn't take our relationship any longer, and I phoned Emory to ask if I could still come. The school said yes. Three days later I was on a plane for Atlanta. But I hated law school and soon dropped out. I had continued to write the man in Paris. I went back and we resumed our relationship.

I wanted to turn Frank's diary into a book. It was my way of seeing that something he wrote got published. Kathy Sawyer was in Paris and she took some of the diary back to the States. John Seigenthaler of the Nashville *Tennessean* arranged for her to show it to Evan Thomas, the editor of a publishing house in New York. The diary was published as *The Heart of a Man*. I took the title from Robert Frost's poem *Reluctance*. The reviews were pretty good, amazing in fact, considering that nobody wanted to read about the war at the time.

The ceasefire was signed. The prisoners of war returned home. My casualty assistance officer arranged for me to talk to several POWs who were in Paris. The wife of one of them had gotten remarried while he was gone. He thought it admirable that I hadn't. I think women who did that didn't have a very good marriage to start with or were so lonely they couldn't stand it. It didn't mean that I was nicer than they were. You do what your constitution and psychological makeup make you believe is right or wrong. Maybe I was a little more in love, I don't know. My mother never gave me any advice on what to do, but I'm sure my father would have been terribly disappointed if I had given up on Frank.

One of Frank's best friends from his hometown was an air force pilot shot down a few months after him. He survived as a POW and later came to visit me. He made me nervous because he was so gung ho. I kept trying to get him to see the war with a little more perspective. One afternoon, we'd been out really late the night before, and I said, "I'm going to take a nap and here's a copy of *The Best and the Brightest*. Why don't you look through it?"

He said, "No, I've got to get back to the base to practice flying bombing patterns." I was not as warm to him as he wanted me to be, and I've never spoken to him since.

With the war over and the POWs home, there was no reason for me to stay in Paris, and I wanted to break with the man I was seeing. "Okay, I'm thirty years old," I said. "I've been a widow long enough. I've been involved with someone who is a shady character at best, someone I would not marry, but I think I want to be married and maybe have children. Let's go back to the world where we know the language." I moved to San Francisco, where I became the West Coast marketing director for Helena Rubinstein.

The first person I got involved with in San Francisco was recently divorced and very bitter. Then I met someone who, it turned out, was seeing somebody else the whole two years I dated him. After that came a brief but intense relationship with a friend of Jack and Shirley, a pilot who had been in Vietnam and who had a bit of a drinking problem.

Sexually? I didn't have any problems there. I just seemed to find people who didn't want a commitment no matter what I did. If that happens repeatedly, of course, it may be what you are looking for instead of the other person's fault. In each instance after we broke up, the man came back and said, "I'm sorry, I made a mistake; would you reconsider?" And I said no. So I didn't suffer a personal rejection in that sense. I was simply involved in a series of dishonest relationships.

I decided to take four months off and travel and not date anybody. I went to the Galápagos, to Peru, climbed mountaintops, and did all sorts of strange things. Then I returned to San Francisco and got involved with an Englishman I saw for a full year and who asked me to marry him, only to find out he was already married and his wife was at home in Britain.

After that I dated somebody who had a son I loved. He had one of those California divorces where he kept the kid three days a week and the mom the rest of the time. We had been seeing each other for eight months. Then he decided to go by himself to a Club Méditerranée. I'd already been to the Club Med in Tahiti and the one in Bora-Bora. I didn't participate in what went on at the clubs but I knew it was widespread.

When he got back, I asked, "Did you?"

"I don't think I want to talk about it," he said.

Later he told me he had slept with somebody who lived in Chicago. "It didn't mean anything," he said. We were driving down the freeway. Suddenly I started screaming. This was not my normal reaction. I realized that I needed help. I asked him to take me to Letterman, a navy hospital. "I must be going crazy or something," I said. "I can't seem to stop crying."

"No," he said. "You'll be okay."

But I didn't stop and he took me to the hospital. By the time I was admitted to see the psychologist I was fairly under control. I felt better ten minutes after I talked to him. His name was Cliff. He was short and had a beard, not very attractive, but he had kind eyes. I decided to undergo therapy once a week. I had been intimately involved with people who were unacceptable to me. It had become a pattern and was something I knew I had to face. Another thing, I found I had a hard time speaking about Frank using the past tense. I'd say, "My husband, he's . . ." or, "Frank's birthday is . . ." Even though I was aware of the problem, I still did it subconsciously.

Cliff was transferred and replaced by a psychiatrist. I saw him for a year, but I've blocked his name because I didn't like him. He was younger than I, seemed to be naive and to operate strictly from book knowledge and was sexist without being able to see it. Still, the therapy sessions helped. What works is what you hear yourself saying aloud the things you never thought about before.

I continued to see the man who had taken me to the hospital. I admired him very much for the love and care he gave his son. Then came a time when we decided to stop seeing each other. I was going to Mexico over Christmas. He called and said that he'd made a mistake and that he wanted me to spend the holidays with him. I told him I would think about our relationship while I was in Mexico.

When I returned to San Francisco, I called and learned that he was in Hawaii with an ex-girlfriend. I did something I had never done before. Frank once told me that he was involved with a woman who obviously didn't care about him and he decided to cure himself of the relationship by making such a fool out of himself, doing something so embarrassing, that he could never have anything to do with her again. So I wrote this guy all sorts of nasty letters. I phoned and left messages all over town while he was in Hawaii. Just harassed him to death. Oh yeah, I felt rejected. I knew he would come back and want to see me again—that's the way it worked. I'll be as theatrical as possible, I thought, the world's worst bitch, and I'll never have to worry about being treated this way again.

It basically worked. I got in touch with him recently. Enough time had passed and I wanted to see how he was.

"Have you gotten married since we last saw each other?" he asked.

"No, have you?"

"Yes, we just filed for a divorce yesterday."

I was getting tired of California. I dated another guy who had been through *est*, the psyche training program. "If you go through *est* we'll get married," he said. "But you've got to do it."

"Ugh, I can't," I said.

I knew it was time to leave. I started looking around. I wanted a career, either in writing or teaching. I found a job teaching English at a New Orleans high school for the academically gifted and moved there.

TO SAY I was psychologically damaged by my experiences and probably will never get married again would be an overstatement. But it would also be lying to say I wasn't affected. The truth is somewhere in between.

I feel sorry for some of the Vietnam veterans. They have had a rough deal. I cannot say I have. I could not live on my monthly checks from the government, but neither could I teach school and travel and live the way I like without them. I am happier with my life than ever in terms of the things I do. Besides teaching wonderful kids, one of every three of them a National Merit finalist, I also coach the debate team.

The Vietnam era was a crazy time. A bunch of us, wives of pilots who were shot down, got together once and sat around exchanging stories. Everybody had to tell the craziest thing she did during that period. "I could have sworn my husband was in our bedroom closet talking to me," one wife said. "It went on a month. I couldn't tell anybody he was there, because I was afraid they might come and take him away."

Another wife told about going to a spiritualist to try to find out about her missing husband. The medium went into a trance and started mumbling, "Yes, I see your husband. He is . . . he's . . ." She was getting excited. Then he put his hand on her thigh. That was when she realized she was going slightly crazy. She ran out. "The next day I went to see a shrink," she said, "and I've been better ever since." Her husband didn't come back, and she remarried.

I did not do anything like that. But my mother tells me now that she couldn't get me to leave the house. I was afraid the phone might ring. I expected to see Frank come tap dancing out of the jungle at any moment.

My mother-in-law has never recovered. She still thinks Frank is alive. She doesn't say that, but I know she does. She does lots of memorial things, gives songbooks to the church and a scholarship or award each year in his name.

I don't know if I have totally accepted the fact of his death. I guess I have. I say I have. I really don't know. I held a memorial service after his status was changed by the navy in 1977 from missing to killed in action. In a final touch, the Pentagon sent me the telegram informing me of the change on October 31, so that Halloween is now officially Frank's date of death for all the forms that must be filled out.

It's much more difficult, I think, when you don't know for sure somebody is dead. You see no body. No casket. You have no feeling of finality. You can't even talk about it right. You get mad at yourself for not being braver about it. And you get mad for being so brave. If you start dating somebody else, you are angry for having the desire to continue living. By the time it is decided that your husband is dead, it's too late to mourn, to shut yourself up and cry, which is probably what you need to do. You have missed the time. It doesn't fit anymore. It's not something you get well from easily. And it hurts, a lot.

5

JOHN HELLMAN finished praying. He could feel the ship turning into the wind. He still felt shaky, but praying had given him the courage to face the Co Trai strike. It was important that his men not see how nervous he was. He wondered how many times since 1965 the *Oriskany* had struck the small bridge. As if in answer, the carrier suddenly sighed, riding a trough in a choppy sea. The *Oriskany* was on her seventh combat tour and showing the fatigue of battle. During a night underway replenishment, the carrier had bumped into the ammunition ship USS *Nitro* and lost an elevator. But the ship continued flight operations, as if determined to see the war through.

The Co Trai bridge had taken on a greater importance than ever because of Nixon's decision to mine North Vietnam's harbors. On May 8, 1972, squadrons from three carriers sowed mine fields in Haiphong, Hon Gai, and Cam Pha in the north, and Thanh Hoa, Vinh, Quang Khe and Dong Hoi in the south. Two weeks later the operation was judged a success. Twenty-seven foreign ships were caught at Haiphong and stuck there, since the North Vietnamese made no attempt to clear the mines. After all the warnings by Johnson administration officials over the years about a strong Soviet reaction, none was forthcoming.

"What happened was that all traffic into Vietnam, except across the Chinese border, stopped," said Vice Admiral Wiliam P. Mack, the Seventh Fleet commander. "Within ten days there was not a missile or shell being fired at us from the beach. The North Vietnamese ran out of ammunition, just as we always said they would."

It was only temporary. The flow of supplies was drastically reduced. North Vietnam's logistics system came under heavy strain. But as the Central Intelligence Agency had predicted, the mining did not dry up supplies but simply caused the North Vietnamese to rearrange their lines of communication. Ships were diverted to Chinese ports and from there supplies were moved across the border by rail or truck. An oil pipeline was constructed from China to Hanoi.

With the heavy pressure imposed by Nixon's strategy, it was imperative that the North Vietnamese keep transit points like Co Trai open. They had added more missile sites to the area, bringing the number of SAM installations in the country to three hundred. Many of their antiaircraft guns were now equipped with sophisticated radar. New MiG-21s were received, and North Vietnamese pilots began launching surprise attacks on American strike groups. In June and July 1972, the Americans lost a plane for every one they shot down.

John Hellman and his squadron were assigned to knock out the flak sites around the bridge. They were ordered to carry the same kind of antipersonnel weapons they had used five years before, called CBUs or cluster bombs. The standard five hundred–pound bomb was not very effective against gun emplacements. It made a crater thirty feet in diameter and fifteen feet deep and sent shrapnel over a zone two hundred feet wide. But bomb shelters made of sandbags or even bamboo could protect gunners from all but a direct hit.

The CBU was another matter. One bomb contained about six hundred bomblets the size of tennis balls, each of which had a two-ounce charge of explosive and three hundred shotgunlike pellets. Compressed gas blew the casing of the cluster bomb open at five hundred feet above the ground, and the six hundred bomblets, containing a total of one hundred and eighty thousand projectiles, exploded on impact, covering a wide area. Yet the CBU was not as deadly as it sounded, nor quite the horror weapon critics made it out to be, not when used against North Vietnamese gunners. They countered the bomblets by building beehive defenses, constructing iron works around an antiaircraft gun, leaving only the barrel sticking out. A CBU bomblet rolled off the iron to explode harmlessly. The gunners did not bother to duck until they saw the puff of gas as the casing of the main bomb popped open to release the bomblets.

The only new thing on Yankee Station was the laser-guided bomb. A laser sensor was inserted in the nose of a bomb, enabling it to guide itself to a target illuminated by low power laser energy. The illumination was handled by attaching a pod beneath an aircraft containing an optical viewer and a laser transmitter. The system was used in two-man planes. The backseat operator located the target and illuminated it with his laser equipment. The laser bomb represented a quantum jump in accuracy and spelled the beginning of the end for the clumsy gravity bomb, used since World War One, which had killed countless numbers of unintended victims. The laser-guided bomb also put an end to American frustration at not being able to drop the Dragon's Jaw at Thanh Hoa. Seven years after the air war began, fourteen air force planes carrying twenty-four laser bombs and other conventional bombs were sent to hit the bridge. The attack was successful. Finally, the Dragon's Jaw was put out of commission—temporarily, at least.

John Hellman didn't know if the strike group would use laser bombs against the Co Trai bridge. Probably not. The new bombs, still in short supply, were used selectively. All Hellman knew was that he would be facing the deadly eighty-five-mm flak guns around the bridge. The six to eight guns in an eighty-five-mm site had firing sequences electronically controlled. One gun fired for a second and a half—*rruup!*—then a brief pause and another gun went *rruup!* The North Vietnamese knew the angle of attack the Americans would have to use to hit the bridge. All their fire would be concentrated in a cone of exploding shrapnel. After seven years, they could do it blindfolded.

John Hellman walked to strike operations and took a seat removed from the others. He looked around him. The pilots were smiling and bantering. Nobody seemed to feel the way he did, or if so, they concealed it well. No, he thought, most of them had not been on Yankee Station in 1966 and 1967. They did not understand what Co Trai meant. They'd not lost two close friends there.

The briefing started. John Hellman was listening but not really. Suddenly he realized the other pilots were getting up to leave. He wondered why. Then the words of the briefer penetrated his daze: "Gentlemen, the Co Trai strike has been canceled due to bad weather."

6

BOB PUNCHES was flying MiG cover on December 18, 1972. It was his job to protect the rear area of the B-52 bombers that were attacking Hanoi and Haiphong in what was to become known as the Christmas bombing. Punches, who had been John Hellman's roommate on the *Oriskany* in '67, was now flying off the USS *Ranger*. He had liked Hellman, whom he considered a serious Catholic and an overall good guy, but he had not been sorry to see, as he said, "some of the old party guys leave." His next roommate on the *Oriskany* had been as religious as himself and they had put a book rack outside their room containing tracts and Bibles. The complexion of the squadron had changed for the better and became more subdued, he thought, after Black Mac and Dick Wyman moved on to other assignments.

After he finished his tour on the *Oriskany*, Punches studied political science in graduate school. His major was Southeast Asian history. Frankly, he conceded, he was not terribly interested in the subject. He wanted to see the war end—that was his main concern. Today it looked as though he might get his wish. He could see the devastating effect the B-52s were having on Hanoi and Haiphong. "This is it," he said, watching the B-52s. "No way they can survive that bombardment. They'll have to capitulate now."

That was what Richard Nixon and Henry Kissinger were counting on. Nixon had launched this final air assault, the heaviest of the war, in an attempt to conclude the conflict and bring the POWs home before an angry Congress returned to Washington in January and forced its end by cutting off funding for the war. The Christmas bombing, which was provoking outrage at home and abroad, had come about after a peace agreement was all but signed in October and then torn up amid charges of duplicity and treachery by both sides.

Restarting the bombing in April 1972, as Nixon had done, played an important role in bringing Hanoi to negotiate the October agreement. The use of air power, especially in the South, stopped the North Vietnamese grab for territory. The Saigon government recaptured Quang Tri, and the battle of An Loc was concluded. These events, combined with domestic antiwar pressure on Nixon in an election year, caused Henry Kissinger and Le Duc Tho to intensify their secret peace negotiations in the summer of 1972.

With the peace agreement seemingly locked up and scheduled to be signed eight days later, Nixon stopped the bombing of North Vietnam on October 23, except in the southern panhandle region. The North Vietnamese then tried to steal a march on Washington, early October 26, by broadcasting a summary of the agreement, giving certain clauses that purposefully had been left vague the most favorable interpretation to themselves and revealing an account of the secret talks in Paris.

Nixon and Kissinger had negotiated the accords without consulting the Saigon government headed by Nguyen Van Thieu. The week before, Kissinger flew to Saigon to brief Thieu and his advisers and was confronted with their displeasure. After hearing the North Vietnamese broadcast, Thieu was outraged, believing that the Americans had sold out South Vietnam in order to get their POWs back. He told Washington he wouldn't go along with the deal. Nixon was not ready to use muscle on Saigon to force the issue and risk getting into a public fight with his ally a week before the presidential election. A last-minute attempt had to be made to accommodate Saigon's reservations about the peace agreement and to assure the South Vietnamese that the U.S. was not leaving them in the lurch to get out of the war.

Henry Kissinger held a news conference on October 26, after Hanoi's broadcast. He was trying, he would say in his memoirs, to accomplish two things: "One was to reassure Hanoi that we would stand by the basic agreement, while leaving open the possibility of raising Saigon's suggested changes. The second was to convey to Saigon that we were determined to proceed on our course." Kissinger told the assembled journalists and the world, "Peace is at hand." As he could not have been unaware, his misleading statement gave a coup de grace to the already crumpling presidential campaign of George McGovern, the Democratic candidate who was running on a pledge to end the war.

Though Kissinger's statement helped win the election for the Republicans, or at least to increase their sizable margin of victory, Nixon later said that it boxed him into "a bit of a corner." The American public believed the war was over and felt deceived when it became clear after the election that such was not the case. The North Vietnamese, for their part, realized how anxious Washington was to conclude the war and stiffened their resistance to accepting any changes in the October agreement to accommodate Saigon. They could read as well as Nixon the growing sentiment in Congress for cutting off the funding for the war. Once again, they believed, time was on their side.

Nixon and Kissinger blamed the breakdown of the peace process on Hanoi. The North Vietnamese were indeed guilty of duplicity by unilaterally broadcasting their version of the agreement, a tactic designed to stir up trouble in Saigon by rubbing Nguyen Van Thieu's nose in the accords as an accomplished fact. But Nixon and Kissinger too were guilty of bad faith in trying to reopen the negotiations to mollify Saigon after a date for signing the agreement had been set.

By the end of November, Nixon had reached a decision on how he would handle the problem. The October agreement called for the Saigon government to share power with the Viet Cong. Nixon decided to assure Thieu that regardless of what the accords said, he would continue to consider him the sovereign head of South Vietnam. Thieu seemed unlikely to concede the point, anyway. He would also promise him massive supplies and assure him that American bombers would react if the North Vietnamese launched an offensive. Meanwhile, he would make it clear to the North Vietnamese that he would react strongly if they continued to resist modifying certain aspects of the October agreement.

Neither Saigon nor Hanoi gave in. Thieu wanted, at rock bottom, an assurance of his sovereignty written into the accords. The North Vietnamese refused to accept any changes and began to retract concessions already made. On December 6, 1972, as the impasse grew, Kissinger cabled Nixon from Paris two possible options. They could, he said, make a minimum demand on the North Vietnamese, something less than what Thieu wanted, and thus risk a public break with Saigon if it was accepted. Or they could provoke the North Vietnamese into breaking off the talks by making unacceptable demands and then resume the bombing until Hanoi agreed to return the POWs in exchange for a U.S. withdrawal from South Vietnam.

Nixon declined to follow either course. He told Kissinger to keep working toward a compromise. But his patience was wearing thin. The media was hammering at the belief that the October agreement had been killed by Saigon and Nixon was caving in to Thieu. Kissinger remained in Paris until December 14, but the North Vietnamese in the form of Le Duc Tho continued to stall, and the talks were broken off.

It was then that Nixon decided to unleash the giant B-52 bombers. He said that he told Admiral Thomas Moorer, chairman of the Joint Chiefs: "I don't want any more of this crap about the fact that we couldn't hit this target or that one. This is your chance to use military power effectively to win this war, and if you don't, I'll consider you responsible."

His decision represented the coincidence of two factors. Nixon wanted to give Hanoi a hard knock and he had grown partial to the B-52s, ordering their use against the upper part of North Vietnam when he restarted the bombing in April 1972, something Lyndon Johnson had never done. But even if Nixon had been squeamish about using the bombers, weather conditions would have dictated his choice of aircraft. The B-52 was the best all-weather bomber available, and during the eleven-day Christmas bombing (a misnomer, since no bombs were dropped on Christmas day) there was only one twelve-hour break in the monsoon weather that permitted the concentrated use of tactical bombers like those on the *Oriskany*.

Even the B-52s had problems with the bad weather. The bomber was designed to carry nuclear weapons, where it made little difference if the bombs did not land exactly on the aiming point. General John Vogt concluded that it was impossible to strike a target with an accuracy of under five hundred feet when conventional bombs were used in B-52s. Efforts were made to minimize civilian casualties. Only legitimate military targets were authorized and laser-guided bombs were used by tactical aircraft when the weather permitted. The White House refused to allow a B-52 attack on a SAM assembly plant in the middle of Hanoi that was producing missiles overnight to knock down the bombers, fearing it might cause large numbers of civilian casualties.

Inevitably, though, civilians were killed, perhaps as many as sixteen hundred. The North Vietnamese, sensing the attacks were coming, had evacuated their children from Hanoi two weeks earlier, and once again their bomb shelters served them well.

How many civilians were killed in North Vietnam during the entire air war was impossible to pinpoint. But extrapolating from figures made public by Hanoi, it seemed likely that the total was somewhere around five thousand, including the Christmas bombing—not a figure Americans could take pride in, but hardly the definition of genocide, which was a word frequently used by antiwar opponents. (More than five hundred thousand civilians were killed in air raids on Japan in World War Two.) That the number wasn't greater was due partly to the ingenuity and resilience of the North Vietnamese, who, after several decades of near continuous warfare, were experts at dodging one kind of shrapnel or other. It was also due to the restraint shown by the Americans, who refused to order the bombing of North Vietnam's dikes, for example, which would have crippled Hanoi's war effort but resulted in thousands of civilians killed by the flooding.

Still, the Christmas bombing was heavy enough. Day and night attacks took place against power plants, broadcast stations, railroads and yards, port and storage facilities, and airfields. Tactical fighters were used during the day; B-52s, along with F-111s, at night. Smaller planes led the big bombers to Hanoi, dropping chaff to confuse the radar. Electronic aircraft orbited off the coast trying to jam missile sites.

But despite the electronic warfare, the B-52s proved vulnerable. They were too big and awkward to attempt an evasive maneuver like a barrel roll to avoid the missiles. The missile radars were jammed, but the North Vietnamese brought down fifteen B-52s by visual sighting. They fired 1,242 Sams in a machine-gunlike barrage. Another twelve air force and six navy planes were lost.

With its heavy aircraft losses and press reports of massive civilian casualties, the Christmas bombing stirred an angry public reaction unequalled since the 1970 Cambodia invasion. Nixon came under tremendous pressure to stop the attacks. The day after the bombing began, his press secretary told reporters that the raids would "continue until such time as a settlement is announced." Several days later, the administration secretly began backtracking. Kissinger cabled Hanoi that Washington was ready to stop the bombing and reopen the negotiations on the basis of the October agreement, which represented no gain for the U.S.

Nixon and Kissinger decided to push aside Nguyen Van Thieu and his objections to the agreement. Nixon was particularly irritated when Thieu leaked word to reporters that Washington tried to force an ultimatum on him and he had refused. But, in reality, Thieu and the South Vietnamese were given a take-it-or-leave-it choice, which Nixon sugarcoated with secret assurances that were worthless in the long run. The bombing was stopped on December 29. The talks were restarted in Paris on January 8. The ceasefire came three weeks later, on January 27, 1973.

Did the Christmas bombing, as Nixon and Kissinger claimed, cause the North Vietnamese to capitulate? Examined from the most favorable angle, it might be said that the bombing ended whatever thoughts Hanoi may have had about stalling to see if the U.S. Congress, scheduled to reconvene on January 2, 1973, would make it easier for them by cutting off spending for the war. The possibility of congressional action, which worried Nixon, was strong, as demonstrated by the resolution that the Senate and House Democratic caucus passed the first week of January to cut off funds as soon as the return of the POWs had been arranged. Admiral Thomas Moorer called the Christmas bombing a catalyst in getting the negotiations restarted. That was probably the best that could be said. Certainly the bombing did not cause a capitulation in the sense that Washington won new concessions. The North Vietnamese essentially wound up with the same agreement they had been ready to sign in October, plus a secret commitment from Nixon, never carried out, to pay them billions of dollars in war reparations. The tough-talking Nixon, under heavy public pressure and the threat of congressional action, suffered, it appeared, a loss of nerve and stopped the Christmas bombing before he had intended.

Ultimately, then, air power had failed the test every time it was used to achieve limited political aims. From McNamara's "credible threat" to Nixon's "the-bastards-have-never-been-bombed-like-they're-going-to-be-bombed-this-time," the results had been abysmal and the cost high: nine hundred and twenty-eight planes lost over North Vietnam. On the other hand, air power had proved its worth on numerous occasions when used in the traditional military sense. Air power had prevented the U.S. Marine base at Khe Sanh from being overrun in 1968 and had helped stop Hanoi's 1972 conventional offensive. Saigon's collapse in 1975, in the face of an offensive of the type turned back in 1972, came not coincidentally after American planes were withdrawn from Indochina.

A DUBIOUS ENDING or not, Bob Punches was glad to see the ceasefire signed. He had often prayed for members of Squadron 162, and he continued to pray that Chuck Rice would make it home safely. After his ship docked at Cubi Point, Punches asked for permission to go to Clark Air Base, to greet the first prisoners of war to return. He stood on the ramp and watched the C-141s land and discharge their dazed but happy cargo.

The POWs had greeted the end of the war in muted fashion. After the North Vietnamese made the announcement, there was no cheering, just anxiety that something might go wrong at the last moment. The shouts of joy came when the plane was wheels-up. Chuck Rice was stunned to see the crowds and the placards with his name on them, welcoming him home. He felt a little guilty. He was no hero, he knew. The soldiers who went through hell in the South would never get that kind of reception. Still, he was grateful.

It was over.

7 · *Dick Wyman*

HINDSIGHT SAYS Vietnam wasn't worth it. Yet look at Southeast Asia today and you see that a lot of things we came to think of as false actually turned out to be true. The domino theory worked in Indochina. The warlike communists proved not to be peace-loving nationalists but warlike communists. The port of Cam Ranh Bay, once used by the U.S. Navy, now plays a key role in the Soviet Union's increasing show of force in the Pacific. No bloodbath occurred, but there was a drownbath, as countless thousands of men, women, and children died in the South China Sea trying to escape a system they found intolerable. Concentration camps, politely called reeducation camps, exist a decade after the fall of Saigon. And whatever happened to the National Liberation Front, once thought by some to be the true, freedom-loving representative of the people? "Ho Ho Ho Chi Minh. The NLF is going to win." Well, they did. Great.

I believe it's fair to say that we did not really go in to win, especially so far as the air war was concerned. The government tried to persuade the public that we were going to have an air war but were not going to hurt anybody. And that was dishonest. If you make the terrible decision to go to war, you must be willing to tell people the truth—that war is a nasty, mean, shitty business. Unfortunately, we lost, so nobody wants to talk about it. But there's a lesson to be learned. You either do it or you don't. And if you do, you go to win, pure and simple. You don't send intellectualized threats or signals to your enemy to try to persuade him to change his ways. He'll be kicking your ass in the meantime.

Everything about the war was screwed up. The last straw for some of us came when the POWs were treated as heroes. There were a number of exceptions like Jim Stockdale, men who deserved it in every way. But a sizable portion of the POWs were fuckups. They got shot down either because of their fear or out of stupidity. They were simply piss-poor pilots. Then they returned home to cheers and were promoted over the heads of everybody else and given their choice of duty assignments. If you had been on Yankee Station beating your brains out every day, you were forgotten. But of course you couldn't complain out loud, because it would sound like sour grapes. I lay awake more than a few nights, though, and whispered, "Hey, wait a minute. What the shit is going on?"

Still, Vietnam gave me a tremendous education in human response. In that respect I think I came out the winner. I learned more about people in a short time than I would've learned in ten or twenty years. Life took on a different meaning. I began to appreciate things I had taken for granted. A sunny day in the countryside gave me a thrill I'd never experienced, just the joy of living. I was at peace with myself. I had confidence in who I was and what I could do.

I was going to play golf one day and my wife Arydce said, "Do you realize you have a family, Dick? You don't spend much time with us. But we exist."

I started paying attention.

It was hard to let go of the fighter pilot image. I screened early and was given command of an F-4 squadron on the USS *Independence*. I loved to get a guy who was a weak aviator and help build his confidence and see him improve and take off. I realized that you probably needed one aspect of the image. Night flying on a carrier is a killer. It's so goddamn small down there and the element of fear comes in and it's just a ballbuster. You needed to think you were something special, a little better than the rest—that kept a guy going.

But I began to disagree with the part that tacitly said you couldn't be a good fighter pilot unless you went out and drank and raised hell. When I got my squadron, I promoted the idea that if a pilot did not want to party or attend happy hour, that was fine. Nobody would be judged on the basis of his social inclinations.

Other things began to change in my thinking. For years I thought nothing could happen to me. Then the awareness started creeping in that a guy could kill himself. I worked harder on my flying while still trying to appear nonchalant about it. If my shipboard career hadn't ended when it did, I would have probably experienced problems in controlling my fear. What happened, I suppose, was that I grew older and more mature. For the first time, I recognized my family as a unit and how valuable it was to me. My two sons were getting to an age where we could do things together. One weekend we went on a fishing trip and had a great time. Then, just as we were about to return home, I was climbing a river bank, and I felt a crushing pain in my chest. I couldn't get my breath. I eased over to a tree and leaned against it.

When we got home, Ardyce asked, "What's wrong, Dick?"

"I don't know," I said. "I've got a pain right here. Probably job stress."

"Let's go to the hospital."

"No, it's better now."

I did not want to admit what had happened. I put it off and went to the hospital the next morning. Ardyce was right. I'd had a goddamn heart attack.

A heart attack! And I was forty-one years old. The left ventricle was virtually blocked. I was put on the medically disabled list. The doctors are waiting to do a bypass, because I'm young for this sort of thing. Another blockage could occur if the operation is done too early. I take medicine but I'm functioning fine. I can't play racketball or tennis, which I loved, and I'm not supposed to drink beer, which I decided was asking too much of a guy. Aviators normally suffer more stress and have a shorter life span than many professionals. Add two combat tours to that and you've got a potential problem.

"You are like an old Indian pony," one of my doctors told me. "You have been run hard and put to bed wet."

That could be said about a lot of us who served in Vietnam.

Epilogue

DICK WYMAN and I settled down on his sun deck with our boots propped up and watched Spruce Creek reflect the last golden light of an autumn day in 1984. Wyman's house in Maine, not far from where he was born, was set amid tall pines about twenty yards from the creek, which led to the ocean a half mile away. His boat was moored to a wood pier. He had ten lobster traps, which he checked every other day, and he and Ardyce spent a lot of time fishing, when he wasn't helping his brother Harry, a contractor, renovate old farmhouses being bought as vacation homes along the Maine coast.

I had turned off the tape recorder. We sat without talking. Dick was drained. He had made a determined effort to put the war behind him and bringing it back was hard on him. There were no mementos of Vietnam in his home, not a picture of an airplane. With his wind-burned face, his mottled gray beard, Dick could have been taken for someone who'd never traveled far from his fishing village, and that was the way he wanted it. He was a respected member of his community and his interests had turned to protecting the environment, especially Maine's lobsters, which he believed to be overfarmed. He had a good pair of binoculars and we used them to search for birds in the fading light—something he enjoyed, he told me, not unaware of the irony of his becoming a birdwatcher.

I had met Dick Wyman and the other members of Squadron 162 on July 19, 1966. I'd flown to the *Oriskany* from Da Nang to do a story for *Time* on Rick Adams, who became the first American to be shot down and rescued twice. During the five years I spent in Vietnam, I visited a number of U.S. Navy ships, including five aircraft carriers, a cruiser or two, nearly a dozen destroyers, and the salvage tug assigned to shadow the Russian spy boat on Yankee Station. Never did I meet any group more interesting than Squadron 162. They were as handsome, intelligent, brave, and skilled as any unit of men to serve in the war.

I returned to Saigon after interviewing Rick Adams and Frank McCulloch, my bureau chief at *Time*, read my file before it was cabled to New York. McCulloch was an ex-marine and a former managing editor of the L.A. *Times* with long experience covering the war.

"Damn good story," McCulloch said, after he finished.

He was, we both knew, speaking not about Rick Adams's rescue—though that was interesting enough—but about the squadron itself, which was not the kind of story suitable for a weekly newsmagazine. It was at that moment that I decided to write about the squadron some day as a way of telling about the air war. I stayed in touch with the ship while I remained in Vietnam. When a photographer friend asked for advice on which aircraft carrier to visit, I sent him to the *Oriskany,* and he was there on October 26, 1966, to take pictures of the fire that appeared in *Life* magazine. I met Commander Bellinger again when he came to Saigon to describe his MiG shootdown.

Then in 1971 I began to research the book seriously. The Pentagon gave me the duty stations of the former members of the squadron, and I traveled around to interview a number of them. Others flew to Washington and dropped by to see me. Cal Swanson was assigned to the Pentagon. For several months, I went to his office in the evenings after he finished working and we talked about the squadron. Swanson had a large knowledge of aircraft carriers, and he patiently taught me, a nonpilot, a great deal.

After I completed my research, however, the time did not seem right to do the book. The war was still going on, and probably nothing was more controversial than the bombing. Though my views on the war were a matter of record (I'd left *Time* in early 1968 to write for *The New Republic*), I did not want to do a book that might be taken simply to add to the polemics of one side or the other. The pilots, after all, whatever one may have thought about the air war, were Americans risking their lives to carry out the assignment given them by their commander-in-chief; and my primary interest was to write about them in human terms, not as symbols of a controversial government policy. So I packed my research in boxes that followed me to Spain and then France.

Thirteen years later, I called Anna Urband at the U.S. Navy's magazine and book branch, and told her I believed it was time to tell the story of the squadron. The *Oriskany* held a special place in her heart, she'd told me years before, and she began speaking enthusiastically about the project, as if only a day or two had passed since we last talked. With her help, I was able to get back in touch with the squadron members.

I would not have been able to write the book, I discovered, if I hadn't done my earlier research. The pilots' memories had dimmed over the years. I was the repository of the squadron history. Using my early research, I was able to jog their recollections and bring out other information of a personal nature that they had been reluctant to disclose while still on active duty.

Cal Swanson was again helpful, even though he knew that some of the pilots remembered him in a critical light. He gave me his interpretation of what had happened on Yankee Station, but he did not try to suggest that I should see it his way. After Vietnam, Swanson enjoyed a career that put him in the top segment of naval officers. He kept his air wing longer than most and later was given command of the naval air station in Norfolk, Virginia, considered a plum of an assignment. But he missed making admiral—by a hair, he said—and retired as a captain.

He and Nell kept up with Richard Bellinger through Norma, who, divorced from Belly, was loyal to the end. Cal and Nell made a trip to the veterans hospital in New England where he was confined. Bellinger, dressed in slacks and a shirt, came to greet them in the reception area. Though Cal had steeled himself, he was shocked. Bellinger had lost weight, was gaunt; he looked disheveled and a front tooth was missing. He grinned at Cal and gave a sign of recognition, but said nothing. The attendant dressed in white began to speak casually, including Bellinger in the conversation although he was not responding. Cal picked it up, telling Belly what had happened to him and the squadron in the intervening years.

Bellinger seemed to be struggling painfully to get something out. Finally he blurted, "You CO at Norfolk?"

"Yes," Cal said. "But that was some time ago."

"Lots of good-looking women in Norfolk!" Belly said, his eyes filling. He cried as Cal and Nell took their leave. He died not long afterward. The autopsy revealed Alzheimer's disease.

Swanson bought a house in San Diego while he was in the war. That was where he and Nell settled down. Unlike Dick Wyman's home,

Swanson's contained plenty of reminders of his career. A large wood-carving of naval aviation wings dominated his fireplace. A plaque on the wall, dense with acronyms, listed his navy assignments after Vietnam. Cal was installed as a member of that vast service community in San Diego, made up of active duty and retired personnel, military bases and defense-related industry, that is a world unto itself.

As always, Cal stayed busy. He was president of the La Jolla Kiwanis Club and a deacon in his church. He held two part-time jobs, one with an airline, the other as an accountant for a chain of income tax consultants. Nell was on the board of directors of the San Diego Light Opera Association. Their relationship had grown firmer, though Nell continued to get angry when Cal, ever the perfectionist, gave her overly explicit instructions about some minor matter. Still, she said, he had mellowed and no longer found it necessary to be the last to leave a party.

I arrived at the Swansons at a moment of family crisis. Rhoda, their daughter, had been selected as Miss San Diego of 1984 and then forced to abdicate after it was discovered she'd recently posed for an eleven-page spread in *Penthouse* magazine under the name of Nina Lee, revealing all of her considerable charms. Nell and Cal had not known about Rhoda's posing for *Penthouse*, and the ensuing scandal, Nell told me, had almost caused Cal to have a heart attack. Though embarrassed by the affair, Nell seemed to take a secret pleasure in Rhoda's success as a model.

Ron Coalson walked in one day while I was there and saw a picture of Rhoda, and said, "Skipper, your daughter turned out to be a fox!" That was the traditional way fighter pilots talked about females, but now, when those words were applied to his own daughter, Cal's face fell to his socks, and Nell and I later enjoyed kidding him about it.

For all of that, the Swansons seemed, as one might have predicted, to be doing well in their life after the war.

Ron Coalson told me that he was also on the right track and happy, after experiencing some ups and downs. His spiritual quest ended when he joined the Church of Religious Science, which he described as a metaphysical new-thought movement. Ron had left the navy and returned to work with the reserves, and finally ended his service career completely. He worked for a while as a craps dealer at a casino in Lake Tahoe, then took a job flying for an airline. His life began to come together when he met his wife and they joined an Edgar Cayce study group. "I began to learn there is something to life other than what you see," he told me. "The problems we have stem from the misuse of our own freewill. Life is a unity and we are all individualized points of the whole. I would not go to war today if somebody were to attack this country. I could not take another life. I don't believe in it anymore."

John Hellman, Coalson's former flight leader, owned an avocado farm in southern California and worked for a defense contractor. The day that the Co Trai strike had been canceled, saving him, he was certain, from death, remained close to his thoughts. He considered it the ultimate time of testing and was still amazed he stood ready to do his duty. His squadron never returned to Co Trai. John Hellman had done well in the navy, retiring as a captain. But when he looked back at his time on Yankee Station, he was not sure he liked himself. "I don't think I was very understanding of my wife and family. I didn't pay much attention to them, and that was a mistake." After his wife suffered a nervous breakdown, she recovered and was the stronger for it, he said. "My wife and I seldom talk about the war," Hellman said. "It's a closed book."

Bob Punches retired from the navy and two weeks later started working for a charter company, taking high-rollers to Nevada or well-heeled tourists to Mexico. In April 1983, he was flying a San Diego businessman who'd just made four hundred million dollars to celebrate in Puerto Vallarta. When Punches dropped the wheels of the Learjet, he smelled smoke. The plane was on fire and he lost control. The multimillionaire and his wife, thinking they were dead, reached across the aisle to hold hands during their final moments. "I was approaching the runway so fast that it felt like I was coming down on an aircraft carrier," Punches said. "My navy training saved me. I knew if I landed straight ahead and kept my wings level I had a good chance."

Everybody believed that Punches had pulled off an incredible save. He was written up by the San Diego city magazine, and the multimillionaire, who suffered only minor injuries, bought him a chicken dinner in appreciation of his brilliant flying, which Punches, if anything a stronger Christian after the war, accepted humbly. *

Chuck Rice flew to see Ron Coalson shortly after he returned from

---

* Bob Punches was killed in 1986 after this book was written. Flying under civilian contract, he was making a simulated attack on a U.S. Navy ship in a Learjet and had a midair collision with another plane. There were no survivors. Also, around the same time, Hanoi returned the remains of Rich Minnich to his family—eighteen years after he was shot down over North Vietnam.

Hanoi and greeted him by saying, "Ron, I think I owe you some money." He paid off the poker debt incurred the night before he was shot down more than five years earlier. When I talked to him, Chuck was working for an airline but at the moment was one of the last holdouts in a strike action against his employer. The strike was not a matter of pay but of principle, he said. The glint in his eye added that after being tortured in Hanoi there was no question of which was the more important to him.

The lives of the other pilots had taken unexpected turns. Black Mac, the plain-talking realist, did not figure he was going far in the navy, and he didn't, but he found it humorously surprising that he wound up laying tiles in Florida. Dick Leach, after sweating it out on Yankee Station, was killed while larking in a small assemble-it-yourself aircraft. Jim Nunn retired as a commander to sell real estate.

I saw no indication that any of them suffered from what psychiatrists called the post-traumatic stress disorder, fairly common among soldiers who'd served on the battlefields in the South. No one claimed to have had nightmares after he left the war. They had suffered the predictable letdown that made peacetime flying seem dull after the excitement of combat. But as Dick Wyman pointed out, theirs was a "clean" war—no blood seen, no real feeling for the damage inflicted, with friends shot down simply disappearing; nothing, then, to provide the material for the horror flashbacks that foot soldiers experienced. And though they were given no victory parades either, they were men with a well-regarded skill as aviators and thus, unlike the average soldier, enjoyed public esteem as pilots, if not as warriors, when they returned home.

Yet there were visible signs that they too had been marked by the war. They looked old, much older, all of them, than their contemporaries. And stress-related medical problems among squadron members, considering their small number, seemed high even for aviators. Dick Wyman . . . heart attack at forty-one. Pat Crahan . . . heart attack at forty-nine. The officer called Goodpaster . . . dead of a heart attack at fifty. The pilots who flew in the war did not get off easy.

Perhaps the ones who suffered the most were the families of the missing in action. I knew that Marilyn Elkins would be my hardest meeting, and I flew to New Orleans with a slight feeling of dread. By an accident of scheduling, I arrived on the eighteenth anniversary of

Frank's being shot down. That date was always difficult for her, she said, and she usually tried to make it pass quickly by staying busy. But I brought everything back, sometimes not as gently as I should have, and she cried.

A few years before, I'd served as the staff investigator for a committee of journalists headed by Walter Cronkite who tried to free the twenty newsmen captured in Cambodia during the war. We collected enough information to hold out the hope, never fulfilled, that some of them might be released. I watched at close hand the agony of uncertainty that the newsmen's families, particularly the wife of a friend of mine who was among the missing, went through during that period. Her emotional reaction and Marilyn's were almost identical; and I suspected that it was the same for many of the relatives of the more than two thousand Americans who remained unaccounted for after the war. My friend's wife and Marilyn tended to speak of their husbands in the present tense. Marilyn made a conscious effort not to do it while we talked, like someone trying to control a stammer, but her lapses were frequent. They both spoke with what one first took to be an undercurrent of hostility but then realized was more a conviction on their part that nobody could truly understand how they felt.

Marilyn was an attractive woman in her early forties. Her home not far from the French Quarter reflected intelligence and taste. She told me she would not mind getting remarried. But it seemed to me that Frank was still there. Not only there, but he had not lost any of his hair or grown slack in the belly or had to deal with aging parents or been weathered by job problems or experienced sex that was anything less than breathless. He was still young, handsome, dashing, and brave. And I left New Orleans wishing her well but fearing that it would not be easy to find someone who could live up to that.

I arrived back in Washington in time for the unveiling ceremonies of the statue at the Vietnam Veterans Memorial. The capital was full of Vietnam vets. They looked as I imagined a reunion of veterans from my native South might have looked ten years after their defeat in the Civil War. Whether the war was right or wrong, they were defiantly proud of having served and determined to show their fallen comrades the respect and honor that they themselves had been denied. Many of the vets wore remnants of uniforms getting too tight. I knew this probably would be one of the last outpourings of passion, for I felt that all the emotions stirred by Vietnam were entering that simple but over-powering monument to those who died and finally being stilled.

I found the name of Frank Callihan Elkins on the Wall. I touched it and stood for a moment in silence. I thought of the poem by Robert Frost that Marilyn had chosen to remember him by. The final lines seemed to me a fitting benediction for all—those who opposed the war and those who served.

> Ah, when to the heart of man
> Was it ever less than a treason
> To go with the drift of things,
> To yield with a grace to reason
> And bow and accept the end
> Of a love or a season?

Source Notes

As is readily apparent, this book is not intended to be a formal history of the air war. Nevertheless, I have tried to be as accurate as possible, and a word on sources is in order. Most of my research came from tape-recorded interviews with naval aviators and from notes and files collected during my five years in Vietnam. But I have also used a number of outside sources that should be noted, along with my deep appreciation and grateful acknowledgement to their authors.

Of first importance was a long essay on the air war by Rear Admiral Malcolm W. Cagle, which was made available to me through the intercession of Cal Swanson when I first began researching this book in 1971. Cagle's work later appeared in modified—and gelded—form in the U.S. *Naval Institute Naval Review* ("Task Force 77 in Action off Vietnam," vol. 98, May 1972), but at the time I received his manuscript, it was considered too hot to print because of "security" reasons. The security was clearly political, not national. Navy officials gave me a copy of Cagle's essay after making numerous deletions with a black marking pencil, which I, of course, promptly held to a strong light and restored to the original. That may have been the idea all along. Cagle made the case, backed by never before published facts and figures, that if the air war had failed it was civilian government officials, specifically Robert McNamara, who had made a botch of it. The military was not as blameless as Cagle suggested, nor was it self-evident that the air war would have been won if it had been fought differently, but many of his conclusions about the odd way civilian officials had run the war were hard to challenge. Compared to the air war in the North, the ground war in the South appeared to be a model of coherent military strategy.

Cagle's thesis was amplified by Admiral U. S. Grant Sharp in his memoirs *Strategy for Defeat* (San Rafael: Pacific Press, 1982). Sharp's memoirs are lumpy soup compared to those of a smoothie like Henry Kissinger—which makes the admiral's report all the more interesting to anyone looking for the unmilled truth. Sharp was no great thinker and his anti-McNamara bias goes farther than the facts justify, but he was smart enough to know from the beginning that the air war was going to turn into a fiasco if civilian officials pursued their course of ambivalence and hesitation.

Sharp's work should be read in tandem with Jon Van Dyke's *North Vietnam's Strategy for Survival* (Palo Alto: Pacific Books, 1972) to get an idea of what was happening to the people facing American bombs. The book is developed mainly from secondary sources, such as speeches by North Vietnam's leaders and articles taken from Hanoi's newspaper, *Nhan Dan*. The author sometimes seems to take at face value the kind of information that I suspect he would have scoffed at if it had come from official U.S. government sources, but *North Vietnam's Strategy for Survival* remains nonetheless a valuable work under the circumstances.

For technical aspects of the air war, *The United States Air Force in Southeast Asia, 1961–1973* (Washington: Office of Air History, 1977) and *The Naval Air War in Vietnam* by Peter Mersky and Norman Polmar (Annapolis: Nautical and Aviation Publishing Company of America, 1981) were helpful, as were *Command and Control and Communications Structures in Southeast Asia* by John Lane (Washington: Superintendent of Documents, 1981) and *MiG Master: The Story of the F-8 Crusader* by Barret Tillman (Annapolis: Nautical and Aviation Publishing Company of America, 1980), a fine work. Jim Stockdale's Tonkin Gulf incident appeared in *In Love and War* by James B. Stockdale (New York: Harper & Row, 1984). *The Heart of a Man*, the journal of Frank Elkins, edited by Marilyn Elkins (New York: W. W. Norton, 1973), showed his sensitivity and talents as a writer.

I have drawn from the political works of four authors who together would make up a formidable bridge party: Richard M. Nixon, Henry A. Kissinger, Seymour M. Hersh, and Harrison E. Salisbury. Nixon's retrospective look at the war, *No More Vietnams* (New York: Arbor House, 1985), is interesting, even if it doesn't live up to its title; and I realized while rereading Henry Kissinger's two-volume memoirs, *White House Years* and *Years of Upheaval* (Boston: Little, Brown, 1979 and

1982), that probably no two other closely linked government figures have produced such readable works. It has often been noted that Kissinger writes well, but Nixon's memoirs, too, stand, in literary terms, above most presidential memoirs—a fact that is, for some reason, seldom remarked upon by critics. After reading their works published as nonfiction on the Vietnam War era, however, one can only hope that Nixon and Kissinger will turn their talents to writing a historical novel about that period. Seymour Hersh set out to correct what he perceived to be certain misapprehensions about the former secretary of state and Nobel Peace Prize winner in *The Price Of Power: Kissinger in the Nixon White House* (New York: Summit Books, 1983), and his book contains a dizzying amount of information ferociously flung together, which saves anyone researching the subject an awful lot of shoe leather. Harrison Salisbury's *Behind The Lines—Hanoi* (New York: Harper & Row, 1967) stirred quite a bit of controversy when it was first published and was denied a Pulitzer Prize by "higher authority" after the Pulitzer jury voted for it. No work was more influential in forming opinions about the air war, and one finds it hard to remember—at least until one reads it a second time—that his book was based on a two-week stay in North Vietnam.

I have used Robert McNamara's legacy to history—the Pentagon Papers, Gravel edition, which are, I must say, unfortunately for such a crucial source work, too often bruised by their authors' prejudices. Perhaps that was inevitable, given the nature of the war. I also read or dipped into one hundred and twelve other books in preparation for writing this work. I have decided not to include a bibliography, since the Library of Congress in Washington, D.C., where I did my basic research, has ended the back pains and eyestrain that used to be the consequences of days spent poring over the card catalog. The library's collection on the Vietnam War is fully computerized, and somber-faced but efficient staffers are on standby to help the reader call up a bibliography on the air war literally in seconds. I suggest that anyone interested in reading further on this subject take advantage of the library's service—one of the more praiseworthy examples of the taxpayers' money at work that I can think of. Please tell them I sent you.

Index

Index

Index

Index

About the Author

ZALIN GRANT worked for the Associated Press as a stringer covering the civil rights crisis before graduating from Clemson University in 1963. After completing his military service as an army officer in Vietnam, he reported from Saigon for *Time* and was later Southeast Asia correspondent of *The New Republic*. He was in Indochina for five years and was one of only several American journalists to cover the war who spoke Vietnamese. He spent more than a year on a writing assignment driving overland from Singapore to Paris, where he now lives. He is the author of *Survivors*, which has been called a Vietnam War classic.